Short Escapes from Bengaluru

This guide is researched and written by
Supriya Sehgal, Puneetinder K Sidhu and Bikram Ghosh

CONTENTS

Plan Your Trip 6

Short Escapes from Bengaluru 8
10 Top Experiences 12
Getting Around 18

Hill Escapes 20

1. Nandi Hills 22
2. Yercaud 28
3. Madikeri & Around 36
4. Adventure in Coorg 44
5. Ooty 52
6. Coonoor 62
7. Kotagiri 70

Heritage Escapes 78

8. Nrityagram 80
9. Lepakshi 86
10. Talakad 90
11. Somanathapura 94
12. Mysore 98

13. Belur–Halebidu 108
14. Chitradurga Fort 116
15. Tirupati 120
16. Pondicherry 130
17. Hampi 142

Nature Escapes 150

18. Ramanagaram 152
19. Bheemeshwari 156
20. Yelagiri Hills 162
21. Hogenakkal 170
22. Sakleshpur 174
23. Chikmagalur 182
24. Wayanad 192
25. Brahmagiri Trek 202
26. Tadiandamol Trek 206
27. Kudremukh Trek 212

Wildlife Escapes 218

28. BRT Wildlife Sanctuary 220
29. Bandipur 226

30. Kabini–Nagarhole 232	38. Gorukana, BR Hills 274
31. Masinagudi 236	39. Kabini River Lodge 280
	40. Amanvana Spa 286
	41. Orange County 290

Escape to a Resort .. 242

32. Angana – The Country Inn 244	42. The Windflower Resort & Spa 294
33. Soukya 250	43. River Tern Lodge 300
34. AyurvedaGram 256	44. Destiny 306
35. Shreyas Yoga Retreat 260	45. Oland Plantation 312
36. Galibore Fishing & Nature Camp 266	
37. Georgia Sunshine Village 270	

Route map 318
Index 320
Acknowledgements 322

HOW TO USE THIS BOOK

Find Your Interest
Sections are colour-coded for easy use

○ Escapes are categorised under hills, heritage, nature, wildlife and resorts.

Boxes & Symbols
To quickly find the information you need

Special Boxes

Look for these boxes to help you get the most out of your trip:

- ✓ *Top Tip* – helpful advice
- ♥ *If You Like* – themed suggestions
- ₹ *Value for Money* – money-saving tips
- ◈ *Detour* – off-beat trips
- 📷 *Snapshot* – interesting facts

Symbols

These symbols indicate:

❄ AC	≋ Pool	📶 Wi-fi
P Parking	☎ Phone	🚌 Bus
🚗 Car	🚆 Train	⛴ Ferry

Accommodation

₹	Budget	below ₹3000
₹₹	Mid-range	₹3000–7000
₹₹₹	High-end	over ₹7000
s		single rooms
d		double rooms
ste		suites
dm		dorms

Eating

₹	Budget	below ₹200
₹₹	Mid-range	₹200–500
₹₹₹	High-end	above ₹500

Trip Planner
At-a-glance information for each destination

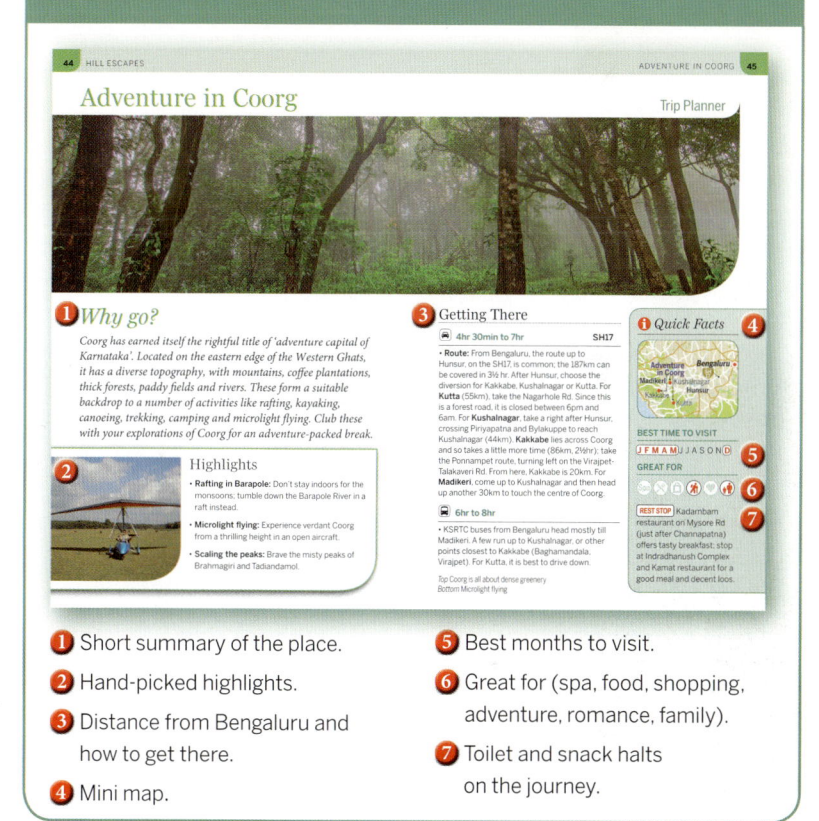

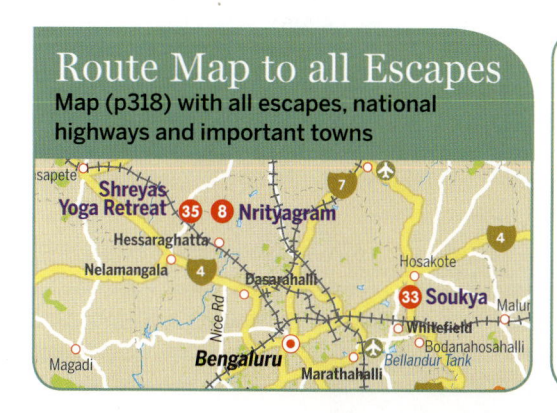

Adventure in Coorg
Trip Planner

❶ Why go?
Coorg has earned itself the rightful title of 'adventure capital of Karnataka'. Located on the eastern edge of the Western Ghats, it has a diverse topography, with mountains, coffee plantations, thick forests, paddy fields and rivers. These form a suitable backdrop to a number of activities like rafting, kayaking, canoeing, trekking, camping and microlight flying. Club these with your explorations of Coorg for an adventure-packed break.

❷ Highlights
- **Rafting in Barapole:** Don't stay indoors for the monsoons; tumble down the Barapole River in a raft instead.
- **Microlight flying:** Experience verdant Coorg from a thrilling height in an open aircraft.
- **Scaling the peaks:** Brave the misty peaks of Brahmagiri and Tadiandamol.

❸ Getting There
4hr 30min to 7hr — SH17
- **Route:** From Bengaluru, the route up to Hunsur, on the SH17, is common; the 187km can be covered in 3½ hr. After Hunsur, choose the diversion for Kakkabe, Kushalnagar or Kutta. For **Kutta** (55km), take the Nagarhole Rd. Since this is a forest road, it is closed between 6pm and 6am. For **Kushalnagar**, take a right after Hunsur, crossing Piriyapatna and Bylakuppe to reach Kushalnagar (44km). **Kakkabe** lies across Coorg and so takes a little more time (86km, 2½hr); take the Ponnampet route, turning left on the Virajpet-Talakaveri Rd. From here, Kakkabe is 20km. For **Madikeri**, come up to Kushalnagar and then head up another 30km to touch the centre of Coorg.

6hr to 8hr
- KSRTC buses from Bengaluru head mostly till Madikeri. A few run up to Kushalnagar, or other points closest to Kakkabe (Baghamandala, Virajpet). For Kutta, it is best to drive down.

Top Coorg is all about dense greenery
Bottom Microlight flying

❹ Quick Facts
BEST TIME TO VISIT
J F M **A M** J J A S O N **D**

GREAT FOR

REST STOP Kadambam restaurant on Mysore Rd (just after Channapatna) offers tasty breakfast; stop at Indradhanush Complex and Kamat restaurant for a good meal and decent loos.

---

❶ Short summary of the place.
❷ Hand-picked highlights.
❸ Distance from Bengaluru and how to get there.
❹ Mini map.
❺ Best months to visit.
❻ Great for (spa, food, shopping, adventure, romance, family).
❼ Toilet and snack halts on the journey.

Route Map to all Escapes
Map (p318) with all escapes, national highways and important towns

OUR REVIEWS
Lonely Planet writers have visited every hotel, restaurant, shop and activity in this book. They don't accept any freebies and favours, so you can be sure our recommendations are unbiased.

PLAN YOUR TRIP

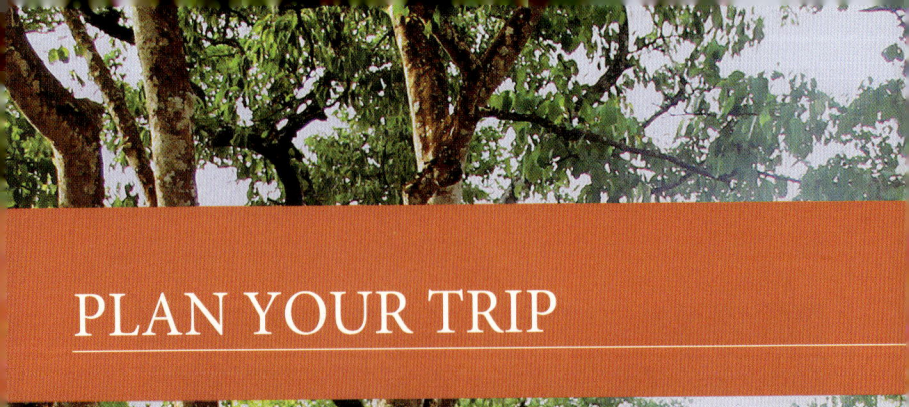

- Short Escapes from Bengaluru.....8
- 10 Top Experiences......................12
- Getting Around............................18

A forest road in Bandipur

Short Escapes from Bengaluru

In Bengaluru, it's easy to escape from your cubicle and into a different world altogether. Scattered around the city are rolling hills rife with plantations, wildlife reserves, medieval temples and grand ruins, not to speak of hiking trails, rafting trips, yoga retreats and luxurious resorts.

Hill Escapes

The Nilgiri and Brahmagiri hills offer a range of holiday experiences. Wander among coffee plantations in **Madikeri** (p36) or soak in picturesque views in **Coonoor** (p62), a garden-fresh cup of tea in hand. If you're looking for more action, head to **Coorg** (p44) for whitewater rafting or buckle your hiking boots to navigate the Nilgiris at **Kotagiri** (p70). If ease of travel is a priority, **Nandi Hills** (p22) – the former summer retreat of Tipu Sultan – is less than two hours away.

Heritage Escapes

Culture vultures needn't travel far from the ultra-modern silicon city to step back in time. The historic town of **Mysore** (p98) is adorned in brocaded regal splendour, the medieval carvings and sculptures of **Belur** (p108), **Halebidu** (p108) and **Somanathapura** (p94) attest to the Hoysala kings' passion for temples and the formidable **Chitradurga Fort** (p116) is the stuff of epics. Stand in the shadows of the Vijayanagar Empire at the melancholy ruins of Hampi (p142), which dot an unearthly landscape. At seaside **Pondicherry** (p130),

Boulders form a dramatic backdrop to Hampi's ruins

take in the distinctly French vibe, join throngs of pilgrims at **Tirupati** (p120) and experience the rhythms of the dance school of **Nrityagram** (p80).

Nature Escapes

Lovers of the great outdoors can trek, climb and raft in the various outdoor locations. **Ramanagram** (p152) – where *Sholay* was shot – is a popular rock-climbing destination near Bengaluru. The Kaveri River offers a smorgasbord of watery adventures – go rafting at **Bheemeshwari** (p156) or take a coracle ride along waterfalls at **Hogenakkal** (p170). For a more sedate experience, visit the coffee plantations of Sakleshpur (p174), Chikmagalur (p182) and Wayanad (p192). The trekking trails in **Brahmagiri** (p202) and **Kudremukh** (p212) also provide an enjoyable challenge.

Wildlife Escapes

With the Nilgiri Biosphere of the Western Ghats (a World Heritage Site) at their doorstep, Bengaluru residents are almost neighbours with herds of Asian elephants, leopards, gaurs, wild dogs, hyenas, spotted deer and many bird species – all of which inhabit the **BRT Wildlife Sanctuary** (p220) and the reserve forests of **Bandipur** (p226) and **Nagarhole** (p232). There are a fair number of eco-savvy accommodation options in these forests and plenty of things to do by the side.

Escape to a Resort

If you're looking for an all-in-one getaway from Bengaluru, you're in luck. We've sought out a number of boutique resorts, wellness spas and even homestays that offer not only accommodation and meals, but also activities and experiences to keep you engaged for an entire weekend. For a combination of world-class luxury and traditional mind-body healing, **Soukya** (p250) and **Shreyas Yoga Retreat** (p260) are your best bets. Other resorts focus on specialised themes such as fishing (**Galibore**, p266), wildlife (**Kabini River Lodge**, p280), farm experiences (**Destiny**, p306) and plantation living (**Orange County**, p290). If fun with the family must include your pets, try **Georgia Sunshine Village** (p270).

A herd of elephants at Nagarhole National Park

10 Top Experiences

1 Wellness at Shreyas

Shreyas Yoga Retreat (p260) presents plush living tempered with meditation, organic vegetarian food and the feel of life on a farm. The immaculate facilities, personalised treatment and ashram-like ambience soothe you even before your rendezvous with Ayurveda starts. Here, you can expect massages of all kinds, guided yoga and an open Jacuzzi by the pool. The packages can be customised to suit your therapeutic needs. For instance, the full body massage is done by an expert after a detailed consultation and an understanding of your physical state.

2 Bouldered Hampi

The forlorn ruins of the Vijayanagara Empire at Hampi (p142) dot a surreal landscape that will leave you spellbound the moment you cast your eyes on it. Heaps of giant boulders perch precariously over miles of rolling terrain, their rusty hues offset by jade-green palm groves, banana plantations and paddy fields. Climb the 600-plus steps to the top of Anjandri Hill to soak in the mesmerising view of the ancient towns split by the Tungabhadra River. Another superb viewing spot is on top of the Matanga Paravath: for a bird's-eye view of the bustling surrounds, walk down the main bazaar and climb this low hill that houses a small temple. Hampi is a treasure trove of architectural brilliance; the exceptional workmanship comes alive in important shrines like Virupaksha, Vijaya Vittala and Achyutaraya, and the Lotus Mahal.

3 Mysore Dasera

The heritage city of Mysore (p98) is at its vibrant best during the 10-day Dasera festival, which continues a tradition started by the Vijayanagar kings in the 15th century. The festival starts with a procession of decorated elephants led by the Maharaja of Mysore – a grand spectacle. Every evening, the Maharaja's Palace is dramatically lit up, while the town is transformed into a gigantic fairground, with concerts, dance performances, sporting demonstrations and cultural events. On the last day, Vijayadashami, the celebrations are capped off with a dazzling torchlight procession.

4 Wildlife Experience, Kabini River Lodge

Kabini River Lodge (p280) charms with its old-world appeal, and offers a range of authentic wildlife and nature experiences. Among the list of activities here is a short ride on a coracle, a round basket-like boat. Your boatman will point out resident birds of the region as you rock and roll along with the rhythms of the river in your seemingly precarious vessel. If boating isn't for you, take a safari into Nagarhole Forest, the erstwhile hunting ground of the Maharaja of Mysore, or set off on a nature walk.

5 Eco Stay, Oland Plantation

Tucked away in a thickly-forested valley off Ooty, this 120-acre organic plantation of tea, coffee and spices, is exceptionally welcoming to certain non-paying guests – herds of bison and elephants that saunter in for a mud bath or a nibble. Oland Plantation (p312) effortlessly matches the best of modern comforts and rustic charm in its plush cottages. Right from the mud block construction of the house to the solar lighting, bio mass water heaters and rainwater harvesting devices, Oland offers a charming ecofriendly vacation ideal for nature lovers.

6 Village of the Blinded Eyes

The creation of the Lepakshi temple complex (p86), with its impressive murals, art and displays of skilful sculpturing, almost emptied the coffers of the Vijayanagara Empire. It is said that the far-from-frugal treasurer of the empire, Virupanna, was blinded for being too loose-fisted with his budget in constructing this marvellous work of art. And it is this harsh punishment that earned Lepakshi its name, which translates to 'village of the blinded eyes'.

7 The Nilgiri Toy Train

For locomotive aficionados, a trip on the historic Nilgiri Mountain Railway (p57, 67) is essential. This toy train, a Unesco World Heritage Site, is steeped in charm. Be prepared to jostle your way to a window seat, and enjoy the ride from Ooty (p52) to Mettupalayam as the train snakes over bridges, through tunnels and past small and picturesque stations. The journey from Coonoor (p62) to Mettupalayam (41km) also affords delightful views; you can choose to do only this stretch.

8 Stone Chronicles in Belur & Halebidu

The Hoysala temples at Belur and Halebidu (p108) are South India's answer to Khajuraho and Konark, and represent a high point in ancient Hindu architecture. The intricate carvings on the Chennakesava Temple (Belur) and Hoysaleswara Temple (Halebidu) are hallmarks of the most prosperous period of Hindu culture in Karnataka. Keep an eye out for exquisite sculptural details ranging from meticulously carved monkey teeth to bangles that still rotate around the wrists, and the depiction of see-through clothing on dancers. Besides scenes from the *Ramayana* and *Mahabharata*, the sculptures also throw light on daily life all those centuries ago. Do take a guide along for a deeper and more nuanced understanding of the temples.

9 Get Coffee Savvy in Chikmagalur

Chikmagalur's (p182) significance as one of India's key coffee destinations has a lot more to it than the presence of coffee conglomerates, or recent large-scale production. For travellers, it's more about history – this is the place where coffee first arrived in India. Follow the mountain trail of Baba Budangiri and Mullayangiri, an area into which a 17th-century saint (Baba Budangiri) smuggled coffee beans. Enjoy astounding views of the coffee- and cloud-covered valley below from these peaks and stay on a plantation to complete the experience. If you want to combine your coffee buzz with an adrenaline rush, you can go rafting on the Bhadra River or head for a bracing trek on Chikmagalur's high mountains.

10 Fun at Destiny

Combining the rough-and-tumble of a farm with all the creature comforts of a luxury hotel, Destiny (p306) off Ooty provides a wonderfully well-rounded experience for the entire family. You can indulge yourself (indoors in the spa) and get your boots muddy and hands soiled (outdoors on the farm). Prepare to have waves of satisfaction sweep over you as you commune with nature amid rustic surroundings; there is nothing more gratifying than picking fresh veggies for dinner, netting a catch or giving a helping hand to tend the horses at this fun place.

Getting Around

Bengaluru is one of the few metros that can boast of a truly wide range of escapes close to the city. Efficient bus services and reliable highways make short breaks even more doable.

Buses

Karnataka has an impressive fleet of KSRTC (Karnataka State Road Transport Corporation) buses. From basic to luxury Volvos, these buses ply between destinations within Karnataka and adjoining states; they are a comfortable and convenient mode of transport for short distances. The five major bus terminals in Bengaluru are: Majestic, KR Market, Shivajinagar, Shantinagar and Banashankari. Book online at www.ksrtc.in.

NH 7 connects the city to Tamil Nadu

Cars

Most Bangaloreans are excited by driving since the highways (barring a small stretch on the Mysore Road) are smooth and easy to navigate. The four major national highways (NH4, NH7, NH48, NH209), and one state highway (SH17), which exit through the city, are conveniently dotted with loos and eating stops, making rides easy and comfortable for families.

Cabs

Cabs are handy if you want to travel in comfort. Taxi charges vary from ₹6.50 per km to ₹12 per

ⓘ *NICE Road*

The Nandi Infrastructure Corridor Enterprises Limited (NICE) Road, four to six lanes, is a tolled and fenced expressway that was developed to connect Bengaluru to Mysore, to alleviate traffic congestion in South Bengaluru. The road also exits on NH7 (Hosur Road) at Electronic City, NH4 (Tumkur Road) near Nelamangala, Banerghatta Road in Bengaluru, NH209 (Kanakapura Road) and SH17 (Mysore Road).

Expert Recommendation
Tips for Long Drives

Santosh Kumar is behind a number of travel ventures: Getoff Ur Ass, Photography Onthemove, First Sunday Rides and more. Here are some tips from someone who surely knows the roads well:

• **Vehicle essentials** – Ensure that your tool kit, documents, hazard indicator, spare tyre, coolant and oils are in place before you head out on a long drive. Most cars supply a suggested tyre-pressure limit for highways, which is different from that for daily use. Get your tyres checked for air a day before leaving. Mechanic help may not be available for long stretches, so invest in a ready-to-use puncture liquid for emergencies.

• **The Ghats section** – Driving out of Bengaluru, one soon hits the mountains, especially towards the Nilgiris. Use lower gears to manoeuvre on winding roads and always be alert for any burning smell – it could be the brakes or the clutch. Stay on your side and sleep well the night before. Try and head out early in the morning for better visibility.

• **Wildlife sections** – Bengaluru's proximity to wildlife hubs (Bandipur, Mudumalai, Wayanad) means that there is bound to be some spill over of wildlife onto highways, when the animals are crossing roads. Though many of these highways are closed at night, evenings are a sensitive time for visibility. Be extra alert and wary of deer, wild boar, sambars and snakes on the roads. Avoid night driving.

km, depending on the type of car you choose. Toll expenses and air-condition should be clearly discussed beforehand. The minimum number of kilometres in a day is 250. There's also an additional driver fee called 'bata', which varies between ₹200 and ₹300 per day.

Trains

Most destinations around Bengaluru are connected by train, but this may not be the most practical way to travel due to odd arrival and departure times. However, places like Hampi or Mysore, can be reached by train to save travel time. Bangalore City, Cantonment and Yesvantpur stations are the three main hubs from where trains depart. Tickets can be booked on www.irctc.co.in.

HILL ESCAPES

- Nandi Hills 22
- Yercaud 28
- Madikeri & Around 36
- Adventure in Coorg 44
- Ooty 52
- Coonoor 62
- Kotagiri 70

■ The stunning Ketti Valley on the way to Ooty

HILL ESCAPES

Nandi Hills

Why go?

Discover the remnants of Tipu's empire and monuments of earlier eras at Nandi Hills, once home to the Tiger of Mysore's impregnable fort. Nandi Hills is a great option for a day trip or even an overnight stay. Sprawling gardens stretch across the hill and offer unparalleled views of the surrounding countryside; there is a restaurant and picnic grounds for day visitors.

Highlights

- **Shri Bhoga Nandeeshwara Swamy Temple:** A masterpiece of temple architecture.

- **Amrita Sarovara:** This ancient temple tank greets visitors to the fort.

- **Shri Yoganandeeshwara Swamy Temple:** Peaceful shrine on the crown of the hill.

NANDI HILLS

Trip Planner

Getting There   56km

🚗 **1hr 20min**   NH7

- **Route:** Drive past Devanahalli (NH7) till you reach Rani Cross (or Nandi Cross). Take a left onto Nandi Hills Rd. Turn left again at Karahalli Cross. Approximately 4km ahead, turn right onto the road leading up to Nandi Hills.

🚌 **1hr 45min**

- There are regular buses from the Majestic bus terminus to Chikballapur, via Bellary Rd. From Chikballapur, buses and autos are available to Nandi Hills, though not so frequent on the return journey.

🚆 **2hr 30min**   Chikballapur

- Direct passenger and local trains to Chikballapur from Bangalore City station. The 8.40am train is the most convenient on the way out, while for returning, opt for the 3.55pm or 7.55am trains.

Top Aerial view of Nandi Hills *Bottom* Nandeeshwara Temple

ⓘ Quick Facts

BEST TIME TO VISIT

J F M A M J J A S O N D

GREAT FOR

Spa · · · · · ·

REST STOP Restaurants at Karahalli Cross and at the Nandi Hills turning (4km) are the best places to stop.

Picnic Paradise

Highlights
1. Shri Bhoga Nandeeshwara Swamy Temple
2. Amrita Sarovara
3. Shri Yoganandeeshwara Swamy Temple
4. Tipu's Summer Lodge
5. Nellikai Basavana
6. Tipu's Drop

Nandi Hills sits safe within the ramparts of the Nandidurg Fortress, overlooking vast tracts of chequered farmland. It is an idyllic garden paradise: teeming with a variety of flowering shrubs, cooled by hilly breezes even in summer, and scattered with monuments and shrines in the most unexpected of places.

The hill is also home to a number of birds, from common tailorbirds, thrushes and babblers to cuckoos, flycatchers, and birds of prey like the Brahminy kite and the rare Egyptian vulture. However, with the steady traffic of visitors, they are not as easily sighted as one might expect.

The Cholas considered this place sacred and called it Ananda Giri, the hill of joy. Around its crown, Tipu Sultan built his famous fortress, and within its walls he built a summer home. The British conquered the fort in 1791, and having discovered for themselves the simple pleasures of being atop this pleasant hill, they turned it into a resort.

Nandi Hills; ₹5; parking two-wheeler/car ₹15/60; 6am–6pm

The stepped tank at Amrita Sarovara

❶ SHRI BHOGA NANDEESHWARA SWAMY TEMPLE

Situated in Nandi village, the temple was built by Ratnavali, consort to the Bana king, Vidhyadhara, around AD 810. However, there is evidence of the contribution of at least three other dynasties – Chola, Hoysala and Vijayanagara – lending the architecture their own inimitable styles. Judging from the intricacy of the carvings on the pillars in the inner sanctum, to the statues overlooking the stepped tank, the monument appears to have been well looked after. The temple grounds are extensive.

Nandi Hills Rd

❷ AMRITA SAROVARA

This ancient stepped tank reveals its true depth only in the dry season, when the water level drops to just a few feet. Almost hidden by a canopy of tree tops, the tank provides a tranquil welcome to the Nandidurg Fort, but is often ignored by visitors because of its proximity to the entrance, and its distance from other attractions on the hill.

❸ SHRI YOGANANDEESHWARA SWAMY TEMPLE

Sitting on bare rock at the summit of the hill, this temple is surrounded by the sky. The absence of intricate carvings

---

♥ *If You Like: Historic haunts*

If you enjoy visiting ancient sites and secret passageways, Nandi Hills offers a number of such attractions. Most of the older sights on the hill are away from the more popular areas, 'hidden' near the fortress walls and often on different sides. It takes a fair amount of walking to discover them.

- **Brahmashrama:** Reputed to be the cave in which the sage Ramakrishna underwent a prolonged period of meditation. Despite the darkness, verses in Kannada can be seen etched into the rock walls.

- **Horse Way:** This path, to allow horsemen easier access to the fort, is at the edge of the northeastern wall.

- **Secret Passage:** A hidden route for the sultan or his soldiers to enter or leave the fort, the passageway is located on the western side of the fort.

- **River Sources:** Steps around the sources of four rivers, Arkavathy, Penner, Palar and Ponnaiyar, can still be found on the hill. In one instance, a tiny room, the purpose of which is a mystery, has been built above the source.

underlines the sturdiness of the stones that went into building the temple (although some isolated eroded figures can be seen protruding from the walls at certain intervals). Look out for the interesting etchings, 'hidden' in the floor of the surrounding walkway, visible to the eye only from particular angles.

4 TIPU'S SUMMER LODGE

A modest dwelling for a sultan, the lodge is tucked next to a gate, and surrounded by trees that throw their shade across it for much of the day. This is generally a quiet spot, away from the fort's more popular attractions. You're restricted, for the most part, to studying the details of the lodge's façade, since it is closed to the public. Nevertheless, some visitors find even the external view of the lodge quite evocative of its past.

5 NELLIKAI BASAVANA

This statue of Nandi is 3m long and 1.8m high, and carved in the Chola style. It is so called because in front of the basavana (bull) is a nellikai tree, adorned today with numerous pieces of plastic ritualistically knotted around its trunk and branches. On festival days dedicated to Shiva, rituals are performed at this shrine and the statue is covered in garlands, colour and sweets. The basavana can be reached by taking the rocky path downhill past the Mayura Pine Top hotel.

Tipu's Drop: not for the faint-hearted

6 TIPU'S DROP

Beneath a stark expanse of rock looking out over farmland is the place where Tipu Sultan is said to have executed criminals by having them thrown off the fortress walls. The view from the edge is steep and guards are posted at the 'drop' at all times now. The spot, however, has lost some of its sinister edge, being frequented by assorted groups of tourists and couples seeking the shade of trees nearby.

NANDI HILLS

🛏 Accommodation

Mayura Pine Top — KSTDC Hotel ₹
📞 081-56250906; Nandi Hills, Chikballapur, Kolar; d ₹600 No other accommodation on the hill surpasses this hotel's view of the landscape below. Despite a few cosmetic changes, Mayura Pine Top retains its modest and unfussy air. Only three rooms are available, each well-kept in season, but prone to be under-serviced during off-season. The staff is friendly but work at their own pace.

Nehru Nilaya — Heritage Hotel ₹
📞 081-56278621; Nandi Hills, Chikballapur, Kolar; d ₹1000 Once known as Cubbon House, this was the summer residence of Lord Cubbon (erstwhile commissioner of Mysore), and later of Jawaharlal Nehru. The building is modest by colonial standards, but with its rounded pillars, wide balconies and high ceilings, it still possesses a certain grandeur. There are only three rooms here, but Nehru Nilaya is the best option if you're partial to old-world charm.

Horticulture Department Cottages ₹
The Horticulture Department provides accommodation in cottages spread across the fort area. **For reservations,**

Nehru Nilaya, formerly Cubbon House, offers decent staying options

contact: Director of Horticulture (15 March–15 July) 📞 080-26579231, 26577366, Lalbagh, Bengaluru; Special Officer, Nandi Hills (16 July–14 March); 📞 081-56278621; rooms ₹250, cottages ₹300; VIP cottages ₹500; VVIP suites ₹1000

🍴 Eating

Mayura Pine Top ₹
10am–8pm Currently, the only restaurant in Nandi Hills. The full menu is not available on most days, and the food is passable. It does, however, serve liquor throughout the day, besides offering an impressive view to enjoy along with your beer.

✓ *Top Tip: Booking ahead*

All accommodation in Nandi Hills is government run. Rooms are limited, though more are being added (and renovated). Book ahead if you plan to stay overnight.

HILL ESCAPES

Yercaud

Why go?

Renowned for its coffee plantations, fruit orchards, missionary schools and seminaries, travellers to Yercaud arrive at a hill station already bustling with life. Nevertheless, in its world, there is time enough to stretch one's legs, take in the sights, enjoy a few good meals, and breathe in the fresh mountain air. In a manner of speaking, it is a place tailor-made for holidays.

Highlights

- **Botanical Gardens:** A layered jungle of nurseries and giant trees.
- **Kiliyur Falls:** A stunningly steep waterfall surrounded by natural beauty.
- **Emerald Lake:** The only natural lake of its size in the Nilgiris.

YERCAUD

Trip Planner

Getting There — 231km

🚗 **4hr 30min** — NH7/Yercaud Rd

• **Route:** Drive down Hosur Rd to Krishnagiri. Turn right at Krishnagiri and follow the NH7 past Dharmapuri to Salem. Do be careful, however, when negotiating the sharp hairpin bends leading up to Yercaud from Salem.

🚌 **6hr**

• Buses to Salem are available from Bengaluru's Majestic bus terminus, though the ride takes around 5 hours. There are regular buses from Salem to Yercaud.

🚆 **5hr 45min** — Salem

• Local trains to Salem are available from Bangalore City and Yesvantpur stations. There are regular buses from Salem to Yercaud.

Top Bird's-eye view of Yercaud *Bottom* Emerald Lake

❶ Quick Facts

BEST TIME TO VISIT

J F M A M J J A **S O N D**

GREAT FOR

REST STOP Freshen up at Krishnagiri before getting onto the highway. Stretch your legs at Salem before the steep uphill drive.

King of the Eastern Ghats

Highlights
1. Botanical Gardens
2. Horticulture Farm
3. Emerald Lake
4. Viewpoints of Yercaud
5. Kiliyur Falls
6. Rajarajeshwari Temple
7. Servarayan Temple
8. Kottachedu Teak Forest

Yercaud is a place of arresting natural beauty. The town is surrounded by forests of tall silver oaks, with black pepper vines crawling up their thin white trunks, and legions of tropical fruit trees and coffee bushes lining the lower slopes. The views that can be enjoyed from its numerous vantage points, stretch far into the distance, presenting the Nilgiri Range like no other place.

Emerald Lake, the largest natural lake in the Nilgiris, occupies the centre of town, and is clearly the most touristy locale, with parks, roadside eateries and crowded souvenir stalls. Attempts by the government to step up tourism in Yercaud have unfortunately resulted in commercialism and pollution around the main attractions. But we recommend short walks (or car rides) to explore the quieter side of this plantation town. Yercaud promises a plentiful holiday for those with restless feet, as well as for those seeking a restful getaway.

1 BOTANICAL GARDENS
Spread across a steep terraced slope, is an artificial jungle created by the Botanical Survey of India, housing some rare specimens, as well as local ones like the Shevaroy Bombax. The Botanical Gardens also runs a prized **orchidarium** with seasonal blooms, and besides a number of native varieties, it displays the Lady's Slipper, a rare insectivorous plant.
Loop Rd; ₹3; camera ₹10; 9am–4pm, Mon–Fri

2 HORTICULTURE FARM
Housing both the famous **Rose Garden** and **Silk Farm** within its compound, the Horticulture Farm offers visitors winding walks through gardens and nurseries growing a wide variety of the bloom: from flat-button roses to many layered giant roses, and even the exotic green rose, seen only during the

warmer months of the year.
Lady's Seat Rd; ₹10; camera ₹10; 8am–5pm

❸ EMERALD LAKE
The only natural lake in the Nilgiri Hills, the Emerald Lake – or 'Big' Lake as the locals call it – is in the centre of Yercaud. Boats can be hired from the boathouse, which has the **Anna and Deer Parks** situated on either side. The latter is primarily for children, and though it houses no deer, it has enclosures for guinea pigs, rabbits and birds, including peacocks.
Town Circle

❹ VIEWPOINTS OF YERCAUD
Among the many viewpoints at Yeraud, we recommended the southern-most called **Tipperary Point**, a short distance from the Town Circle. The most remarkable sight it offers is of the White Elephant's Teeth, a pair of tall white quartz crystals contrasted against the black rock surrounding them. They are said to be the remnants of a crashed meteor. **Pagoda Point** is another attraction, which was marked by an ancient pile of stones placed by tribal worshippers. However, a modern temple has been built at the spot, obstructing some of the view, and sadly, many of the ancient stones have been vandalised. A much-visited viewpoint is **Lady's Seat**, but it's better avoided in peak season if you do not want to be jostled by touristy crowds.

The scenic twisting road leading up to Yercaud

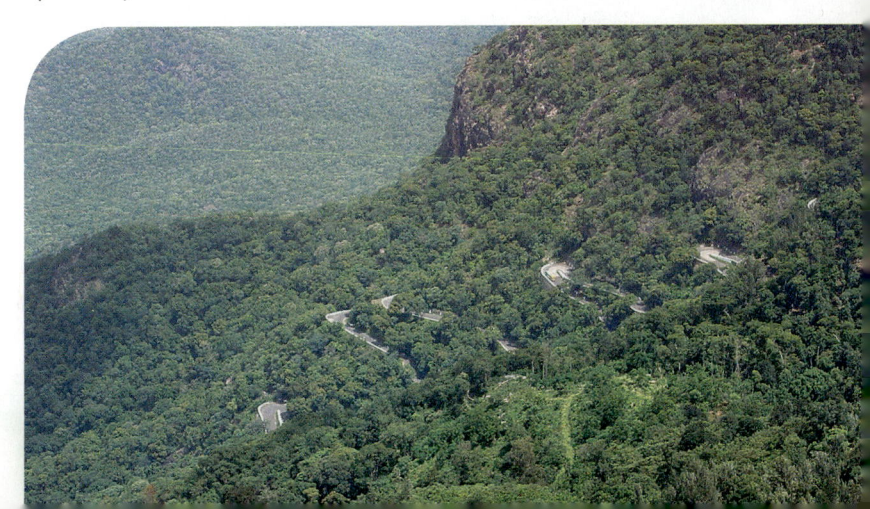

5 KILIYUR FALLS

The falls are a wonder to behold, including a sweeping view of the valley below and the hills above. They can only be experienced between the months of September and January, after the monsoons. Visiting Kiliyur is a bit of a trek, since rocky paths and steep stairs lead you down to the viewing area. The climb is not advisable for children and the elderly.
Kiliyur Falls Rd

6 RAJARAJESHWARI TEMPLE

This is a modern temple just over 30 years old. A meditating Shiva sits in the middle of a tiny pool, while another five-headed Ganesha idol is of artistic value. Also of interest is a small shrine outlining the link between the gods and astrology.
Loop Rd

7 SERVARAYAN TEMPLE

The temple was built at the site of this sacred cave a hundred years ago. It houses the idols of the god Servarayan and the river goddess Kaveri. The locals believe that the cave reaches deep into the mountain, to the source of the River Kaveri. Despite the modern constructions around the temple, the cave can seem quite primal, and is under the care of the local women of the hills.
Servarayan Temple Rd; ₹10

The rare Lady's Slipper found in the Botanical Gardens

8 KOTTACHEDU TEAK FOREST

Approximately 11km from Yercaud town, the Vanniyar River flows through the teak forest down to the Vaniam Dam. Said once to be inhabited by the hill tribes, till plague struck them down, the teak forest today is full of birds, insects and small mammals. Bison are also spotted every now and then. You can drive through the forest in your own vehicle as no permission is needed to enter it.

YERCAUD

Accommodation

Hotel Shevaroys — Hotel ₹
📞 04281-222288, 222383; www.hotelshevaroys.com; Hospital Rd; villas from ₹4200–5200, d from ₹1100–2800; 🅿 Centrally located, with landscaped gardens, a children's playground, bar and three restaurants, the hotel is the most convenient place to stay in Yercaud. Rooms are spacious and well-kept, affording guests their privacy. However, the food is average and the service can be inconsistent.

The Grange Resort — Resort ₹
📞 04281-222180, 222181, 316055; www.grangeresort.com; Cockburn Rd, Five Rds; cottages from ₹2100–3200; 🅿 Set amidst 100 acres of coffee plantation, orange orchards and pepper vines, this resort boasts plush individual cottages and a restaurant that serves homely meals. There's a playground for children, and adults can explore the estate on foot or indulge in a bout of dirt-biking. Good place for a private holiday.

Greenberry Resort — Family Resort ₹
📞 04281-222180, 222181, 316055; www.greenberryresort.com; Pagoda Point Rd; d from ₹2250–3000; 🅿 A newer resort, Greenberry promises modern comforts far away from the bustle of the town. The rooms are large, with a private sit-out with views of the sky through a transparent ceiling. The cafe looks out over the forest. With its bright playground, the hotel is suited to families with kids.

Hotel Grand Palace — Spa Resort ₹₹
📞 04281-223481, 223486; www.grandpalaceyercaud.com; Kiliyur Falls Rd; rooms from ₹3700–6500; 🅿 With panoramic views, a pool and spa, Grand Palace promises a luxurious stay. Rooms are well equipped and some have verandas with hammocks, from which you can watch the sunset and the lights of Salem twinkling below.

GRT Nature Trails
Sky Rocca — Luxury Resort ₹₹
📞 04281-225100; www.grthotels.com; 20th Hairpin Bend, Salem-Yercaud Main Rd, Ondikadai; d from ₹5000–7000; 🅿 Sky Rocca offers luxurious rooms, and also hosts a series of adventure activities. The restaurant overlooks Salem town and serves well-cooked meals. The bar is open from 11am to 11pm, and the bakery's always good for a snack.

✓ Top Tip: Getting around

The easiest way to get around Yercaud is in a car or an auto. Local autos and taxis are available from the Town Circle. If you have the stamina for it, though, walking around Yercaud can be a real pleasure. One can often find isolated viewpoints and hidden forested areas just wandering the roads behind the town.

❤ *If You Like: Nature holidays*

If you prefer quieter holidays in more forested areas, consider this set of camps and hotels, situated just a short distance away from Yercaud town. Bookings can only be made through their website, and charges are levied per head rather than per bed, room or tent. (📞04281–226767, 9442146266; www.stayatyercaud.com.)

• **Heaven's Ledge** Set on a cliff, this campsite is for more adventurous folk. Offering forest treks, rough-terrain cycling, and three large communal tents for sleeping (but with clean, well-constructed toilets), this is definitely the most 'natural' of all stays in Yercaud. **Adults/children (below 12 years) ₹1906/953 (incl taxes)**

• **Plantation Camp** Only has dormitories on offer and accepts bookings exclusively for large groups of 15–30 people. Situated in the middle of a coffee plantation, its a great place for birdwatching. **Adults/children (below 12 years) ₹1317/659 (incl taxes)**

• **The Last Shola** In an effort to preserve the native habitat of Yercaud, this hotel provides isolated cottage-stays amongst one of the largest coffee plantations, 15km away from town, near the Woodlands Lake. **Adults/children (below 12 years) ₹2584/1292 (incl taxes)**

Lake Forest Heritage ₹₹
📞04281–223217, 9444028132; www.indecohotels.com; Ondikadai; d from ₹4000–15,000; P Perhaps the most sophisticated hotel in Yercaud, each room is unique and features antique furniture and fixtures. All the wood used is restored or recycled, a testament to the hotel's commitment to nature. The staff are indulgent and quite friendly.

🍴 Eating

Henrietta Indian/European ₹₹
📞04281–223217, 9444028132; Lake Forest Hotel, Ondikodai; 7am–10pm The restaurant at Lake Forest is perhaps the best in town when it comes to menu and service. Serving both Indian dishes and contemporary European cuisine, no efforts are spared in preparing meals. It is decorated with antique items providing old-world splendour in a modern setting.

Salem Heights Multi-Cuisine ₹₹₹
📞04281–225100; GRT Nature Trails, 20th Hairpin Bend, Salem-Yercaud Main Rd, Ondikadai; 7am–11pm Salem Heights prides itself on its excellent service (though one might take issue with the price). The menu includes Indian, Chinese and Continental dishes. Overlooking the valley, one has a clear view of the road leading down to Salem; after sunset, the lights from vehicles can be seen tracing this route in the dark.

Saravana Bhavan Elite — South Indian ₹
📞04272-22777; Manajkuttai Rd; 7am–10pm Serving delicious south Indian food, this self-service restaurant is close to the Town Circle, near the 'Big' Lake. In spite of its limited menu and seating, it's an ideal lunch home, though the staff can be a bit brusque at peak hours.

Eggetarian — Cafe ₹
Town Circle; 10am–8pm This cafe is great for snacks, serving burgers, sandwiches, rolls and even rice-based dishes, but of three (sometimes four) basic varieties: vegetarian, egg, chicken (and cheese). Along with soft drinks, Cafe Coffee Day coffees and teas are available.

Pear Tree Cafe — Cafe ₹
Small Lake Rd, opp Montfort School; ₹150–250; 8am–6pm Opposite the 'Small' Lake, next to Montfort School, the Pear Tree Cafe is a homely establishment offering sandwiches, pizzas, pasta, milkshakes, and assorted fried snacks. It's the perfect stop for a quick bite during the daytime in that part of Yercaud town. The cafe is shut after dark.

🍸 Nightlife

Salem Rocks — Lounge Bar
📞04281-225100; GRT Nature Trails, 20th Hairpin Bend, Salem-Yercaud Main Rd, Ondikadai; ₹500–800; 11am–11pm Salem Rocks at the Nature Trails Hotel is a split-level lounge bar that serves a range of liquor, both Indian and imported. Offering great views of the hills and the valley, it's a nice place to relax at any time of the day.

🛍 Shopping

Perfume Paradise — Perfumed Oils
📞04281-222346, 9443244055; www.perfumeparadise.in; Lady's Seat Rd The name of the shop is deceptive because its most popular items are not perfumes at all but rather natural oils, recommended for regular use for their fortifying properties, or as remedies for various ailments. Perfumes are available as well, sold in little vials. The shop has an extensive item list and also delivers products to out-of-town locations (as long as the postage is paid).

Sunny Brook Nursery
📞04281-223076, 9944449009; Town Circle Located opposite the 'Big' Lake, the Sunny Brook Nursery extends over quite a substantial area under white fibreglass. It houses a number of exotic flowers and plants, from button roses and epiphytes to palm trees and a few hybrids, all neatly labelled. The staff are pretty diligent and helpful. One has to pay a fee to take pictures.

HILL ESCAPES

Madikeri & Around

Why go?

Busy Madikeri (Mercara), the chief town and transport hub of Coorg (Kodagu), is spread out along a series of ridges. An imposing fort, Omkareshwara Temple, the royal tombs, lush coffee and spice estates, and stunning panoramas of verdant valleys from Raja's Seat, are ample reason to visit this old-world hill station surrounded by dense rainforests.

Highlights

- **Coffee Plantations:** Privately-owned estates set amidst lush rainforests.
- **Golden Temple:** Buddhist temple harbouring gorgeous statues of Buddha and Padmasambhava.
- **Nalnad Palace:** Former summer home of the Kodava rulers.

MADIKERI & AROUND 37

Trip Planner

Getting There 250km

🚗 5hr SH17

- **Route:** Use the excellent Bengaluru–Mysore Expressway (SH17) till you reach the Mysore Ring Rd. Turn right here, and then again at the Atal Behari Vajpayee Circle, for Hunsur and onward to Madikeri.

🚌 6hr

- Volvos, plying three times every day, depart from the Mysore Rd Satellite bus stand near the Gopalan Mall. The buses leave Bengaluru at 7am, 10am and 2pm, arriving in Madikeri at 1pm, 4pm and 8pm respectively. The tickets cost ₹450.

Top Forests around Madikeri
Bottom A coffee bush

❶ *Quick Facts*

BEST TIME TO VISIT

J F M A M J J A S **O N D**

GREAT FOR

Spa

REST STOP Indradhanush Complex near Maddur, for toilet break and meals; Cafe Coorg on Hunsur Bypass.

Boundless Green

Highlights
1. Raja's Seat
2. Madikeri Fort & Palace
3. Omkareshwar Temple
4. Abbi Falls
5. Royal Tombs
6. Igguthappa Temple
7. Nalnad Palace
8. Golden Temple
9. Dubare Elephant Camp

Madikeri, the administrative headquarters of Coorg district, lies in the Western Ghats in southwestern Karnataka. Once the seat of the Kodava rulers, and named after Mudduraja, its many attractions, hidden amidst modern-day expansion, are ample testimony to an imperial past.

This hill station has pleasant weather all year round (only interrupted by heavy monsoon downpours from July to September). Consequently, the town, and its surrounds, have been bestowed with a rich canopy of teak forests, and acres of coffee and spice plantations.

You can pack much into your trip to Madikeri. A good plan is to stay at one of the many cosy homestays, which are growing in number. From here, visit the town and the scattered sights around it. Whether it's the Abbi Falls, the Buddhist settlement at Bylakuppe, the Igguthappa Temple in Kakkabe, or the elephant camp at Dubare, you are never more than 1½ hours away from any attraction, at any point.

Omkareshwar Temple, dedicated to Lord Shiva

Snapshot: Talakaveri

Located 50km from Madikeri, on the Brahmagiri Hill near Bhagamandala, Talakaveri is the origin of the Kaveri, southern India's most sacred river. While there is no visible source of water, a perennial spring is said to swell the water in the holy tank at the temple here, before emerging as the river some distance away.

Come mid-October, on the day of Tulasankramana, thousands of pilgrims converge to witness the gush of water from the spring. Talakaveri is a longish, yet doable, day-trip from Madikeri. Combine your visit with a walk or drive up to the Brahmagiri peak, 8km away, for awesome vistas of the Western Ghats.

❶ RAJA'S SEAT

A well-maintained garden used by the Kodava rulers, it offers stunning views of the Coorg Valley below. Visit in the evening to see the sun descend behind rolling hills; after sunset, the musical fountains are switched on. Easy to find, Raja's Seat is located at the western end of Madikeri.

₹10; fountain show 7pm Mon–Fri, 6.45pm and 7.30pm Sat, Sun and festivals

❷ MADIKERI FORT & PALACE

The original mud fort here was replaced by the present one built by Tipu Sultan. The stone ramparts enclose the palace of the Kodagu rulers, which now houses the offices of the deputy commissioner. Within the sprawling complex is a former church doubling as a museum and a temple. Two large elephant statues stand alongside the double-storied colonial palace. Though the fort and palace aren't as impressive as they sound, a visit is a good way to kill time.

Museum 10am–5pm; photography not allowed

❸ OMKARESHWAR TEMPLE

This temple was built by King Lingarajendra in 1820, as penance for killing a brahmin. It is dedicated to Lord Shiva (the shivlinga was reportedly brought from Kashi). Located in the heart of Madikeri, the complex encloses a large water tank across from the steps that lead to the main shrine.

6.30am–12pm, 5pm–8pm; photography not allowed

❹ ABBI FALLS

An 8km drive beyond Madikeri, through cardamom and coffee plantations, will bring you to a little short of the falls. A brief walk down a paved path from here takes you to a hanging bridge opposite the wide cascade of water. Watch out for teeming crowds; it is preferable to visit in the mornings and afternoons. Swimming is dangerous and best avoided, and the place is infested by leeches during monsoon.

❺ ROYAL TOMBS

Also called Gadduge, these early 19th-century mausoleums of the Kodava rulers are located just short of the Abbi Falls. Built in the Indo-Saracenic style, the domes and minarets of these structures tower over the town of Madikeri. The caretaker lives just outside the premises, and may be requested to show you around.

9am–5pm

❻ IGGUTHAPPA TEMPLE

Dedicated to the main deity of the Kodavas, this temple, the warrior race's holiest shrine, is located in Kakkabe, a small village about 40km from Madikeri (said to be southern Asia's largest producer of forest honey). Igguthappa Temple, another name for Lord Subramanya, is also considered to be the rain god. Every March, during the Kaliyarchi festival, his idol is taken around in a procession before being reinstalled in the shrine.

✆8272238400; 5.30am–12.30pm, 6.30pm–7pm; Kakkabe

> ### ✓ Top Tip: Rain alert
>
> If you're planning on visiting Madikeri during its stunning monsoon, be well-equipped; for it doesn't just rain here, it pours. Light and quick-dry raingear should include hooded jackets and pants, hiking boots (ankle high, if not higher) and plenty of socks. You can also throw into your daypack an all-encompassing poncho for those emergencies.

❼ NALNAD PALACE

This former hunting lodge and summer home of the Kodava kings is also in Kakkabe, at the base of Tadiyandamol, Coorg's highest peak. The low-slung double-storey structure, built in 1792, is embellished with intricate wooden friezes and frescoes,

MADIKERI & AROUND

while a pavilion crowned by Nandi adorns the garden.

Nearing the palace, do not turn left into the gate at the Karnataka Tourism sign; for the main access, go further to the fork then turn left into the clearing in front of the government primary school. A caretaker will let you into the palace for free.

9am–5pm; near Palace Estate, Kakkabe

❽ GOLDEN TEMPLE

This Buddhist temple is located in Bylakuppe, the largest Tibetan settlement in southern India, some 30-odd km from Madikeri. It gets its name from the three magnificent gilded statues of the Buddha, Padmasambhava and Amitayus in the cavernous prayer hall. Nearby, two monasteries, Namdroling and Tashilunpo, stand cheek-by-jowl with Sera, an educational monastic institution where thousands of monks and nuns receive instruction.

To reach the Golden Temple, take a left at Kushalnagar on the Mysore-Madikeri Highway; from here, it's roughly 10km.

7am–8pm

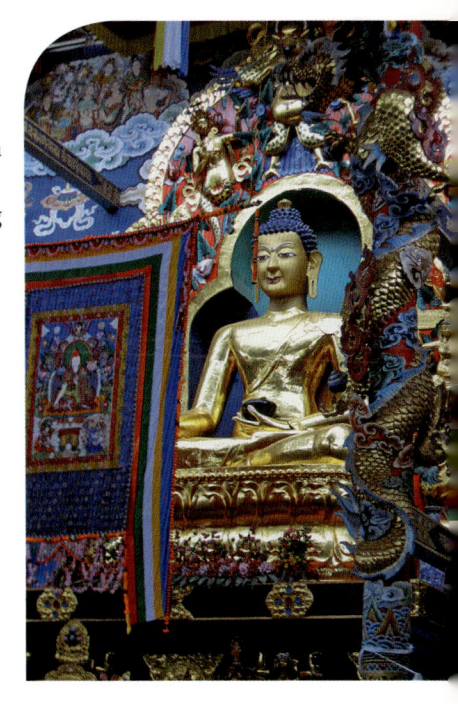

The stunning Buddhist shrine in Bylakuppe

❾ DUBARE ELEPHANT CAMP

This unique facility, managed by Jungle Lodges and Resorts, is located on an island in the Kaveri River. Providing visitors with an intimate interface, trained naturalists help you observe, learn and participate in numerous elephant-centric activities. A short boat ride takes you across to the camp, where you can watch the pachyderms being bathed, groomed and fed; this is followed by an elephant ride. Extremely touristy, it will earn you brownie points with the kids.

8.30am–12pm; ₹300 onwards (depending on choice of activities); 14km from Kushalnagar, 40km from Madikeri

🛏 Accommodation

Sayuri   **Heritage Homestay** ₹
☏ 8272225107, 9448190990;
Munishwera Temple Rd; d ₹2000; P
This 100-year-old Kodava house may well be that proverbial home away from home. Quaint, comfortable and lived-in, the resident help (speaking only the local language) understands and takes care of your every need. Their traditional breakfast (included in the tariff) of rice-flour roti and curried beans is highly recommended.

Palace Estate   **Plantation Homestay** ₹
☏ 8272238446, 9880447702; www.palaceestate.co.in; Kakkabe; d ₹2000–2500 (all meals extra); P Overlooking Nalnad Palace, this plantation home has astonishing views of densely forested mountains. Set at the base of Tadiyandamol peak, the 50-acre coffee and spice estate is a solitude seeker's haven. The ride to Palace Estate is uncomfortable in stretches but the destination makes the journey worth your while.

Gowri Nivas   **Homestay** ₹₹
☏ 9448493833, 9448193822; www.gowrinivas.com; New Extension; d ₹3800, children under 12 years/above 12 years ₹500/1000; ❄ P
This tastefully done up modern Kodava house set in a lush garden, offers an independent two-room cottage, and one room in the main family unit. Hospitable and helpful, the owners are mostly at hand to provide insightful information about all things Coorgi. They also serve delicious home-cooked meals. To get here, ask for the New Extension auto-rickshaw stand.

Jade Hills   **Homestay** ₹₹
☏ 9916618829; Kaloor Rd, Galibeedu village; d ₹3000; P Located on a hilltop, this privately owned cottage of recent vintage is accessed through verdant forest slopes. The gazebo out front reveals the most stunning views of the valley beyond. Quiet, clean and comfortable.

Berry Lane   **Plantation Homestay** ₹₹
☏ 8274252978, 9448721460, 9343631236; Ontiangadi Rd, Ammathi; d ₹2500–3500; ❄ P If relaxing in wooded coffee and spice-rich environs is foremost on your mind, head for this private estate. Located in the plantation-rich region south of the Kaveri River, its crowning glory is a

| An elegant room at the
| Gowri Nivas

MADIKERI & AROUND

large veranda that opens onto a dense verdure of pepper-vines, papayas and plantains. A walk around the plantation is recommended.

Eating

Pause, The Unwind Café ₹
☏9343076006, 9341380456; Shop No. 4, Kodava Samaj Building, Main Rd; 11am–8pm On offer here is a limited-item menu, yet enough to appease hunger on the go. Popular for coffee, and cakes on order, the quick bites here are tasty too. In meals, the home-style chicken biryani is delicious (and the helping hearty).

Neel Sagar Vegetarian ₹
☏8272220477, 9141226975; Kodava Samaj Building, near Police Station; 7am–10pm A pure vegetarian restaurant, Neel Sagar offers north and south Indian meals and snacks, and also Jain food. It's spacious, with utilitarian interiors, and can get rather noisy. But if you're looking for well-prepared vegetarian fare, look no further. Not, however, for those seeking a leisurely experience.

Coorg Cuisinette Coorgi ₹₹
☏9448127358, 9449699864, 9480208933; Yelakki Krupa Building, opp Head Post Office, Main Rd; 12.30pm–4.30pm, 7.30pm–9.30pm Drop by for traditional Kodava dishes (mainly non-vegetarian) if you are not in a rush; it takes 20–30 minutes for your meal to arrive. Sip on their fresh

> ### Value for Money: Food blessed by gods
>
> If you find yourself at the Igguthappa Temple in the forenoon, with time to spare, wait around for the clock to strike one, when a simple yet scrumptious lunch is offered free of cost to visitors daily.

passion-fruit juice with honey, a great way to bide your time. Located on the first floor, it is easily missed; keep a sharp lookout.

Raintree Multi-Cuisine ₹₹
☏8272220301; www.raintree.in; 13/14 Pension Lane, behind Town Hall; 11am–3pm, 6pm–10.30pm Mon–Thurs, 11am–11pm Fri–Sun A multi-cuisine fine-dining restaurant, Raintree occupies the many spaces of a former house. Their exhaustive menu features generous helpings of delicious, well-prepared seafood, tandoori, Mughlai and Coorgi cuisine. Try the ghee roast items, especially the prawns.

Shopping

A browse around the old market in the heart of Madikeri will yield almost anything produced in Coorg. Coffee, honey, cardamom, pepper, cinnamon, cloves, vanilla, ginger, nutmeg, cashews, areca nut, are all up for grabs. Coming in packets of different sizes, the prices are comparable.

Adventure in Coorg

Why go?

Coorg has earned itself the rightful title of 'adventure capital of Karnataka'. Located on the eastern edge of the Western Ghats, it has a diverse topography, with mountains, coffee plantations, thick forests, paddy fields and rivers. These form a suitable backdrop to a number of activities like rafting, kayaking, canoeing, trekking, camping and microlight flying. Club these with your explorations of Coorg for an adventure-packed break.

Highlights

- **Rafting in Barapole:** Don't stay indoors for the monsoons; tumble down the Barapole River in a raft instead.
- **Microlight flying:** Experience verdant Coorg from a thrilling height in an open aircraft.
- **Scaling the peaks:** Brave the misty peaks of Brahmagiri and Tadiandamol.

ADVENTURE IN COORG

Trip Planner

Getting There

4hr 30min to 7hr SH17

- **Route:** From Bengaluru, the route up to Hunsur, on the SH17, is common; the 187km can be covered in 3½ hr. After Hunsur, choose the diversion for Kakkabe, Kushalnagar or Kutta. For **Kutta** (55km), take the Nagarhole Rd. Since this is a forest road, it is closed between 6pm and 6am. For **Kushalnagar**, take a right after Hunsur, crossing Piriyapatna and Bylakuppe to reach Kushalnagar (44km). **Kakkabe** lies across Coorg and so takes a little more time (86km, 2½hr); take the Ponnampet route, turning left on the Virajpet-Talakaveri Rd. From here, Kakkabe is 20km. For **Madikeri**, come up to Kushalnagar and then head up another 30km to touch the centre of Coorg.

6hr to 8hr

- KSRTC buses from Bengaluru head mostly till Madikeri. A few run up to Kushalnagar, or other points closest to Kakkabe (Baghamandala, Virajpet). For Kutta, it is best to drive down.

Top Coorg is all about dense greenery
Bottom Microlight flying

Quick Facts

BEST TIME TO VISIT

J F M A M J J A S O N D

GREAT FOR

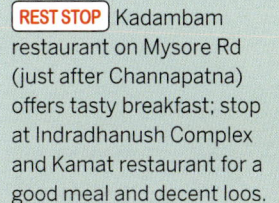

REST STOP Kadambam restaurant on Mysore Rd (just after Channapatna) offers tasty breakfast; stop at Indradhanush Complex and Kamat restaurant for a good meal and decent loos.

Tap Your Adrenaline

Highlights
1. **Rafting (off Kutta)**
2. **Microlight Flying (off Kutta/Gonikoppa)**
3. **Brahmagiri Trek (off Kutta)**
4. **Kayaking & Canoeing (off Kakkabe)**
5. **Tadiandamol Trek (off Kakkabe)**
6. **Quad Biking & More (off Kakkabe)**
7. **Camping & Kayaking by the Harangi (off Kushalnagar)**
8. **Hike to Manangeri (off Madikeri)**

Spread over 4100 sq km, the whole of Coorg is impossible to cover in a short duration. Base yourself at any one of the regional hubs listed below for your choice of activity:

Kutta: Serves well as base camp if you want to climb the Brahmagiri Peak (p192), tumble down the white waters of the Upper Barapole River in a raft, or experience flying in a microlight. It is also closest to Bengaluru, if you are taking the Nagarhole route.

Kakkabe: Tadiandamol, the highest peak in Coorg, is just next door here. You can also indulge in kayaking or canoeing on the Kakkabe River, or book yourself for half-day adventure activities like quad biking and the jungle gym with Now or Neverland (p48).

Kushalnagar: Pitch tents by the Harangi Dam and go kayaking in the still waters of the reservoir. You can also climb the Kotta Betta (the third-highest peak in Coorg).

Madikeri: Most central to all the regions; stay here for a total experience of Coorg. Explore sightseeing options around town (p36), or indulge in your chosen adventure activity.

1 RAFTING (OFF KUTTA)
Experience the monsoon by getting soaked in the gushing waters of the Upper Barapole (Kithu-Kakkatu River), and manoeuvre the rapids (1–4 class) with Coorg Whitewater Rafting. Their base camp is located in the Ponya Devarakad Estate. The camp is well organised, with hot showers, a bonfire, and a quiet stretch where guests are oriented and trained before setting out. Arrive here in T-shirt, shorts and floaters to get briefed and to sign the indemnity bond,

before you start. Enjoy the 2.8km stretch, where you bounce across rapids of varying difficulty; for nervous first-timers, be assured that you are guided by experts, and a safety kayak is always close by for rescue.

☏9481883745; www.coorgwhitewaterrafting.com; Ponya Estate (off T Shettigeri); ₹1200 per head (3–4 hours, including jeep pick-up, gear, tea, use of base camp); photography with own camera free (additional ₹100 for professional photographs and video); 9am, 11am, 2pm & 4pm; weight limit 120 kg; children above 14 years only

❷ MICROLIGHT FLYING (OFF KUTTA/GONIKOPPA)

Experience a 'wind in your face' adventure with Muthanna of Coorg Sky Adventures, in a two-seater open plane which takes you to a height of 3500 feet. This activity is extremely sensitive to the weather and time of day. Before experiencing the adrenaline rush of flying in a microlight, you have to sign an indemnity form – and arrive at 7.30am or 3.30pm sharp, in sturdy footwear, to cross the paddy-field runway; these are the only two time slots available owing to the wind conditions. The most suitable weather for flying is between November and May. Use your discretion if you are a heart patient or have an altitude-related disorder.

☏9448954384; www.coorgskyadventures.com; Ponnampet (off Gonikoppa); ₹2250 per head (10min), ₹5000 per head (30min, 50 km), ₹8000 per head (60mins, 100 km); weight limit 90kg; children above 7 years only

Rafting in Upper Barapole

❸ BRAHMAGIRI TREK (OFF KUTTA)

The forested Brahmagiri range is a challenging trek that varies from moderate to difficult and is suited for the physically fit. The trek involves an overnight stay and offers an excellent opportunity to spot wild animals and delight in Coorg's impressive biodiversity (p192).

❹ KAYAKING & CANOEING (OFF KAKKABE)

Enjoy the more tranquil side of the Kaveri River with Jungle Mount Adventures at their seven-acre campsite, flanked by paddy fields. Experience, with the aid of instructors, a ride on a kayak (3-man) or a canoe (2-man) on this 20ft-deep stretch of the river at the edge of the camp. The facility offers stay in basic camp rooms, food, gear and a bonfire at the end of the day. Ideal for a day trip. Only guests with bookings allowed.
☎ 9845831675; www.junglemountadventures.com; Kakkabe village, Yavakapady Post; d incl full board ₹3200

❺ TADIANDAMOL TREK (OFF KAKKABE)

The highest peak in Coorg offers a short but demanding trek of 5km. It can be covered in a day, and is suitable for trekkers from of intermediate level, although physically fit beginners may take a shot at it too (see p196 for details).

> Manangeri is an easy trek for families

❻ QUAD BIKING & MORE (OFF KAKKABE)

Indo-British company Now or Neverland presents a host of adventure activities, including quad biking, jungle gym, paintball and mountain biking. The most exciting of these is to take a 250cc quad bike off road through forests and slushy tracks on a 1km circuit. Supervised by instructors and with top-notch safety equipment, this makes for a safe family outing. Soar above the forest canopy on ropes, zip lines and strong wires for a tree-top aerial assault on an obstacle course speckled with walkways, bridges and tunnels.
☎ 08274-323023; www.noworneverland.com

ADVENTURE IN COORG

❼ CAMPING & KAYAKING BY THE HARANGI (OFF KUSHALNAGAR)

Wake up to a misty stretch of water and the sound of the forest, if you camp in the backwaters of the Harangi Dam. An extension of Eco Habitat Homestay (14km from this spot), this three-acre personal camping site is a massive hit with outdoor enthusiasts. A coffee estate and bamboo stands skirt the property.

> ✓ *Top Tip: Roads*
>
> Be conservative about covering distances in Coorg. Roads from one location to another can be quite bumpy and do not, in any case, match the regular time-distance ratio. A small stretch of 20km could well take an hour given the road conditions.

Few places in Coorg allow camping and this one definitely tops the list with its beautiful view of the backwaters. Kayaking and canoeing are also available here (under supervision). Though day trips can be organised, it's recommended that you take in the whole experience by starting in the afternoon from Eco Habitat, indulging in a bit of water sport, and camping by the water. There is a small utility area with a basic loo close to the camping spot. Packed food, a barbecue and wood for a bonfire can be made available at an additional cost.

📞9448127245; www.ecohabitat.in; Narkur village; ₹500 per tent (with sleeping mats and air pillows – carry your own sleeping bag; deposit of ₹2500 refundable); ₹1500 for group of 4 for barbeque; ₹100–₹300 for full night bonfire; ₹500 for watchman; ₹100 for phone hire (BSNL); ₹250 kayaking/canoeing, per head (weight limit 200 kg, children above 5 only)

❽ HIKE TO MANANGERI (OFF MADIKERI)

Take the Madikeri–Mangalore Road, 10km off the toll junction, to the small village of Manangeri. Enjoy an exhilarating four-wheel drive (5km) up the hill on the right (just by a small tea shop) and then hike up to the Manangeri ridge. The hike is only 2km and is easy for children as well. The view from the ridge is gorgeous. This hidden trail is not on the tourist map but is one of the most beautiful in Coorg. Hire a jeep from Madikeri (₹1000 one way); ask the driver to wait a couple of hours so you can be dropped back. If you have time, you can hike up the entire 7km.

Accommodation

STAY OFF KUTTA

The Jade — Heritage Homestay ₹
☎ 8274244396; www.thejadecoorg.com; Manchalli, Kutta; d incl full board ₹2700 (lunch not included) Experience an exclusive stay in this old Coorgi-style house with low wooden doors, after crossing a bright green patch of paddy fields. The Brahmagiri Peak base camp is just 2km away, making The Jade a convenient choice for trekkers.

Narikadi — Homestay ₹
☎ 9972232400; www.narikadihomestay.com; Narikadi Estate, Kutta; d incl full board ₹2600 (old rooms), ₹3000 (new rooms) Choose between the newly-built four rooms overlooking the coffee-drying yard, or the two snug rooms, over 100 years old (and still kept intact), attached to the house. The splendid view of paddy fields here will keep you enthralled.

Culmaney — Homestay ₹₹
☎ 9448469659; Faith Cinchona Estate, Kutta; d incl full board from ₹4000 Stay at Prabhu and Maya's estate house for a complete orientation on Coorgi history and culture. You won't be leaving the dining table in a hurry (after having finished your meal), for conversations here lead from one topic to another. Culmaney's hosts truly represent Coorgi hospitality, and most guests leave as friends of the couple.

Bison Manor — Nature Retreat ₹₹
☎ 8105118877; www.bisonmanor.com; New Grand Estate, Kutta; d incl full board ₹3900 You'll enjoy spending time at Bison Manor, run by Hugh and Vivian. The ambiance of this old Coorgi home has been kept intact by preserving the paintings of the original owner. The nine spacious rooms, aesthetically done up in warm hues, overlook the Brahmagiri range (the view from the upper-floor rooms is the best). Nature trails within the estate, friendly dogs on the property and a serene backdrop make Bison Manor a wonderful choice.

Machaan — Resort ₹₹
☎ 9900437002; www.machaan.com; Churikad, K Bagada village, Kutta; d incl full board ₹3500 Tucked away on a coffee plantation, Machaan is one of the few luxury options to stay in Kutta. Comfortable wooden cottages, enthusiastic staff and in-house activities for guests make this a good choice for families.

STAY OFF KAKKABE – SEE TADIANDAMOL (P201)

STAY OFF KUSHALNAGAR

Bel Home — Plantation Stay ₹₹
☎ 9880908135; www.belhome.co.in; Bellarimotte Estate, Madapura Post; d incl full board ₹4200 The

breezy sit-out areas of this 1928 cottage, access to the faraway coffee plantation crossing the Madapura River and proximity to Kotta Betta (the third-highest peak in Coorg) make Bel Home a very attractive choice. Get a real taste of Coorg here, with a 'bean to cup' coffee experience, local food and a spot of birdwatching. Families seeking less strenuous adventure activities, like an easy hike to Kotta Betta or a picnic by the placid stream (Madapura) close to the property, should stay here.

Eco Habitat   Homestay ₹₹
☏9448127245; www.ecohabitat.in; Chikbettagere village, Guddehosur Post, Kushalnagar; d incl full board ₹5000 (lunch and dinner ₹250 per meal per head) Eco Habitat has two exclusive cottages, with personal 'splash' pools attached. Immaculately furnished, the cottages are spacious enough for extra beds. Stay here for Chethana's delicious lemon-grass tea and food (each meal is better than the previous one) along with Som's engaging penchant for taking guests to unexplored parts of Coorg. Eco Habitat offers privacy as well as the hosts' fantastic company.

STAY OFF MADIKERI
Victorian Verandaz   Homestay ₹
☏9448059850; www.livingcoorg.com; Modur Estate, Kadagadal Post; d incl breakfast ₹2500 The two rooms and a dining area here are neatly kept and personal – perfect for a family unit. This homestay offers a view of the valley below, a jeep drive through the thick coffee plantation and delicious homely food. It is just off Madikeri, and conveniently central for reaching other parts of Coorg for adventure activities.

Silver Brooks   Homestay ₹₹
☏8272200107; www. silverbrookestate.com ; Kadagadal village; d incl breakfast from ₹3300 The wide verandah, spacious rooms, handpicked collection of wooden furniture and small library of Silver Brooks make it a delight to stay in. A small winding road leads to this pleasant homestay with an alluring garden and wide, sunny sit-outs. The stone pillar bases are designed as board games – they're a hit with children.

See P36 for more Madikeri accommodation

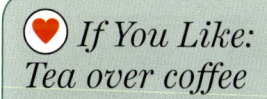

> ### ♥ *If You Like:*
> ### *Tea over coffee*
>
> It's no blasphemy to want a hot cup of tea in the land of coffee! KT Tea in Hotel Green Land, at the toll junction in Madikeri, should not be missed.
> **☏08278–224820; Near IB, Mangalore Rd; ₹15 per glass**

Ooty

Why go?

Immortalised by Bollywood, Ooty's (Udhagamandalam) reputation as 'Queen of the Hills' is hard to beat, despite the tourists milling around. With many 'tick off the list' things to do, it's an engaging destination with the toy train, Botanical Gardens, Boat House, and more. Stay on the outer fringes to get a taste of old-world charm, still lingering in refurbished colonial bungalows.

Highlights

- **Nilgiri Toy Train:** World Heritage Site.
- **Botanical Gardens:** One of the best of its kind in the country.
- **Tea Gardens and Museum:** All you ever wanted to know about tea.
- **Colonial bungalows:** Relive the Raj by staying in one.

Trip Planner

Getting There 265km

🚗 6hr SH17, NH181

- **Route:** Keep to the Mysore Highway (SH17) all the way till Mysore city. After this, take the NH181 on to Nanjangud, Gundlupet, Bandipur and Masinagudi till you hit Ooty.

🚌 7hr 30min

- Multiple KSRTC buses start from Kempegowda bus stand in Bengaluru. The forest part of the highway (Bandipur) is closed between 9pm and 5am. However, you can opt for the 10.15pm or 10.45pm bus (deluxe and luxury, ₹349 onwards) if you want a non-stop, overnight ride. These buses have special permission to travel at night.

Top The hill-scape of Ooty
Bottom Fresh blooms at the Botanical Gardens

❶ Quick Facts

BEST TIME TO VISIT

J F M A M J J A S **O N D**

GREAT FOR

Spa · 🔒 · 🚶 · ♥ · 👪

REST STOP For good food and reasonably clean loos, Mysore Rd has Kadambam (just after Channapatna), and later Indradhanush Complex and Kamat.

Sullivan's Muse

Highlights
1. **Doddabetta Peak**
2. **Tea Factory & Museum**
3. **Botanical Gardens**
4. **Boat House**
5. **Thread Garden**
6. **Rose Garden**
7. **St Stephen's Church**
8. **The Nilgiri Mountain Railway (Toy Train)**
9. **Tribal Research Centre Museum**

Tea plantation-clad hills, strewn with bright Lego-like houses, are your first glimpse of Ooty. Interspersed with lush patches of fern and eucalyptus, the hills immediately put you in a good mood after leaving behind the heat of the plains.

John Sullivan, Collector of Coimbatore, set foot in Wotokymund (Ootacamund) in 1821 and chose it as the perfect sanatorium for English soldiers. Thus began the shaping of this nondescript village into a buzzing hill station. Till date, Sullivan's discovery is dotted with English reminiscences.

Though the destination itself has a repertoire of travel clichés, which ensures a typical hill-station experience, it cannot be missed. Enjoy simple pleasures like the sight of fresh carrots and turnips temptingly lining the roads, and the whimsical weather, specially nearing the monsoons. This place is a delight for shutterbugs but the innocent bystander will have to duck quite a bit to stay out of other people's pictures.

❶ DODDABETTA PEAK
The peaceful 9km stretch of fern and eucalyptus-lined bumpy road off Ooty, ends in a bevy of snapping tourists making a beeline for the lone telescope, worn out children's swings and snack food joints. The reasonably well-kept Doddabetta Peak itself offers a great view of the Hecuba, Kattadadu and the Kulkudi summits. A short stop is enough to stay away from a chartered holiday experience. An unfrequented trek with complex permissions is possible from the city.
₹5; 8am–5pm

❷ TEA FACTORY & MUSEUM

A commendable educational effort which caters to a variety of travellers – one cannot really brag about the museum or the presentation of the loud speaker-enabled guide – but the limited information on tea brewing is enough for mass consumption. There is a channelled walk through the factory that ends in a small sampling of tea. There is also a counter to buy spices and chocolates, as well as, of course, varieties of Nilgiri tea.

Doddabetta Rd, Ooty; children/adults ₹2/5; camera ₹10; 9am–6pm

❸ BOTANICAL GARDENS

Established in 1847, the Botanical Gardens of Ooty are less appreciated for the horticultural experience and more for a pleasing backdrop for photo enthusiasts. One cannot help join the frenzy with temptingly beautiful varieties of flowers and the large cacti in the glasshouse. Its vast expanse even allows one to find a lone bench to absorb all the cheer around. The crumbling plants at the sales counter are a sad contrast to the lush gardens outside.

Government Botanical Garden; children/adults ₹10/20; camera/video ₹30/75; 7am–6.30pm

Botanical Gardens, repository of the Nilgiris' fauna

Take a joyride in the iconic Toy Train

❹ BOAT HOUSE
This is a single stop for a full day of entertainment if you have an appetite for boating, horse riding and carousels. Especially recommended if you are travelling with children, for whom the cotton candy stands, fruit vendors, food court, mini train and the rest of the activities can be engaging. Given the amount of tourists that visit the Boat House, it has been well maintained.
₹5; camera/video ₹10/100; boating ₹320 onwards; horse riding ₹50 onwards; 8am–6pm

❺ THREAD GARDEN
The Thread Garden is a laudable effort to replicate flower varieties in thread. The brainchild of Antony Joseph, six crore metres of thread have been put to use by 50 ladies over 12 years, to create this mind-boggling array of 150 varieties of flowers. However, the dimly-lit presentation in a shed-like enclosure tends to dampen your interest a bit.
☎ 0423 2445145; www.threadgarden.com; opp Boat House; children/adults ₹10/15; camera ₹30; 8am–6pm

❻ ROSE GARDEN
Paler in comparison to the grand Botanical Garden, this too winds up as a photography destination for most people. There are over 1000 varieties of roses, out of which a green one is bound to catch your attention.
Ooty Centenary Rose Garden; children/adults ₹10/15; camera/video ₹30/75; 7am–6.30pm

❼ ST STEPHEN'S CHURCH
Established in the 19th century, this historic landmark is one of the oldest churches in the region and stands testament

to the colonial past of the city. Walk around to the back of the church to see the cemetery, and trace the graves of John Sullivan's wife and daughter.
9.30am–4.30pm

❽ THE NILGIRI MOUNTAIN RAILWAY (TOY TRAIN)
The Unesco-listed World Heritage Site is worth every jostle once you have squirmed your way into a comfortable position along with all the other tourists. Started in 1908, the train still runs partially on steam locomotive engines (on the Coonoor–Mettupalayam stretch), and chugs its way from Ooty to Mettupalayam in 3½ hours. It twists and turns over 250 bridges, through 16 tunnels and deep gorges, across forests and tea plantations. Book ahead to ensure a ride, though having a ticket is no guarantee of a great seat.
www.irctc.co.in; first class/second seater ₹155/23; 2pm–5.35pm

❾ TRIBAL RESEARCH CENTRE MUSEUM
Though not extensive, the Tribal Research Centre Museum does give you an idea about the history and current life of the tribes of the Nilgiris. Engross yourself in the decent collection of artefacts and items of daily use of the tribes before moving on to the rest of the displays at the museum, which may seem somewhat cheerless and unrelated.
M Palada; 10am–5pm; Mon–Fri

✓ *Top Tip: How to buy tea*

Claims of 'best', 'most fragrant' and 'international quality' tea leaves at most shops in the city can be slightly perplexing, if you're looking to buy some. With estates moving towards branding their own product, the advertising hullaballoo is even stronger. Here are a few tips on making a reasonable decision about which kind of tea to buy. Depending on taste, there are multiple flavours available. Besides that, you should be checking for freshness in the smell (not musty), uniformity in colour, and also check that no colour additives are present. Rub a little between your fingers; if it comes onto your skin immediately, then the tea is sure to be adulterated. Some tried and tested brands include Tranquilitea (only online purchase), Chamraj and Glendale. Also see p317 for more tips.

Accommodation

I-India   Heritage Cottage ₹
0423-2448959; www.iindiaecolodge.in; 273 Grand Duff Rd, Valley View; d incl full board from ₹2400-3000 This newly furbished 100-year-old cottage, away from the city, has a comforting hill station feel about it. The establishment is great value for money with clean 'no frills' rooms, a cheerful common area with wide French windows, and a fantastic view of the valley. Run by a small team, the personalised attention is a welcome change.

Lymond House   Homestay ₹₹
0423-2223377; www.serendipityo.com; 77 Sylks Rd; d incl full board from ₹4094-4747 The British style cottage (1855) still retains a colonial air in its high ceilings, fireplaces, lush garden and a small driveway. Sit out in the gazebo to enjoy the Ooty weather or meet other travellers by the bonfire in the evenings. A handwritten note on laundry details in your room brings a smile to your face. There's also an in-house restaurant.

Tranquilitea   Heritage Bungalow ₹₹
9443841572; www.tranquilitea.in; The Bungalow in Ooty, The Nilgiris, Ootacamund; d incl full board from ₹4000-7500 Proximity to town and a view of the race tracks are the best things about this cosy three-room refurbished colonial bungalow. You can be sure to have your privacy intact as no other room is let out even if you book only one room. Ideal for a group.

King's Cliff   Heritage Cottage ₹₹
9487000111; www.kingscliff-ooty.com; Havelock Rd, Ooty; d incl full board from ₹3568-5846 Slide back in time at this 1920s 'Shakespearean' themed cottage, complete with elaborate tapestry, fireplaces and wooden floors. It's

> I-India is perfect for those on a shoestring budget

delightful to see that the management has painstakingly tried to match the upholstery from an old photograph. Dig into the baked goodies and be pampered by the well-trained and attentive staff.

Sherlock Themed Cottage ₹₹
☏9487000111; www.littlearth.in/sherlock; The Nilgiris, Ootacamund; d incl full board from ₹2500–5846
The Sherlock Holmes-themed cottage sits tucked on a hill at the far end of Ooty. Apart from the great view, a sprawling garden and frequent visitors like deer and bison, the century-old cottage gives you a chance to indulge in Holmes-related pictures, books, and little nooks and corners; the dining room is named after Irene Adler.

Red Hills
Nature Resort Heritage Cottage ₹₹₹
☏0423-2595755; The Nilgiris, Ootacamund; r incl full board from ₹7000 Visit Red Hills for a spectacular view of the Avalanche and Emerald lakes from your room. The 1875 property is on the outskirts of Ooty and attracts only those who want to stay away from the city din. The long drive up is worth your while for the vantage location, organic garden, Moby the dog and personalised treks.

Destiny Heritage Cottage ₹₹₹
☏9487000111; www.littlearth.in/sherlock; The Nilgiris, Ootacamund; d incl full board from ₹5358–7886

The 2km bone-rattling truck ride on a forest road ends in a 100-acre farm geared up to ensure you rough it out in luxury. A spa overlooking the hills, horse-riding, bonfires, fishing, zip-lining and other adventure sports ensure an activity-centric holiday. The western farm theme spills over into the names of rooms, creatively christened 'Billy the Kid', 'Butch Cassidy', etc.

Eating
Earl's Secret at
Kings Cliff Multi-Cuisine ₹₹₹
☏9487000111; www.kingscliff-ooty.com; Havelock Rd; 12.30pm–2.45pm (buffet), 7.30pm–10pm (a la carte)
Large spreads of Thai and Continental food (recommended). The restaurant seats 85 in cosy pockets of the heritage bungalow, of which the sunny glasshouse is welcome on a cold, rainy day.

Lymond House Continental ₹₹₹
☏9843149490; www.serendipityo.com; Sylks Rd; 12.30pm–3pm, 7.30pm–10pm The blackboard menu lists the dishes of the day, while some retro favourites and the garden add to the setting for a long lunch. Great homemade desserts and personalised attention by Joe, the restaurant manager, completes an enjoyable experience. Prior booking is required.

Shinkows Chinese ₹₹
☏0423-2442811; 38/83 Commissioners Rd; 12pm–3.45pm, 6.30pm–9.45pm The apparent

nostalgia sweeps one in the 1954 restaurant, even if you are visiting for the very first time. Yellow checked table cloths, chatty waiters and the obvious familiarity of locals make an endearing backdrop. Old timers will tell you that No 5 (chicken and mushroom soup) and No 26 (pork and broccoli dish) is what keeps them coming back to Mr Pao Chun's famous establishment.

Nahar Restaurants   Multi-Cuisine ₹₹
0423-2442173; 52-A Charring Cross; 1.30pm-3.30pm, 7pm-8.30pm A set of restaurants right on the main Charring Cross, the speciality is vegetarian food. Expectedly, it is swarming with crowds in the tourist season. Visit the Sidewalk Cafe for Continental and Chandan for Indian and Chinese fare.

Hotel Blue Hills   Multi-Cuisine ₹₹
0423-2442034; Commercial Rd 1pm-10pm Though nondescript to look at, Hotel Blue Hills serves excellent non-vegetarian food like brain masala and various chicken delights. Good place to catch lunch if you are roaming around Commercial Street.

Shopping

Higginbothams   Books
0423-2442546; Oriental Building, opp Collector's Office; 9am-1pm, 2pm-6pm Visit the century-old building which houses Higginbothams bookshop, bursting with books on old wooden shelves. Fredrick Price's *Ootacamund: A History* is recommended reading for gripping tales of Ooty.

Chellaram   Tea
0423-2442229; New No 47, Commercial Rd; 9.30am-1.30pm, 3pm-7.30pm Buy the best quality Nilgiri tea from here. Apart from tea you can shop for herbs, spices and eucalyptus oil here. Also pick up the regular souvenirs from this age-old establishment.

King Star   Chocolates
0423-2450205; 54, Commercial Rd; 12pm-9pm Homemade chocolates are an essential part of the Ooty shopping landscape with plenty of shops selling a vast array. Pick up a mixed box from the oldest establishment in Ooty (1942), whose ownership, sadly, is now fragmented. The chocolates might taste just the same as in any other shop, but buying from this small, dingy shop is a romantic travel experience.

Modern Stores   Chocolates
0423-2447353; 144 Garden Rd; 9.30am-9pm The cleaner and glitzier Modern Stores up ahead on Garden Road has far surpassed King Star in its popularity to grab a bag of chocolates. This store too is over 50 years old (though it does not look like it).

Mohans   Ethnic Jewellery
☏ 0423–2442376; opp Collector's Office; 10am–1.30pm, 3pm–8pm

A distinct shopping establishment near St Stephen's Church, Mohan's has been around in the city since 1947. Though they claim to sell Toda jewellery, locals are confident that the tribe has stopped making their traditional ornaments, and these might be imitations. The shop is good for other bric-a-bracs which make for interesting souvenirs to take home.

🛈 Activities

This may well, unexpectedly, become a golfing break if you are thus inclined. Two golf courses in the Nilgiris allow non-members to play by paying a green fee.

The Wellington Gymkhana Club   Golf
☏ 0423–2230256; www.wellingtongymkhanaclub.com; Wellington, Barracks Post; 8pm–6.30pm; ₹400 for 18 holes

Established in 1873, the club is spread over 63 acres and has impressive facilities, including a Golf Pro gym and lockers. One must book in advance as weekends are packed with regulars. Note that only guests of members are allowed; you can ask homestay owners for admission.

The Ootacamund Gymkhana Club   Golf
☏ 0423–2442254; www.ootygolfclub.org; Ooty–Mysore Rd; 7am–10pm; ₹1100 for guests of members, for 18 holes

The Ooty Gymkhana has a sprawling 18-hole golf course. Non-members are allowed to play after paying a small fee. Book in advance to ensure a confirmed slot.

> Gorge on the delicious homemade chocolates available at Ooty

Coonoor

Why go?

Tranquil Coonoor, off the beaten tourist track, offers memorable experiences. This tea country is an olfactory paradise for lovers of the cup that cheers. For views of the Coimbatore plains, tea terraces and nearby mountains, choose from a number of superb vantage points around. The locomotive buff will surely enjoy a ride in the heritage Nilgiri Toy Train.

Highlights

- **Sim's Park:** Rejuvenate your senses with a brisk walk amidst nature.
- **Highfield Tea Estate:** Take a tour to savour the aroma and see how the leaf is processed.
- **Picnic at the Droog:** Take the easy trek upto Tipu Sultan's ruined fort.

COONOOR 63

Trip Planner

Getting There 285km

🚗 6hr 30min SH17, NH181

- **Route:** Stick to the Mysore Rd all the way till Mysore city. Then take the road leading to Nanjangud, Gundlupet, Bandipur and Masinagudi till you hit Ooty. From here, avoid the main town and get onto the Lovedale-Coimbatore-Ooty NH181 for about 25km till you reach Coonoor.

🚌 8hr

- Multiple KSRTC buses, starting from Kempegowda bus stand, go to Ooty. From here, you will have to change to a TNSTC (Tamil Nadu State Transport Corporation) bus, which are a dime a dozen, and ply regularly.

Top Misty hills are synonymous with Coonoor
Bottom Tea tips waiting to be plucked

ℹ️ Quick Facts

BEST TIME TO VISIT

J F M **A M J J A S** O N D

GREAT FOR

Spa 🍴 🔒 🥾 ❤️ 👥

REST STOP For good food and reasonably clean loos, Mysore Rd has Kadambam (just after Channapatna), and later Indradhanush Complex and Kamat.

A Carpet of Tea

Highlights
1. Sim's Park
2. Lamb's Rock
3. Lady Canning's Seat
4. Dolphin's Nose
5. The Droog
6. Highfield Tea Estate
7. Ralliah Dam
8. Nilgiri Palette Art Gallery

A popular summer refuge of the British from 1819 onwards, Coonoor was also fostered by India's erstwhile royalty. And time has almost stood still here. Today, the boarding schools, clubs, colonial architecture and plantation life are little different from what they were during the days of the Raj.

Visit Coonoor for a pleasant change from the run-of-the-mill hill station holiday. Enjoy the peaceful bellflower-lined streets (preferably on foot). Around town are numerous viewing lookouts, which are best explored early in the mornings to avoid the rush of tourists. The weather patterns here are starkly different from neighbouring Ooty, with the rains arriving in November. Expectedly, the summer months, from April to September, are the best time of the year to visit.

Historic Coonoor has all the charm, affability and familiarity of a small town, where everyone knows each other. Should you ever happen to lose your bearings, the townsfolk will happily guide you in the right direction.

1 SIM'S PARK
Meet keen morning walkers at Sim's Park. This 1874 creation

Snapshot: Tribals of Nilgiri Hills

A number of tribal groups exist in the Nilgiris: Todas, Kotas, Kurumbas, Irulas, Paniyas and the Kattunayakans. Each group has its unique cultural traits, and is found in different parts of the mountains. Exposure has led to many of these tribes leading urban lives and working in various sectors of trade and industry. Only a few still inhabit the forests, and these pockets are fiercely protected by the government and anthropologists alike. Find out more about them at the Tribal Research Centre Museum in Ooty (p57). Though a little run down, the museum is an educational experience.

of one JD Smith started out as a pleasure resort and gradually developed into a botanical garden. If visiting in May, look out for the annual fruit and flower show. **Adults/children ₹20/10, camera/video ₹30/75; 8am–6.30pm**

❷ LAMB'S ROCK
Eight kilometres out of town, a forest-fringed road leads upto Lamb's Rock, a favourite viewing point that buzzes with tourists. On weekends, the narrow road is packed with cars. From here, you can get a view of the sprawling Coimbatore plains as well as a large jagged rock, at least a few hundred feet tall, buried deep in the forest.

❸ LADY CANNING'S SEAT
Tucked between trees, this viewing point is ahead of Lamb's Rock on the same road. Named after the wife of Lord Canning (one of the British viceroys), the spot commands a brilliant view of the tea estates and distant mountains. Grab a hot cup of tea and take in the view here. Off the main road, it is a short climb to the top.

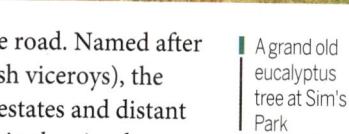

A grand old eucalyptus tree at Sim's Park

❹ DOLPHIN'S NOSE
Another viewing point which has a splendid panorama of the Catherine Falls in Kotagiri. It can, however, be noisy and crowded. Visit in the mornings to avoid the rush – but be prepared to be greeted by the previous day's trash. Dolphin's Nose is 10km from Coonoor town and stands at a height of 1000ft above sea level.

❺ THE DROOG
The weathered 18th-century fort of Tipu Sultan, Droog (also known as Bakasura Malai) can be reached by a combination

> ### 📷 Snapshot: *The 12-year Kurinji bloom*
>
> *Strobilanthes*, the carpety blue flower better known as the Kurinji, crops up in conversations every 12 years in the Nilgiris. Though there are over 40 species of flower across this mountain range, the Kurinji is the most popular. Uniquely, it blooms just once every 12 years, and spreads like sponge over high hillsides. The blooming period is short and tourists excitedly make their way to the hills during this time. The next flowering is in 2018.

of road travel (13km) and a short trek. Though the fort itself is in ruins, the view of the valleys below makes it a picturesque trek. It's a great spot for a picnic lunch – after all, one would need refuelling after the climb up to the spot. Droog is not recommended for older people due to the strenuous nature of the walk involved.

❻ HIGHFIELD TEA ESTATE

This 50-year-old factory off the Sim's Park–Kotagiri Road is one of the few that allows visitors a short tour inside to see the tea-making process. Enthusiastic self-appointed guides latch on quick, but give you a fair idea about what goes into the making of tea. You can also wander around the plantation to click photographs. A heavy scent of tea hangs on to you long after you have left, but the trip is definitely worth it. There is also an in-house store selling tea leaves and herbal oils.

📞 0423–2230840; pay what you feel; 8.30am–6.30pm

❼ RALLIAH DAM

Officially a part Kotagiri, this can be considered Coonoor's secret. A short walk through a thicket leads you to the still waters of the Ralliah Dam, built in 1941 to provide water to the town (a function it still performs). It is an excellent spot for small groups. If you walk along the bank, you reach a small Toda settlement. There is an occasional guard who volunteers as a guide, and can be paid a small amount. Ralliah Dam is about 11km from Coonoor on the Kattabettu–Kotagiri Road. Ask for directions at Elithorai village to reach the dam.

8 NILGIRI PALETTE ART GALLERY

A small, bright art gallery near the main Bedford Junction, the Nilgiri Palette can be comfortably reached on foot. It displays artist Deepa Kern's figurative, abstract and landscape creations in warm hues. The Coonoor-based artist has been painting for over 20 years and has showcased her work internationally.

☏ 9442631717; www.deepakern.com; Abda Building, ICICI Bank Rd, Grays Hill, The Nilgiris; 10.30am–7pm (lunch break 2pm–3.30pm)

Take a picturesque ride across the Nilgiris

♥ *If You Like: Railways – Nilgiri toy train*

The pride of the Nilgiris is the Unesco-World Heritage toy train that runs between Ooty and Mettupalayam (46km). Throngs of peeping heads and cameras are a common sight on the stations in between: Coonoor, Kallar, Addereley, Hill Grove, Runny Mede, Kateri, Lovedale, Wellington, Aruvankadu and Ketti.

It was back in 1889 when the first train chugged through the forests and tea plantations. Today, 12 of the original steam engines still take up the daunting task of lugging the train up the hills. If you're looking at a short ride, board at Coonoor, get down at Kallar and ask for a pick up.

To get a seat book ahead (www.irctc.co.in; first class/second seater ₹135/19; 3.15pm–5.35pm) – though there's no guarantee of a good spot. Stepping out for a quick cup of tea on misty platforms adds to the whole experience.

🛏 Accommodation

Tenerife Tranquilitea   **Homestay** ₹₹
☎9443841572; www.tranquilitea.in;
Tenerife Rosery Tea Gardens; d incl
full board from ₹4000 Guest privacy
is the focus here; no other rooms
are let out if you have booked one. A
sunny garden in front of the room, a
tea lounge, and undivided attention
ensure an exclusive stay. To add to
the experience, the tea-tasting tour is
educational and fun.

De Rock   **Garden Resort** ₹₹
☎0423-2103030; www.de-rock.
com; 2/16 E, Lamb's Rock, Guernsey;
d incl full board from ₹3000–3300
A cosy three-room setup is perched
on the edge of a hill by Lamb's Rock.
The rooms have a brilliant view of the
valley, especially at night. The staff is
endearing and spoils you silly.

180° McIver   **Heritage Bungalow** ₹₹
☎9715033011; www.serendipityo.
com; 1–4 Orange Grove Rd; d incl
full board from ₹3857–5875 A unique
180-degree view of the valley is best
experienced from a wide garden in
front of this 115-year bungalow. The
refurbished wooden floors, high
ceilings and fireplaces ensure a luxury
stay – and the grand bathroom can
become a quick favourite.

Acres Wild   **Farm Stay** ₹₹
☎9443232621; www.acres-wild.
com; 571, Upper Meanjee Estate,
Kannimariamman Kovil Street; d
incl full board from ₹3597–4796
Single and double unit cottages sit
wide apart in this farmhouse, located
on uncultivated land. One can spot a
fair amount of wildlife in the evenings
here. But the most fascinating part of
Acres Wild is the cheese cellar and the
workshop area.

The Gateway Hotel   **Hotel** ₹₹₹
☎0423-2225400; www.
thegatewayhotels.com; The Gateway
Hotel, Church Rd; d incl full board
from ₹6096–9863; 🛜 This colonial
building with an old-world charm
comes with all the contemporary
amenities, as you'd expect from a
5-star Taj Hotel property, including
a spa. Opt for the fireplace room, or
the one with a personal garden. The
Hampton Bar is a decent place to get
a drink.

🍴 Eating

180° McIver   **Multi-Cuisine** ₹₹₹
☎9715033011; Orange Grove
Rd; 12pm–2.45pm, 7pm–9.45pm

Intricate embroidery sold
at Needle Craft

The McIver Villa has an in-house continental restaurant run by French chef, Pierre Mazou who uses organic ingredients only. Long, lazy lunches (with a view of the valley) are the order of the day. Book ahead if you are part of a large group.

Quality Inn   **Multi-Cuisine ₹₹**
☎0423-2236400; www.qualityrestaurant.net; Bedford, Upper Coonoor; 12.30pm-10.30pm If you are roaming around Coonoor town, the slow, laid-back service of Quality Inn might be your best bet. The fare here is moderately good; the large lunch buffet is recommended.

🔒 Shopping

Green Shop   **Tribal Products**
☎0423-2238412; Jograj Building, Bedford Circle; 9.30am-7.30pm An initiative of the Kotagiri-based Keystone Foundation, Green Shop's range consists of products sourced from the local tribes of the region, with a view to providing them with a sustainable means of living. This fair-trade establishment has Kurumba paintings in veg dyes (₹275), organic food, pottery, handicrafts, garments and oils, among other products.

Transcultural Mission   **Handicrafts**
☎9626343774; 28/C Quill Hill; 9am-4.30pm Pamela Bennyalves's nine-year-old initiative to work with mothers of slum children has resulted in a superb range of hand-embroidered products, out of a small workshop in Upper Coonoor. Pick up bed sheets, pillow covers, towels, etc; a large percentage of the proceeds goes back to the women.

Vishal Marketing Co.   **Tea**
☎0423-2232500, ISSU Building, Coonoor; 9.30am-1.30pm, 3.30pm-8pm Owing to the patronage of most resorts and homestays, this otherwise nondescript store on Bedford Circle simply can't be missed if you're shopping for some tea. The owner, Mr Parekh, stocks the best of the region's top-20 brands. The teas range in price from ₹100 to ₹8000 per kg.

Cee Dee Jay's Baker's Junction (Cedrick's Nilgiris)   **Cheese**
☎0423-2222223, 27 Stanes School Rd; 10am-9pm, Sun closed If you are craving for fresh bread and some local cheese, visit this department store just off Bedford Circle. The shop stocks a variety of cheeses from the Acres Wild and Gray Hill farms in Coonoor.

Needle Craft   **Needlework**
☎0423-2230788; Erin Villa, Singara Estate Rd; 10am-5.30pm The beautiful Erin Villa is home to Needle Craft, which stores products from missionary establishments. Look out for delicately made (if slightly overpriced) silk embroidery, handmade lace, cut-work and cross-stitch work.

Kotagiri

Why go?

People visit (and come back to) quaint Kotagiri for three reasons – its largely undiscovered biodiversity; its nostaligic colonial ambience; and its charming weather year-round. Add some fantastic trekking options to that list, and a distinctly untouristy air, and you have the perfect mountain getaway.

Highlights

- **Kodanad Viewpoint:** Offers unusual vistas quite unlike other Nilgiri views.
- **Banagudi Shola:** Forest representing the rich biodiversity of the region.
- **Pethakal Bungalow:** Tracing the tribal and colonial history of the Nilgiris.

KOTAGIRI 71

Trip Planner

Getting There 295km

🚗 **6hr 30min** **SH17, NH209**

- **Route:** Stick to the Mysore Rd all the way till Mysore city. After this, take the road leading to Nanjangud, Gundlupet, Bandipur and Masinagudi till you hit Ooty. From here, head towards Wood Cock Rd on your left, then turn left onto the Coimbatore-Ooty Highway (NH181). Go straight and take a left onto SH15, just before the 5km mark. From here Kotagiri is about 25km; it will fall on your right (after an HP Petrol Bunk on your left).

🚌 **8hr**

- Multiple KSRTC buses, starting from Kempegowda bus stand, go to Ooty. To reach Kotagiri, you will have to change to a TNSTC (Tamil Nadu State Transport Corporation) bus, which are frequent and ply regularly.

Top Kotagiri town
Bottom Kodanad Viewpoint

ⓘ *Quick Facts*

BEST TIME TO VISIT

J F M A M J J A S **O N D**

GREAT FOR

[Spa] [✗] [🔒] [🏃] [♥] [🚹]

REST STOP For good food and reasonably clean loos, Mysore Rd has Kadambam (just after Channapatna), and later Indradhanush Complex and Kamat.

The Nilgiri Chronicles

Highlights
1. Kodanad Viewpoint
2. Toda Shrine
3. Catherine Falls
4. Pethakal Bungalow (Interpretation Centre of the Nilgiris Biosphere Reserve)
5. Nehru Park
6. Kallur Peak
7. Banagudi Shola (Sacred Forest)

If you're keen on learning about the colonial history of the Nilgiris, then Kotagiri should be your first stop. While a few British expeditions had set off earlier, it was only after John Sullivan (collector of Coimbatore) built the Pethakal Bungalow in 1819 that British interest in the mountain region grew. And with them came potato cultivation and tea plantations.

The indigenous cultural fabric of the town, on the other hand, comes from the diverse tribal groups for whom the Nilgiris is home – the most prominent among them being the Badagas. If you are visiting in December, plan around the Hethai Habba, the annual festival of the Badagas at which they seek the blessings of their goddess, Hethai. Going beyond the perpetually misty views of the tidy tea-lined valleys, a visit to Kotagiri offers an experience that's simple and fulfilling.

1 KODANAD VIEWPOINT
A significant spot featuring dramatic views – including that of one of India's largest earthen dams (Bhavanisagar Dam), Tipu Sultan's garrison base (Ali Rani Koli), the meeting point of the Western and Eastern Ghats, and the Moyar River twisting into a horseshoe shape – the Kodanad viewpoint is a pleasant change from the regular hill-station vistas. The viewpoint lies about 18km outside Kotagiri town.

2 TODA SHRINE
On your way back from Kodanad, do not miss a Toda mund (tribal shrine) just off the main road. It has a characteristic small door, thatched roof and carvings on the outside. More interestingly, three large rounded boulders represent the essentials of a marriage proposal made by a man: to lift three stones, eat three ragi (finger millet) balls (each weighing

❸ CATHERINE FALLS

The 249ft-high waterfall is best seen from the opposite Coonoor (p62) hillside (likewise, one can get a clearer view of Dolphin's Nose viewpoint from Kotagiri). Head further than the vandalised spot for a closer look. The point is about 8km outside Kotagiri town.

❹ PETHAKAL BUNGALOW (INTERPRETATION CENTRE OF THE NILGIRIS BIOSPHERE RESERVE)

The centre has a collection of well-kept memorabilia spread over two floors in the original bungalow, presenting a quick

Luke Church, a prominent Kotagiri landmark

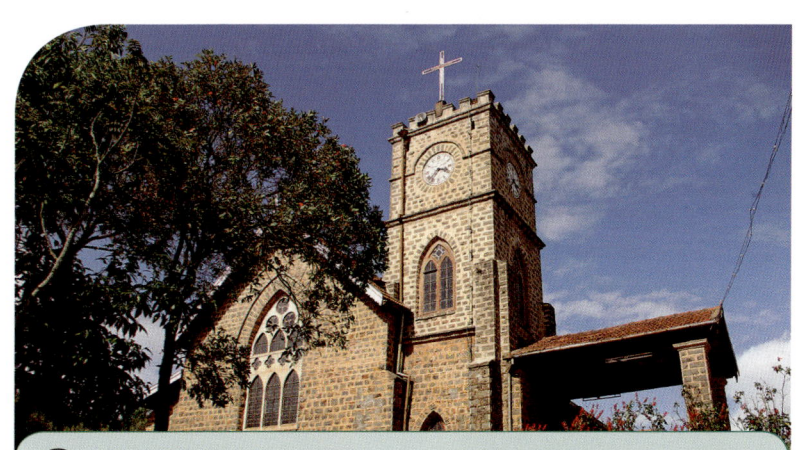

♥ *If You Like: Historic churches*

The three Christian establishments of Kotagiri, **Kota Hall**, **Christ Church** and **Luke Church**, are important landmarks in the town. These are woven together by a common thread of historic incidents that laid and strengthened the foundation of British presence here.

After Sullivan started the advent of British occupation in the region, General Gibson contributed to make the Kotagiri landscape, more British savvy. He lived in Kota Hall and erected Christ Church near where the bus stand is. After an earthquake in 1906, he decided to build another place of worship for the Europeans, Luke Church.

If you happen to see Reverand Mulley, who now heads Luke, don't miss a chance to chat with him and find out about the history of these buildings.

history of the British presence in the Nilgiris, and also of the pre-colonial tribal era. Look out for an identical picture of Ooty taken in 1870, and then in 1970. Even if the door is locked, one can call a displayed number to which an attendant will respond and let you in.

✆9488771571, Sullivan Memorial, Nilgiri Documentation Centre, Kannerimukku; ₹10; 10am–5pm (closed for lunch 1pm–2pm)

❺ NEHRU PARK

A small but pleasant park on the Johnstone (now Kamraj) Circle, it is believed to be the place where a young Jawaharlal Nehru learnt horse riding. Step in to see the ancient Kotha Temple through a locked gate (it is, incidentally, from the Kotha tribe that Kotagiri gets its name).

Johnstone Circle; adult/children ₹5/2, camera/video ₹20/75; 6am–9pm

❻ KALLUR PEAK

The Kallur Peak is a short walk from Adubettu near the Aravenu hill. Apart from the picturesque view of the Mettupalayam plains below, you can see the Nilgiri Toy Train chugging along the meandering track.

Ancient tombstones, or dolmans, in Banagudi Shola

❼ BANAGUDI SHOLA (SACRED FOREST)

This is a sacred forest with ancient shrines still worshipped by the tribals. To absorb the rich biodiversity of this 21-hectare grove, it's best to opt for a guided hike with A Bhoopathy (✆97869 71735) or his team from Nature Watch. Dolmans or burial tombstones which are thousands of years old, a host of birds, reptiles and animal species, and a Kurumba settlement, subsist in this forest area. You'll also come across a village close by belonging to the Toriya tribe.

🛏 Accommodation

Lazy Hills   Luxury Homestay ₹₹
☎9941943921; www.lazyhills.in; 4/657/3, Adubettu, Arvenu; d incl breakfast ₹4510 The earthy and minimalistic architecture of the two dwellings here (a tree house and luxury room) gives just the right amount of intimacy and privacy. At Lazy Hills, you'll be consumed by the silence of the valley. And if the clouds allow, you could be treated to a spectacular sunset. Only guests over 21 years allowed.

Cassiopeia   Guesthouse ₹₹
☎0423–2233323; www.serendipityo.com; Kenthony Rd, Elada, Kodanad; d incl breakfast ₹4228 Newly constructed Cassiopeia sits on the edge of Pristine Valley, overlooking a large expanse of acacias and tea estates. A three-bedroom house, it's perfect for a large group. Admire the Rangaswamy Peak in the distance as you lounge in the flower-lined balcony on the first floor.

The Sunshine Bungalow   Guesthouse ₹₹
☎9486553104; www.thesunshinebungalow.com; Club Road; d incl full board from ₹5900 One of the oldest English properties in Kotagiri, Sunshine Bungalow has been refurbished with modern furniture but has retained its old-world charm. Poster beds, elaborate furnishings and wooden flooring give a grand air to the house. Choose one of the front facing rooms to ensure that you get enough natural light in your room.

Twin Tree   Hotel ₹₹
☎04266–275333; www.twintreekotagiri.com; 5/39-A Corsley Rd, opp Riverside Public School; d incl breakfast ₹3560 Quiet and clean, Twin Tree has a cosy set of rooms away from the busy city junction. There is also an in-house cafe if you are feeling too lazy to step outside. A great view of tea plantations and a pleasant garden make for a comfortable and hassle-free stay.

Masters Garden   Guesthouse ₹₹
☎9486553104; Masters Cottage, Club Rd; d incl full board from ₹11,800 (for 4 adults) Yet another

---

♥ If You Like: Volunteering

Volunteer at the 17-year-old Keystone Foundation, which works with the indigenous communities of the Nilgiris to enhance the quality of life and the environment. Get in touch with the Kotagiri-based organisation only if you want to commit a month or more of your time. Apply for a range of fascinating, on-ground projects undertaken by Keystone.

☎04266–272277; www.keystone-foundation.org; mathew@keystone-foundation.org; Keystone Centre, Groves Hill Rd, PB No 35

renovated old colonial bungalow, overlooking a lush valley, Masters (or Lord's) Garden is an ideal spot if you want to stay away from the town. The guesthouse has two rooms which are let out to a single group only.

La Maison Luxury Homestay ₹₹₹
☏9585471635; www.lamaison.in; Hadathorai, Nihung Post Office; d incl breakfast from ₹6900–8900
French couple Anne and Benoit's cheerful white luxury bungalow is the perfect homestay if you want every meal served 'fresh from the garden' (and also if you want to binge on cheese and wine!). Anne experiments with a host of homegrown veggies and flowers in the food. The open Jacuzzi by the tea plantation is the most coveted spot on the property.

Eating

Orange Pekoe (Spice Inn) Multi-Cuisine ₹₹
☏04266–211000; www.orangepekoeleisurehotel.com; Ooty-Kotagiri Rd; 11am–10.30pm
This new establishment is just off the main road as you enter Kotagiri. Though the mixed cuisine is nothing to write home about, the place is clean, and sufficient for a quick meal.

Hari Mess South Indian ₹
☏04266–272148; Mettupalayam Rd; 12pm–3.30pm, 7pm–9.30pm
Run by a trio of brothers, this is a place loved for its unassuming homemade food and hospitality. It's easy to overlook the dinginess when you have sumptuous non-vegetarian combos prepared by the affable family.

♥ If You Like: Eco adventures

Nature Watch (☏9786971735) is an adventure company with a focus on eco-tourism and conservation. The group has an assortment of backpacking trails across the Nilgiris, catering to all levels. They can customise your package according to your needs: discuss your health and ability in detail and get recommendations from the small but efficient team for the right trip for you. For longer trails through forests, you need to get permission from the government; contact at least eight days in advance.

One Day Package (Beginners)

- **Peaks:** Solur, Hebbanad, Rangaswamy, Darshkal
- Hullikkal Droog
- Rangaswamy Pillar
- Dolphin Nose to Catherine Falls
- Ridge-way trail from Catherine Falls to Mullur
- Bikkapathi peak to Hebbanad peak
- Aderly to Burliar

Special Treks (Advanced)

- Kodanad to Thengumarahada
- Rangaswamy to Aracode
- Garikaiyoor to Kallampallayam
- Solur to Bokkeypuram
- Hebbanad to Anaigatty

KOTAGIRI

Nahar Multi-Cuisine ₹₹₹
☏04266–273300; www.
naharretreat.com; Kota Hall Rd;
9am–9pm The ambience in Nahar's might have a busy and chartered-holiday feel to it, but the food is better than that served at most other hotels. The restaurant prepares multi-cuisine fare but stick with North and South Indian, to be on the safe side. Nahar also serves Jain food.

BS Bakery
Aravenu Rd; 8am–8pm Check out the baked snack, 'varkey', ready to be packed in newspapers and doled out with speed. This crunchy snack is best consumed when slightly warm. Arrive early morning or in the evenings, when the batch is fresh.

🛍 Shopping

Green Shop Local Produce
☏04266–273887; www.lastforest.
in; Johnstone Square; 9.30am–7.30pm An initiative of the Keystone Foundation, the Green Shop is great for buying souvenirs which have been sourced from the local tribes of the region. Paintings, honey, oils, clothes and organic foods are the best picks.

Riverside Tea Promoters Tea
☏04266–272769; Aravenu (PO);
8.30am–7.30pm Though you may want to pick up tea leaves when leaving Ooty, you can also buy a souvenir pack from this shop.

Pick up one of these beautiful Toda embroidery pieces as a souvenir

Women's Co-operative Handicrafts
10am–5pm; Mon–Sat The Women's Co-operative is focused on Toda products, especially embroidered goods like shawls, bags, tablecloths, etc. Honey and candles are also available here. The shop is run-down and dusty, but it is the best place to get a good bargain on these authentic products (instead of the more glitzy shops in town).

HERITAGE ESCAPES

- Nrityagram **80**
- Lepakshi **86**
- Talakad **90**
- Somanathapura **94**
- Mysore **98**
- Belur–Halebidu **108**
- Chitradurga Fort **116**
- Tirupati **120**
- Pondicherry **130**
- Hampi **142**

▌I Sculpted artistry at Chennakesava Temple, Somnathapura

HERITAGE ESCAPES

Nrityagram

Why go?

The serene campus of Nrityagram – started by Odissi exponent Protima Bedi – makes for a refreshing short break, especially, if clubbed with a stay at the Taj Kuteeram. In an experience that's both educational and relaxing, one can learn about a unique gurukul system amid a scenic backdrop, where the nature-inspired architecture merges perfectly with the rural setting.

Highlights

- **Dance Practice:** Watch students of the dance school being put through their paces.
- **Cycling Trip:** Pedal your way from Nrityagram and Kuteeram.
- **Yoga Sessions:** Enjoy yoga with a personalised instructor.

NRITYAGRAM

Trip Planner

Getting There — 35km

🚗 1hr — Off NH4

- **Route:** Take NH4 (Tumkur Rd) and look out for the Reliance building on your right after hitting the Peenya industrial area (at Dasarahalli). Take a right from this building and follow the signs for the next 8km. Once you reach Hessaraghatta village, take the road going to the left.

🚌 2hr

- Though car is the most convenient way of reaching Nrityagram, one can opt for bus number 266 from the city; this goes right up to the dance school. Other buses (253, 253 D, 253 E and 253 J) stop at Hessaraghatta village. From here, one can take an auto, which will charge about ₹50.

ℹ️ Quick Facts

Nrityagram • Dasarahalli
Hessaraghatta • Bengaluru

BEST TIME TO VISIT

J F M A M J J A S O N D

GREAT FOR

Spa · 🍴 · 🔒 · 🏃 · ❤️ · 👥

Top and *Bottom* Nrityagram is all about dance

Culture, Nature & Therapy

Highlights
1. Dance Practice
2. Yoga at Kuteeram

The Nrityagram campus was built by the late Protima Bedi to revive the gurukul system of dance education in seven classical forms (it now only holds Odissi classes). The school was started in 1990 within the earthy spaces conceived by Goan architect Gerard da Cunha. Inspired by simple materials and the beautiful natural surroundings, the structure provides a calming ambience in which to learn dance. Even after Bedi's tragic death, while on a pilgrimage to Kailash, Nrityagram continues to passionately follow her dream of a place where dancers can reach perfection.

A temple dedicated to Bedi's teacher, Guru Kelucharan Mohapatra, stands tall on the edge of a yoga platform as one enters the school. Rock sculptures are strewn all over the vast expanse. And there are organic vegetable gardens, rock benches and plenty of trees to keep you company – look out for the unique 'nagalinga pushpa' tree by the housing complex.

1 DANCE PRACTICE
Guests are allowed on specific days to watch the practice sessions led by famous artistes, Surupa Sen and Bijayani Satpathy. Soft whispers and giggles soon subside as decorum and discipline take over in the spacious practice hall. International and Indian students, women dressed in typical bordered cotton saris and men in traditional dhotis, keep to the rhythm on the wooden floor.
₹50; 10am–2pm, Tues–Sat (dance classes 10.30am–1pm)

2 YOGA AT KUTEERAM
The yoga hall at Kuteeram has been built in a distinctive dome-shaped style, the better to resonate with the sound of chanting. If interested, one can ask for a personal yoga class. You can also use the facility by yourself.

NRITYAGRAM

Taj Kuteeram combines comfort with rustic charm

🛏 Accommodation

Taj Kuteeram   Hotel ₹₹

📞080–28466326; www.tajhotels.com; Hessaraghatta; d incl breakfast standard cottage ₹4777, ste ₹7762

The accommodation wing of Nrityagram, Kuteeram was taken over by the Taj Group in 1999 (though they have retained the name). This adjacent property is also the creation of the same architect, and follows a similar design style as that of the school.

A small bridge over a pond leads to a wide courtyard, overlooked by the restaurant. A bunch of white geese roam unbothered, adding to the charm of the well-maintained garden. The three suites and six cottages here have stone pillars and cement beds in common. Indian motifs, murals and artefacts blend completely with the surroundings. Opt for the deluxe suite No 9 for a wide sit-out and more space.

🍽 Eating

Taj Kuteeram   Multi-Cuisine

The in-house restaurant at Kuteeram is the only dining option available here. A buffet is organised in case there are extra guests on a particular day, but

---

📷 *Snapshot: Vasant Habba*

The free annual spring festival at Nrityagram hosts an impressive line-up of classical dance and music artistes. The three-day event is organised in February every year (the website is updated closer to time). Unfortunately, over the last three years, the festival has had to be cancelled but the administration is confident about hosting it in future years.

Snapshot: Architecture of Nrityagram

Given its rich traditional ethos, Nrityagram was designed by the award-winning architect, Gerard da Cunha with a view to synthesise the simplicity of a gurukul and the strong aesthetics, conducive to the art form. The design follows a vernacular rhythm with use of a symmetrical granite base, airy windows and mortar-less archways. An open yoga platform and an amphitheater built from red earth are the two prominent structures here, apart from the round student cottages. The cottages were inspired by the yurts of nomadic tribes in Central Asia (found in Tibet and Ladakh). De Cunha also left about 10 acres of pleasantly unmanicured cultivation land to grow fruits and vegetables.

---

one can choose from a wide spread of a la carte options. The restaurant has a wonderfully cosy ambience, and the healthy low-fat food – with plenty of local infusion – is appetising. The staff enthusiastically promotes ethnic dishes like home-style country chicken and greens.

A leisurely cycling trip through picturesque country roads

Activities

Taj Kuteeram has an array of activities to choose from, particularly popular with children. You can ask the management to organise archery, nature walks in nearby villages, cycling, magic show, and outdoor games like badminton. The hotel also has a games room, where one can play chess and carrom.

If You Like: Cycling

Art of Bicycling Trips organises one-day excursions to Nrityagram. One can ask for a customised trip or join an existing group. The trip is led by an expert and includes a 21-speed bike with helmet, refreshments, mineral water, lunch at Taj Kuteeram, entry fee at Nrityagram, pottery, shooting, and a support van. Discuss details with the organisers before booking.

📞 9538973506; www.artofbicycletrips.com; ₹3500 per head; Sat

Karnataka's Cultural Calendar

- **Bengaluru Habba** The week-long youthful fest brings a medley of performing arts at venues across the city in January after Sankaranti. Free. www.bengaluruhabba.co.in

- **Chitrasanthe** The Karnataka Chitrakala Parishath hosts an annual one-day art and sculpture festival in late January. www.karnatakachitrakalaparishath.com

- **Hampi Utsava** Classical music and dance, folk arts and crafts come alive before the temples and archaeological site of Hampi. The crème of performers congregate here in November. www.thehampi.com

- **Karavali Utsava** Witness the best of Carnatic and Hindustani music and dance; folk art, crafts and food are add-ons. Held at Karvar, Mangalore each winter.

- **Lakkundi Utsav** In Gadag, located amidst ancient Hindu and Jain temples, the festival hosts classical performances and folk arts. May–Jun

- **Ramanavami Music Festival** The Garden City's classical music fest held at Fort School grounds at Chamrajapet over a month, beginning April. For the connoisseur.

- **Nagamandala** This ritual performance to appease the spirit of a serpent is unique to Dakshina Kannada and coastal districts of Udupi. Dancers dress as serpent maidens or nagakannikas and perform late into the night. Dec–Apr

- **Rangashankara Fest** Karnataka's theatre gurus Girish Karnad and Arundathi Nag host the annual theatre festival. Good drama guaranteed. Nov–Dec; www.rangashankara.org

- **Yakshagana Festival** Yakshagana is a native folk art form of Karnataka that involves dance, music, pantomime, with elaborate costumes. Yakshagana festivals are held in venues across Karnataka including Uttara and Dakshina Kannada, Kasargode, Shimoga, and are gaining popularity in Bengaluru.

*By **Vani Ganapathy**, bharatanatyam performer and cultural exponent, based in Bengaluru.*

| A bharatanatyam performance by Vani Ganapathy

Lepakshi Day Trip

Why go?

A journey to Lepakshi is a pilgrimage, not for the sake of religion alone, but equally for the wonder of its architecture and artistry. In a town as small and unremarkable as any in the area, Lepakshi is distinguished by two extraordinary monuments: the enormous temple complex dedicated to Lord Veerabhadra, and nearby, the gigantic statue of Nandi the bull.

Highlights

- **Shri Veerabhadra Swamy Temple:** An intricately designed temple embodying the Vijayanagara style of architecture.

- **Lepakshi Nandi:** An enormous statue carved from a single block of stone.

LEPAKSHI 87

Trip Planner

Getting There 122km

🚗 **2hr 20min** NH7

- **Route:** The simplest way to reach Lepakshi is to head north up the Bangalore–Hyderabad Highway (NH7), and turn left at the Kodikonda checkpost, towards Hindupur. Roads are good and traffic is generally light.

🚌 **3hr**

- Buses to Hindupur from Majestic bus terminus are infrequent, though buses to Chikballapur and Gauribadinur leave at regular intervals. There are frequent buses from both places to Hindupur, and from Hindupur onwards to Lepakshi.

🚆 **2hr 30min**

- Regular trains from Bangalore City, Yesvantpur and Krishnarajapuram stations for Hindupur.

Top Veerabhadra Temple
Bottom Mural within the temple

❶ Quick Facts

BEST TIME TO VISIT

J F M A M J J A S O N D

GREAT FOR

Spa · 🍴 · 🔒 · 🚶 · ❤ · 👨‍👦

REST STOP Chikballapur, a mid-way stop to use the toilet or pick up a few snacks.

A Testament to Beauty

Highlights
1. **Shri Veerabhadra Swamy Temple**
2. **Lepakshi Nandi**

The monolithic Nandi at the town's entrance

Once a thriving centre of creativity and craftsmanship, Lepakshi today is an open-air museum of genius and beauty – a true testament to the skill and imagination of the artisans and architects of the Vijayanagara Empire. Indeed, the making of the Veerabhadra Swamy Temple is said to have almost emptied the kingdom's coffers.

Even today, Lepakshi bears witness to the care invested by its makers and their attention to detail – from larger questions like the temple's layout, to the finer points of the carvings that cover its walls and pillars, and the paintings that adorn its ceiling. The name 'Lepakshi' today is synonymous with artistry, used liberally throughout the region by a host of craft workshops and boutiques, promising only the best.

1 SHRI VEERABHADRA SWAMY TEMPLE
Constructed around 1538, the temple is a remarkable cultural achievement. Famous for its perfect forms and lifelike detail, not to mention its sheer scale, it attracts students of art and architecture from all over the country. Enclosing five different shrines, ranging from the gigantic Nagalingam – the seven-headed snake – to the diminutive altar of Durga Devi,

Snapshot: The murals on the ceiling

On the ceiling of the Ardha Mandapa, spanning the length of the platform outside the inner sanctum, is what is recognised as the best example of Vijayanagara mural art in existence. Though fading and flaked in places, the murals still boast vivid colours and an incredible eye for detail. It was also, perhaps, a matter of ego, as the builder of the temple, Virupanna (the treasurer of the Vijayanagara Empire), is represented often with his retinue, as if personally witnessing scenes from myth and legend.

📷 Snapshot: 'The Village of the Blinded Eyes'

Virupanna, treasurer of the Vijayanagara Empire, is accepted as the builder of the Veerabhadra Temple, virtually emptying the empire's treasury in his endeavours. When the king came to know about this, he ordered the construction to be stopped and Virupanna blinded as punishment. Hearing of his punishment, Virupanna is said to have torn his eyes out himself and flung them at the temple, leaving two telling stains on the walls near the Kalyana Mandapam. It is this legend that gives the village its name: 'Lepa-akshi' – 'the village of the blinded eyes'.

the temple of the fearsome Veerabhadra is sacred today not only as a place of devotion, but also as a site of ancient, and incredible, beauty.

❷ LEPAKSHI NANDI

Easily the largest Nandi sculpture in India, the Lepakshi Nandi sits a short distance away from the Veerabhadra Temple. Approximately 4.6m high and 8.2m long, the depth of detail on its body reveals the skill of its creators. Legend has it that like the Nagalingam, the Lepakshi Nandi was casually chiselled from a single boulder by workmen waiting for lunch, giving the impression that this kind of thing was all in a day's work for these unknown artisans.

The enormous Nagalingam statue

HERITAGE ESCAPES

Talakad Day Trip

Why go?

Immerse yourself in the ancient beauty of the granite temples from the Chola and Hoysala eras, half buried in sand. Unravel the story behind the sand dunes, curiously dotting the verdure on the banks of the Kaveri River – and find out all about the queen's curse that is supposed to be the cause behind these barren patches.

Highlights

- **Granite glories:** Five magnificent stone temples, and many more half-hidden amidst sand banks.
- **Keerthi Narayana Temple:** Dedicated to Vishnu, it houses an 8ft-tall idol within.

TALAKAD 91

Trip Planner

Getting There 130km

🚗 **3hr** **NH209**

- **Route:** Take the NH209 through Kanakapura and Halagur for Malavalli. Past Malavalli, follow directions to Sargur Hand Post and onto Talakad.

🚌 **4hr**

- Buses for Kanakapura depart regularly from the wholesale KR Market. However, the frequency from Kanakapura to Talakad is fairly erratic.

ⓘ *Quick Facts*

BEST TIME TO VISIT

J F M A M J J A **S O N D**

GREAT FOR

REST STOP Carry a packed meal and use petrol pumps for toilet breaks.

Top The meandering Kaveri defines Talakad
Bottom Polished granite statues are the hallmark here

Shrines among the Sands

Highlights
1. Shiva Temples
2. Keerthi Narayana Temple

A site of historic significance, Talakad is located on a sharp bend in the Kaveri River. The area has been ruled periodically by the Gangas, Cholas, Hoysalas, Vijayanagaras and the Wodeyars, since the 8th century.

Known for its incredibly beautiful granite temples sunk into sand dunes, Talakad exudes a desert-like appearance. Of the 30 temples buried here, five Dravidian-style structures, built during the reign of the Gangas and the Cholas, have been excavated, all within a radius of eight kilometres.

The five temples form the Panchalingam, representing the five faces of Lord Shiva. Of these, the Pataleshwar and Maruleshwara temples, built by the Ganga rulers, are the oldest, while the Arkeshwara, Vaidyanatheshwara (the largest temple) and Mallikarjuna shrines date back to the Chola era.

Not your typical temple town teeming with pilgrims, Talakad makes for an excellent riverside picnic spot. It's a comfortable day-trip from Bengaluru – if you leave before the city wakes up, and return before rush hour.

Snapshot: Panch lingam Darshan

To honour the Panch lingam (Pataleshwar, Maruleshwara, Arkeshwara, Vaidyanatheshwara, Mallikarjuna), said to represent the five faces of Shiva, a fair is held once every 12 years on a full-moon night, in the month of Kartik, overlapping with the months of October and November.

1 SHIVA TEMPLES

The most magnificent of the five Shiva temples (all devoid of any sand) is the Vaidyanatheshwara Temple. Located at the beginning of an intensively undulating walk across the dunes, its main entrance is flanked by sentinels intricately carved in stone. A large, joint-free chain link hangs from a roof edge, ample proof of the craftsmanship of the sculptors of yore. A sheltered path takes you past the other Shiva temples, culminating at the Keerthi Narayana

Temple– all can be visited in a leisurely two hours. There are a few resident priests who still worship here.

❷ KEERTHI NARAYANA TEMPLE

Remarkable also is the Keerthi Narayana Temple, built by the Hoysalas in the 12th century to commemorate their victory over the Cholas. It is dedicated to the god Vishnu. Following excavations, this brick and black granite structure has been rebuilt, stone by ancient stone, on a new foundation close to the original spot. **8.30am–1.30pm; 4.30pm–8pm;** P

> ✓ *Top Tip: Meals*
>
> Remember to pack that picnic basket amply as there are no notable places to eat here, other than street-food stalls.

The Vaidyanatheshwara Temple is the largest

📷 *Snapshot: Queen's curse*

Ancient Talakad's most colourful myth dates back to the 17th century. On defeating Rangaraya, viceroy of Srirangapatna, the victorious Wodeyar ruler of Mysore alleged that Rangaraya's wife, Alamelamma, had in her possession jewels that belonged to the temple of Srirangapatna. When she heard that soldiers were arriving to divest her of the jewels, she is said to have fled to Talakad, where, before drowning herself in the Kaveri, she vent her spleen against king and town. 'Let Talakad be filled with sand. Let the Mysore kings remain childless. Let the river at Malingi become a whirlpool.' The sandy deluge is supposed to have begun soon after, fuelling fertile imaginations and stories. The myth of the sand dunes has metamorphosed into a full-blown legend, echoing through the centuries.

Somanathapura Day Trip

Why go?

If you have a taste for history and architecture, this fabulous shrine is only a day trip from Bengaluru. The famous Hoysala temple trail is incomplete without a trip to Somanathapura. Though not as popular as its contemporaries, Belur and Halebidu (p108), the 13th-century temple here is a remarkable representation of the typical Hoysala style.

Highlights

- **The temple pillars:** Marvel at these gigantic hand-made structures.
- **Nandi bull:** Look out for this bizzare addition on Janardhan's belly.
- **Carvings on outer walls:** Covering a range of topics from myth and folklore to erotica.

SOMANATHAPURA 95

Trip Planner

Getting There 150km

🚗 3hr SH17

- **Route:** Start early to beat the weekend traffic on Mysore Rd. Take a left at Maddur on SH17 to reach Malavalli. Follow the SH33 up to Chamanahalli, after which take a left towards Kethupura. From here, Somanathapura is about 3km. Frustratingly, the distance shown on direction boards is wrong, so rely on help from locals.

🚌 4hr

Choose from multiple KSRTC buses starting from Kempegowda bus stand. Get down at Mandya (this stretch is about 100km). From here, erratic private operators run buses till Malavalli, from where you can take an auto (bargain well).

Top The temple dates to the 13th century
Bottom The deities are carved out of soapstone

❶ Quick Facts

BEST TIME TO VISIT

J F M A M J J A S O N D

GREAT FOR

REST STOP For a good meal and reasonably clean loos, the Mysore Rd has Kadambam (for breakfast; just after Channapatna), Indradhanush Complex and Kamat.

The 13th-century Wonder

Highlights
1. Temple Pillars
2. Temple Platform
3. Three Deities
4. 16 Different Ceilings
5. Carvings on Outer Walls

Given that it is a detour from the popular Belur-Halebidu circuit, people often tend to miss the temple in Somanathapura, which is actually closer to Bengaluru, and less crowded too. Built in 1268 under the patronage of Narsimha III, it is similar, in architectural style and grandeur. This characteristic soapstone Keshava (Vishnu) temple is one of 92 shrines in Karnataka built during the Hoysala dynasty.

Somanathapura was named after Soma, the commander of King Narsimha's army, and the temple was built under his guidance. Soma went on to build many more temples on the banks of the Kaveri River, to immortalise his name.

1 TEMPLE PILLARS
The 16 pillars inside the shrine have been painstakingly made by rolling concrete pieces against wooden platforms to mould them into a cylindrical shape. No pillar is alike, a feature which may not have been deliberate, as this was made in an era where mechanised tools were not available.

The sculptures cover subjects from day-to-day life

2 TEMPLE PLATFORM
The temple stands on a zigzag platform which is 1km in periphery. The base of the temple has elephant sculptures. The artisans created visual interest by ensuring that there was a different element to each carving.

3 THREE DEITIES
The temple is dedicated to the god Vishnu, with statues of Janardhan and Venugopala in the north and south sanctums.

Unfortunately, the original Vishnu was replaced by an earlier excavated statue that does not belong to this temple. The only symbol of Shiva in this otherwise Vishnu-dominated shrine is a rather bold depiction of the **Nandi bull** (Shiva's mount) on the belly of the Janardhan statue. It is said the artisan making this statue was a Shiva devotee, and wanted to incorporate some element to commemorate the god. He did not face any opposition from Narsimha.

❹ 16 DIFFERENT CEILINGS
As you enter the sanctum, look up at the intricately sculpted ceilings representing the different stages of blooming plantains and lotuses. (There is some debate, however, on whether the plants are actually plantains and lotuses.)

❺ CARVINGS ON OUTER WALLS
Since the temple was also a centre of education, folklore and religious stories unfold extensively on its walls. Detailed stories from the *Ramayana* and *Mahabharata* are depicted through carvings; alongside these are hundreds of statues of gods in various incarnations. Opt for a guided tour to get the most out of your visit (recommended government-approved guide, Mr Ramakrishna ✆9945645237).

Eating

Kadambam   **Iyengar Cuisine ₹**
✆9945390120; www.kadambam.in; Channapatna, Mysore Rd; 7am–11pm Stop for breakfast just after Channapatna town at the famous Kadambam restaurant. Enjoy your thatte idli (a flat rice pancake) and the tangy puliyogare (tamarind rice), after a furious battle for the waiters' attention . The place is usually packed so arrive early or you will have to wait to get a seat.

Indradhanush Complex   **Kannada & Fusion Cuisine ₹₹**
✆9945390120; Bangalore Rd; 6am–11pm One of the oldest stop overs on the Bengaluru–Mysore highway, this complex houses KFC, Cafe Coffee Day, Corner House – and the Indradhanush Hotel. The service is fast, to accommodate the many tourists frequenting this place. However, for some authentic Kannada food, give the modern outlets a miss and head to the rear of the complex.

Mysore

Why go?

Steeped in culture and tradition, Mysore is a heritage-rich experience. Savour its art and architecture or simply ride up to the Chamundeshwari Temple for some great views. Keep the kids busy for many an hour at the Mysore Zoo, and drive out to Srirangapatna for some Tipu Sultan lore. Visit the Ranganathittu Bird Sanctuary if you are into birding.

Highlights

- **Mysore Palace:** An architectural beauty, especially when ablaze with lights on holidays.
- **Chamundeshwari Temple:** Splendid views of the city from the temple hill.
- **Mysore Zoo:** One of the oldest in India – and a treat for kids.

MYSORE

Trip Planner

Getting There   150km

🚗 **3hr**   SH17

- **Route:** Follow the well-marked SH17, the main artery from Bengaluru to Mysore, via Ramanagaram, Maddur and Srirangapatna.

🚌 **4hr**

- KSRTC buses from Mysore Rd bus stand leave for Mysore throughout the day. The most convenient timings are at noon, 12.05pm, 1pm and 1.10pm (₹280). A private Volvo bus leaves at 6am from Indiranagar (₹250).

🚆 **2hr**

- The Shatabdi Express (12007) leaves Bengaluru City Junction at 11am, and Mysore Junction at 2.15pm (for the return journey). Operates once daily except Wednesdays.

Top The Mysore Palace facade
Bottom Mysore Zoo is over 100 years old

🛈 Quick Facts

BEST TIME TO VISIT

[J F M] A M J J A [S O N D]

GREAT FOR

Spa ❌ 🔒 🚶 ❤️ 👫

REST STOP Indradhanush Complex near Maddur for toilet break and food.

Karnataka's Culture Capital

Highlights
1. Mysore Palace
2. Chamundeshwari Temple
3. Mysore Zoo
4. Sri Jayachamarajendra Art Gallery
5. St Philomena's Cathedral
6. Brindavan Gardens

Located at the base of the Chamundi Hills, Mysore is the second largest city in Karnataka. It was the capital of the kingdom of Mysore and ruled by the Wodeyar dynasty till 1947. Generous patrons of art and culture, the rulers built many grand palaces that today form a rich component of Mysore's heritage.

The Wodeyars also encouraged traditional crafts such as weaving and painting. Sarees in pure silk and gold (zari) threads are a Mysore trademark, even earning them a Geographical Indication Number (patent number). The Mysore style of painting, with its distinctive gold foil work, goes back to the turn of the 17th century.

The festival of Dasera, however, is the hallmark of Mysore's traditional heritage. The elaborate celebrations continue for 10 days, and Dasera is the top draw for seasonal visitors; it is a tradition that is over 400 years old. The festivities culminate in a majestic procession of bejewelled elephants around the city.

♥ *If You Like: Highway eateries*

The entire stretch between Bengaluru and Mysore is a veritable foodie haven. For those truly delish memories of gluttony on the road, dig into the biryani at **Hotel Taj** (not to be confused with its more famous namesake) near Ramanagaram, or Mysore-style snacks and filter coffee at the **Indradhanush Complex** (falls to your right as you approach Maddur).

Find space for at least one of the famed vadas at **Maddur Tiffanys** (also to your right); sign off with the king fish rava fry or seer fish curry at **Poojari's Fishland**, on your right just short of Mysore. Another regular feature is the military hotels, roadside shacks that serve up (mostly) non-vegetarian delights for diehard carnivores (but not for the pernickety or faint-hearted).

MYSORE

❶ MYSORE PALACE
The domed, three-storey structure in grey granite, surrounded by large gardens, is a fine example of late 19th century Indo-Saracenic architecture. Its multiple-arched façade sports the figure of goddess Gajalakshmi atop a central tower. Also known as the Amba Vilas, the palace is the official residence of the erstwhile royal family, and is beautifully illuminated every Sunday and public holiday between 7pm and 8pm. Photography is prohibited inside the palace; visitors are required to remove their shoes.
📞 0821–2421051; www.mysorepalace.gov.in; adults ₹40, entry free for children under 10 years; 10am–5.30pm

❷ CHAMUNDESHWARI TEMPLE
Located atop the Chamundi Hill, this temple is dedicated to the reigning goddess of the royal family of Mysore. Legend states that she slayed the demon Mahishasura (after whom the city is named) in a fierce fight; the Dravidian-style temple honours her feat. A 1000-step approach to the temple is popular with both devotees and fitness enthusiasts; the Nandi temple at the 600th step provides some relief! For the less adventurous, there is a motorable road, too.
📞 0821–2590027; www.mysorechamunditemple.com; ₹20, ₹100 (fast-track queue for those short on time); 7.30am–2pm, 3.30pm–6pm, 7.30pm–9pm

> Chamundeshwari Temple is an example of Dravidian architecture

❸ MYSORE ZOO
Formally named Sri Chamarajendra Zoological Garden after its founder, the zoo is 120 years old, and was established

under royal patronage in 1892. Starting out as a 10-acre park in the palace grounds, it is today spread over 250 acres comprising large enclosures, a bandstand and an artificial island for birds amidst the Karanji Tank. Along with its celebrated elephants, the zoo houses rhinos, gorillas, bison, giraffes, zebras and a white tiger. It has also introduced an initiative to adopt animals.

0821–2520302, 2440752; Indira Nagar; adults/children (5 to 12 years) ₹40/20, entry free for children under 5 years; camera/video ₹20/150; 8.30am–5.30pm; closed Tues

❹ SRI JAYACHAMARAJENDRA ART GALLERY

Housed in the Jaganmohan Palace, this museum is an art lover's dream: three floors of paintings (including those by Roerich and Ravi Varma), portraits, ceramics, furniture and musical instruments. Despite the indifferent display, spare a good two hours for this enriching experience.

Jaganmohan Palace; ₹20; 8.30am–5.30pm

❺ ST PHILOMENA'S CATHEDRAL

Drawing inspiration from Cologne Cathedral in Germany,

The illuminated fountains at Brindavan Gardens

this neo-Gothic church with its twin spires, stained glass and buttresses is a distinctive landmark of Mysore. Built by the Maharaja in 1933, it is dedicated to a Greek saint martyred in the 3rd century. The crypt houses a reposing marble statue of the saint below the main altar – draped in a silk saree!
Ashoka Rd; 8am–5pm

❻ BRINDAVAN GARDENS

These terraced gardens were created following the construction of the KRS Dam over the Kaveri River. Envisaged along the lines of the Shalimar Gardens in Srinagar, they are replete with fountains, cascades, water channels, lawns, flowerbeds and walkways. A popular tourist spot 20km outside Mysore, it is especially crowded in the evenings when the illuminated musical fountain show is on.

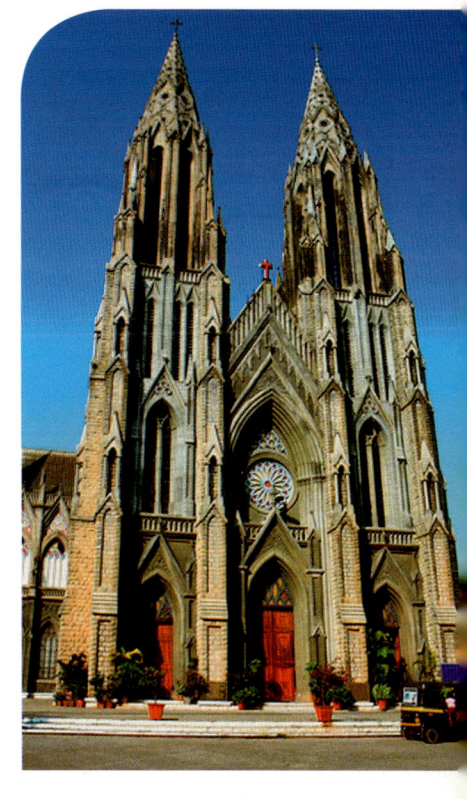

Adults/children (above 7 years) ₹15/5; camera ₹40 (video cameras prohibited); 6.30am–9pm, fountain show timings Jan–Sep (Mon–Fri) 7pm–7.55pm (Sat–Sun) 6.30pm–7.30pm; Oct–Dec (Mon–Fri) 6.30pm–7.30 pm (Sat–Sun) 6.30pm–8.30pm; Dasera 6.30pm–9.30pm

St Philomena, a slice of Cologne in Mysore

📷 *Snapshot: Mysore Ganjifa*

An ancient Indian card game said to have travelled with the Mughals, Ganjifa found patronage by the Mysore royals who commissioned cards made of lac wafers, ivory, mother-of-pearl and tortoise-shell, embellished with precious stones. The hand-crafted cards, painted on leather, paper, palm leaf and fish scales for mass use – once a celebrated art form, vulnerable heritage today – told stories from the *Puranas*, the *Ramayana* and the *Mahabharata* (among other religious and Sanskrit texts).

Detour: Srirangapatna & Ranganathittu Bird Sanctuary

• **Srirangapatna** (adults ₹5, free entry for children under 15 years; photography prohibited; 9am–5pm): Situated 19km north of Mysore on the Bengaluru highway, this town derives its name from the ancient **Ranganathaswamy Temple**, an important Vaishnavite shrine. In recent history, it has been associated with Tipu Sultan's short (albeit heady) reign of Mysore. It is home to the **Dariya Daulat**, his fresco-filled summer palace set amidst sprawling grounds. Nearby is the **Gumbaz** complex housing the tombs of Tipu and his parents; this is open to visitors free of charge from 8am to 6.30pm.

• **Ranganathittu Bird Sanctuary** (adults/children ₹50/25; parking ₹30; boat tour (shared) adults/children ₹50/25, boat tour (for two) ₹1000; 9am–6pm. Check for student concessions): This small sanctuary, comprising six islets in the Kaveri River, is located a stone's throw away from Srirangapatna town. With their riverine reed beds, these isles are the favoured nesting places of painted, openbill and woolly-necked storks, common spoonbills and black-headed ibis, amongst others. The trees are home to colonies of flying fox, while the odd marsh crocodile is routinely spotted. The best season for sighting water birds is June to November, while in December, you can spot migratory birds.

Storks gather at the Ranganathittu Bird Sanctuary

The Ranganathaswamy Temple, one of Srirangapatna's main attractions

📖 Accommodation

Jasmine Apartment Suites — Service Apartments ₹
☎ 0821-2415505, 2415504, 4242632; www.jasminesuites.com; 83, 2nd 'B' Cross, 2nd Main, Vijaynagar 1st Stage; ₹2000 (plus taxes); ❄ 🛜 🅿 Conveniently located in a quiet residential area, these suites are comfortable, clean and come equipped with a kitchenette. Tariff includes breakfast (basic English or south Indian). Cutlery, crockery and toiletries are provided on request.

The Green Hotel — Heritage Hotel ₹₹
☎ 0821-2512536, 4255004, 4255001; Chittaranjan Palace, 2270 Vinoba Rd, Jayalakshmipuram; ₹3250-6750 (plus taxes); 🛜 🅿 This large old mansion, with expansive grounds and al fresco seating, has a quaint feel to it. Rooms in the main building, though small, have retained their old-world charm, as have the spaces leading to them. The spacious new wing comes with basic but modern amenities. For meals, stick to the Indian preparations.

Windflower Spa & Resorts — Spa Resort ₹₹
☎ 0821-2522500; www.thewindflower.com; Maharanapratap Simhaji Rd, Nazarbad; ₹5100-9900 (plus taxes); ❄ 🛜 🏊 🅿 One of the earlier Windflower properties, its sheen has begun to fade. Yet the location, along with well-priced and well-appointed (and reasonably plush) rooms work for this hotel. The popular spa therapies here range in price from ₹700-5000, depending on duration.

Royal Orchid Metropole — Heritage Hotel ₹₹₹
☎ 0821-4255566; www.royalorchidhotels.com; 5 Jhansi Lakshmibai Rd; ₹6000-12,000 (plus taxes); ❄ 🛜 🏊 🅿 A colonial-era heritage hotel in the heart of the city, it comes with a central courtyard and al fresco dining. The lavish rooms are of varying sizes and can get noisy, given their location. The ones at the back, while pool-facing, are somewhat uncomfortably walled-in. But the food at their evening-only BBQ restaurant, Shikari, makes up for the negatives.

Hotel Regaalis — Deluxe Hotel ₹₹₹
☎ 0821-2426426; www.ushalexushotels.com; 13-14 Vinoba Rd; ₹6500-11,000 (plus taxes); ❄ 🛜 🏊 🅿 Located in the heart of the city, the gracious Regaalis is set amidst four acres of verdant landscape. It has well-maintained, spacious and clean rooms, a well-stocked pastry shop, and good food – the kebabs at Charcoals, the hotel's poolside restaurant, are a must-try.

Lalitha Mahal Hotel — Luxury Hotel ₹₹₹
☎ 0821-2526100; www.lalithamahalpalace.in; Lalitha Mahal Rd; ₹6000-50,000 (plus taxes); ❄ 🛜 🏊 🅿 This elegant building, perched on a ridge near the

Chamundi Hills, is another of Mysore's striking landmarks. It was built by the Maharaja in 1927 for the exclusive use of the Viceroy. It is, today, an elite heritage hotel of the government-managed Ashok Group. The palace wing, with its original furnishings and fittings, gives the hotel a sense of history and splendour.

Eating

RRR Hotel   Andhra Restaurant ₹
0821-2442878; 2721/1-2, Sri Harsha Rd; 11.45am-3.45pm, 6.45pm-11pm RRR Hotel is your go-to place if Andhra-style food is the one thing on your mind. Devoid of all frills, this restaurant prepares the most delectable chicken and mutton biryanis, as well as vegetarian thalis. Hearty food served quickly, at this larger, and newer, of the two outlets, in close proximity to the Mysore Palace.

Green Leaf Food Court   Vegetarian Fast Food ₹
0821-6550857, 9731939208; 2813 Kalidasa Rd, VV Mohalla; 7.30am-10.30pm A popular hangout for students, it serves both north and south Indian meals (best to stick to the latter). A great place for breakfast and wake-me-up filter coffee. Tends to get busy given its popularity and location, but the food is well worth it.

Down Town   Fast Food ₹
0821-2513942; Chandra Complex, 42 Kalidasa Rd, VV Mohalla; ₹250 for two; 11am-2.30pm, 5.30pm-10pm This youthful hangout takes you back to the pre-burger-chain era. For over two decades, owners Sagari and Roy have been dishing out comfort fast food to Mysore residents. Their home-style non-vegetarian burgers, rolls and hotdogs score over the vegetarian items.

Malgudi Café   Coffee Shop ₹
0821-2512536, 4255000, 4255001; Chittaranjan Palace, 2270 Vinoba Rd, Jayalakshmipuram; 9.30am-7pm This quaintly named coffee shop is located in the Green Hotel, a former palace for royal princesses. Managed by a UK charity, the cafe dishes out the most awesome filter coffee, and cakes prepared by a local women's self-help group.

Caffe Pascucci   Italian Cafe ₹₹₹
0821-2511125; www.pascucci.in; 2713/1, New D3, Adipampa Rd, Jayalakshmipuram; 9am-11pm Part of a chain, this recently-opened cafe has a decent Italian selection. While pizzas remain the fast-moving choice, give the salads, piadinas and pastas a chance too. Desserts are fine – notably the apple cinnamon pie – and the coffees, many.

La Gardenia   Fine Dining ₹₹₹
0821-2426426, 2427427; 13-14 Vinoba Rd; 6.30am-11pm The multi-cuisine restaurant at the

Regaalis boasts a sumptuous buffet and a la carte selection. Spacious and sophisticated, the staff here are efficient and knowledgeable. Just the place to treat yourself to a leisurely meal.

Activities
Silk Weaving Factory
0821-2481803; KSIC (Karnataka Silk Industries Corporation) Factory, Manandavadi Rd; 9am–11.15am, 12.15pm–3pm, closed Sundays and public holidays Visitors are welcome to stroll through the different sections of this factory, located behind the showroom on Manandavadi Road. Learn how the bobbins and the tremendously loud looms assist a single, almost invisible, thread of pure silk to metamorphose into the beautiful Mysore saree. Entry is free; deposit cameras and collect passes at the office adjacent to the factory gate.

Swaasthya Ayurveda Centre
0821-6557557, 9845913471; www.swaasthya.com; 726/B, 6th Cross, opp Yoganarasimhaswamy Temple, Vijaynagar 1st Stage A consultation and treatment centre, it offers a wide range of wellness and curative therapies. The place is pocket-friendly, fuss-free, and the therapists skilled and efficient. Allow yourself a relaxing Abhyanga, Swedna or Shirodhara treatment under the guidance of Dr Sujatha JR, chief physician. Remember to call ahead for an appointment.

Shopping
N Kauvery Handicrafts Emporium
0821-4262849, 4262759; www.nikauvery.com; 3149, Dawood Khan Street, Five Light Circle, Lashkar Mohalla; 9am–9pm Mysore is synonymous with silk, paintings, sandalwood oil (and its many by-products) and rosewood carvings, most of which can be purchased at this Karnataka Silk Import Export Corporation-run (KSIEC) emporium, near St Philomena's Cathedral.

Devaraj Urs Road   Shopping Area
A kilometre-long stretch flanked on both sides by traditional shops, branded stores and trendy outlets. Scour the narrow alleys leading off for more. Take a break at Bombay Tiffanys Annexe and try the sinfully sweet Mysore pak, a local delicacy.

One of the several processes in silk weaving at a factory in Mysore

Belur–Halebidu

Why go?

The towns of Belur and Halebidu are usually spoken of together since they are located close to each other on the Hoysala temple trail. These magnificent shrines are a delight for the devout, and for architecture and history buffs too. If you are neither, you can always venture out of the towns and enjoy the beautiful countryside. Use Hassan as your base.

Highlights

- **Belur:** Home to the Chennakesava Temple, an architectural masterpiece.
- **Halebidu:** A Shiva temple, depicted with tales from the Hindu epics.
- **Shettihalli Church:** In splendid isolation, and a welcome break from the temples.

BELUR–HALEBIDU 109

Trip Planner

Getting There   185km

🚗 **4hr**   NH48

- **Route:** Exit Bengaluru towards the Tumkur Highway and then in the direction of Nelamangala. NH48 takes you right up to Hassan.

🚌 **5hr**

- KSRTC buses starting from Kempegowda bus stand in Bengaluru stop in Hassan on their way to Chikmagalur. The overnight bus (₹328 onwards) reaches at 3.30am but is a little inconvenient. It is best to drive to Hassan.

🚆   Hassan

- Yesvantpur–Karwar Express (16515), 4hr 10min (7.30am–11.40am); Mon, Wed and Fri.

- Kannur Express (16517), 4hr 40min (8.55pm–1.35am); daily.

Top Chennakesava Temple
Bottom Shettihalli Church

ℹ️ *Quick Facts*

BEST TIME TO VISIT

J F M A M J J A S O N D

GREAT FOR

Spa 🍴 🛍️ 🚶 ❤️ 👪

REST STOP Kamat Upachar on NH4 has relatively decent loos (though you'll have to take a U-turn at Dobbaspet to reach the eatery); the other option is Cafe Coffee Day at Dobbaspet.

Chronicles in Slate

Highlights
1. Belur
2. Halebidu
3. Shettihalli Church
4. Gorur Dam
5. Mosale

The hook for this circuit is the two famous temples of Belur and Halebidu, built during the Hoysala Empire, between the 11th and 13th centuries. These temples are the apex of one of the most artistically flourishing periods in medieval Hindu culture.

Of the 1500 built in the period, 92 temples remain. Out of these, Somanathapura (p94), Belur and Halebidu are the more elaborate and boast of exquisite carvings. Of the three, the Chennakesava Temple in Belur is currently the only one still functioning daily.

The best way to cover the Belur–Halebidu circuit is by following the trail of the Hoysala-specific sites (see map below) sprinkled around these two towns. These are Hiremagalur, Marle, Belavadi, Basadhihalli, Kedhareshwara, Hulikere, Pushpagiri, Adaguru, Kondajji, Koravangala and Dhoddagadhavalli. There's little to see in Hassan itself but the town is the perfect base for exploring the area.

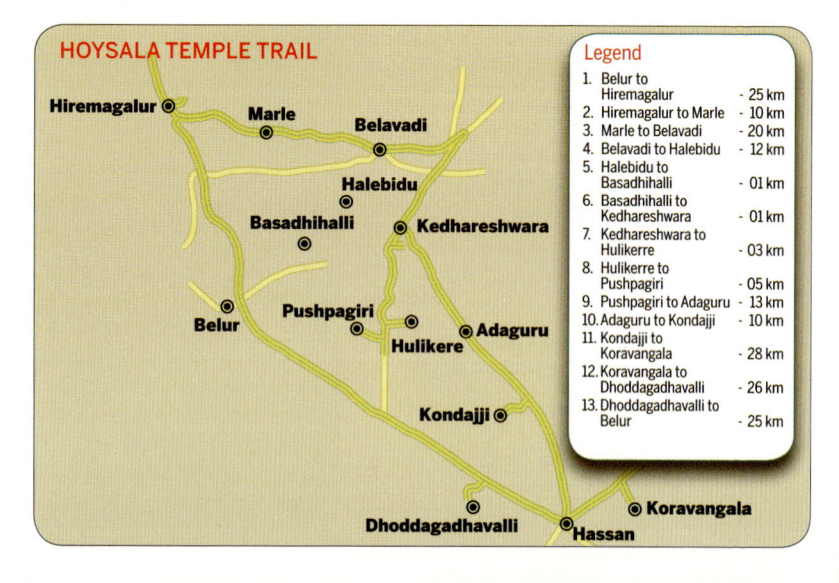

HOYSALA TEMPLE TRAIL

Legend

1.	Belur to Hiremagalur	- 25 km
2.	Hiremagalur to Marle	- 10 km
3.	Marle to Belavadi	- 20 km
4.	Belavadi to Halebidu	- 12 km
5.	Halebidu to Basadhihalli	- 01 km
6.	Basadhihalli to Kedhareshwara	- 01 km
7.	Kedhareshwara to Hulikerre	- 03 km
8.	Hulikerre to Pushpagiri	- 05 km
9.	Pushpagiri to Adaguru	- 13 km
10.	Adaguru to Kondajji	- 10 km
11.	Kondajji to Koravangala	- 28 km
12.	Koravangala to Dhoddagadhavalli	- 26 km
13.	Dhoddagadhavalli to Belur	- 25 km

📷 *Snapshot: Hoysala's cultural flowering*

The Deccan Plateau's most glorious cultural epoch fell between the 11th and 14th centuries. Under the patronage of the Hoysala Empire, led by King Vishnuvardhana, the people of the region were exposed to the fine art of temple architecture. The empire provided a number of artisans a sustainable livelihood and an opportunity to showcase their skill. Slate-stone wonders, giving importance to both Shiva and Vishnu, were crafted over a period of time. The Hoysala temples were more like schools; sculptures depicted not only divine themes but also everyday life.

❶ BELUR

The star-shaped shrine, typical of the Hoysala style, is known as the Chennakesava Temple. It's the main temple in Belur, dedicated to Lord Vishnu. It took 103 years to complete the superb carvings – 4000 in all – in slate stone. Hoysala emblems, statues of dancing ladies and stories of epics unfold in this black stone. Apart from the awe-inspiring sculptures, there's also a monolithic 15m lamp tower in front of the temple, which stands, fascinatingly, without a foundation; one can see the gap between the foot of the lamp and its base.
Temple Rd; shoes ₹2, light inside ₹20; 7.30am–1pm, 3pm–7.30pm

❷ HALEBIDU

Aesthetically, the Hoysaleswara Temple in Halebidu is similar to the one in Belur but it also has a number of distinct features – like the depiction of the mythological 'seven-in-one' animal, Makara, and of tales from the *Ramayana* and *Mahabharata*. Hire a guide to take you through this Shiva temple, with its manicured lawns; spare at least an hour for a rehearsed but informative guided tour.
Temple Rd, Halebidu; shoes ₹2; sunrise to sunset (best to visit between 8am and 5pm)

❸ SHETTIHALLI CHURCH

The remains of Shettihalli Church, 18km from Hassan, look almost fairytale-like in the backdrop of the Gorur Dam catchment area. Though marred by graffiti, the church

stands grandly on the banks while fishermen row their coracles to the middle of the water body. It is said to have been submerged in the waters of the Hemavathi Dam at one point of time. Built by French missionaries in the 19th century, it makes for a good change from an otherwise temple-dominated trip.
Banks of the Gorur village and Hemavathi River

❹ GORUR DAM
While not particularly exotic, the Gorur Dam makes for a good drive from Hassan. The dam gates are opened after the monsoon, which is the best time to visit the spot. After a long walk to the dam area, one can get pretty close to the gushing water below.
10am–5pm

The mythological bird Garuda

❺ MOSALE
About 12km from Hassan, the village of Mosale houses two temples dedicated to Nageshwara and Chennakesava. One passes through a village with bright doors to reach these shrines. They too belong to the Hoysala period but are less intricate. If they are locked, you can invariably ask someone to find the key custodian, who lives in Mosale, to open them.
8am–5pm

✓ *Top Tip: Hire a guide*

Belur and Halebidu have a good number of government-approved guides available to showcase the detailed workmanship and mirrors to point with light. Carvings as minute as the teeth of a monkey, rotating bangles and see-through printed cloths are identified by these guides – take one along (₹200) for they will make your visit more enlightening.

Detour: Shravanabelagola

The massive statue of Bahubali, looking out over the town of Shravanabelagola, is often seen in brochures of the Hassan-Belur-Halebidu circuit. It is certainly intriguing enough to merit a detour. Though the town has no connect with the Hoysala temple trail, it can be conveniently clubbed on the same route. A centre for Jain pilgrimage, Shravanabelagola deserves a couple of hours.

Climb the two temple hills of Chandragiri and Vindhyagiri. The monolithic statue of Lord Gomateshwara (Bahubali), 57ft tall, dwarfs anyone who ascends the steep rock steps of Vindhyagiri. Reach in time for the early morning prayers (8am), when devotees gather to chant. Look out for the Mahamastakabhisheka, a festival celebrated every 12 years. On this day, the statue is bathed in consecrated water, milk, sugarcane juice and saffron paste. The next big day will be in 2018. Chandragiri, which houses an older set of Jain temples, is shorter and easier to climb; it has fewer tourists, so is relatively peaceful.

Apart from the Jain Association guesthouses, the 40-year-old Hotel Raghu is the only place where one can put up for a night. And you'll find a number of 'Jain food only' joints here. Shravanabelagola is best covered on the way back from Sakleshpur or Hassan – if you are driving. It is 12km off the Bengaluru-Mangalore Highway, 158km from Bengaluru.

The huge statue of Bahubali is visible long before you reach Shravanabelagola

Accommodation

HASSAN

Suvarna Regency — Hotel ₹
📞 08172-264006; d ₹1760 (no meals) Newly refurbished, the hotel is at the heart of the city, which makes it a very convenient option. You would wish you were in a quieter place, but the rooms are spacious and clean. But do not expect any fringe advantages. Also, don't choose the non-AC double rooms – these are too stuffy and small.

The Ashok Hassan — Hotel ₹₹
📞 008172-268731; www.hassanashok.com; Post Box No 121, BM Rd; d incl full board from ₹4856–7892 Boasting great ambience and service, The Ashok also has multiple plush rooms. Its green environs make for a pleasant change from the bland options in town. There's also a 24-hour cafe and a bar.

Southern Star — Hotel ₹₹
📞 08172-251816; www.hotelsouthernstar.com; BM Rd; d incl full board from ₹4776–5941; W The spacious reception and polite staff immediately make you feel welcome and relaxed. Rooms are predictably clean and well equipped; some of the bathrooms even have a bath-tub. The property also has a spa (timings 8am–8pm; book in advance).

Hoysala Village Resort — Resort ₹₹₹
📞 08172-256764; www.hoysalavillageresorts.in; Belur Rd; d incl full board from ₹8100–9100;
Set up in 1992, this is the only luxury resort in the region. It gets a steady stream of guests through the year, so book ahead. The kolam (flour patterns made on the ground), Indian motifs and names of the rooms add to the Indian theme in this 34-room property. The cottages and suites are spacious, and come with all the trappings of a good resort. The resort also has a restaurant, a spa (6am–9pm only for checked-in guests) and indoor games.

BELUR

Hotel Mayura Velapuri — Hotel ₹
📞 08177-222209; Temple Rd; d incl full board from ₹950–1800
Surprisingly clean and well equipped, ideal if you're looking to make Belur a base. But very few people choose this

| Hoysala Village Resort is a luxury staying option at Belur

🍴 Eating

HASSAN
Karwar (Southern Star)　　Multi-Cuisine ₹₹₹
☎ 08172–251816; www.hotelsouthernstar.com; BM Rd; 12.30pm–10pm Courteous staff, quick service and superb Indian food – Karwar is a great place to unwind after a hectic day's sightseeing. The perfect restaurant for a hearty meal.

Suvarna (Suvarna Regency)　　South Indian, Vegetarian ₹₹
☎ 08172–264006; www.suvarnaregencyhotel.com; 7am–10pm The largely south Indian fare is prepared quickly to service the milling crowds. Not high on ambience, but a decent place to catch a wholesome breakfast.

Ashok Hassan　　Multi-Cuisine ₹₹₹
☎ 08172–268731; www.hassanashok.com; Post Box No 121, BM Rd; 12.30pm–10pm One of the better restaurants in town, the Ashok Hassan is one place where you can order non-Indian cuisine. It also has a decent bar.

HALEBIDU
Hotel Mayura Shanthala　　Multi-Cuisine ₹₹
☎ 08177–273224; 8.30am–9pm A KSTDC unit, this is the only reasonable place in Halebidu where you can have a meal. Located just opposite the temple, it gets quite crowded at lunch time during the season. The restaurant is basic but clean. Both vegetarian and non-vegetarian dishes are served.

BELUR
Hotel Mayura Velapuri　　Multi-Cuisine ₹₹
☎ 08177–222209; Temple Rd; 10am–8pm Also run by the KSTDC, this is a fairly new establishment. The restaurant serves basic food (vegetarian and non-vegetarian) in a clean environment. Its proximity to the temple makes it easier to cover Belur in a short span of time.

Vishnu Regency　　Multi-Cuisine ₹₹
☎ 08177–222209; Temple Rd; 10am–8pm There are not too many eating options in Belur, but this restaurant serves vegetarian fare in a hygienic environment. Don't, however, go with high expectations – the elaborate menu may not live up to them.

🛍 Shopping
Slate Stone Curios
The only worthy place to pick up a souvenir is from outside Halebidu Temple. A row of women use the same stone as that which went into building the shrine, to make curios like Ganeshas, Buddha busts, etc. Make sure you bargain well.

Chitradurga Fort Day Trip

Why go?

Visit the fort town of Chitradurga whose history goes back a long way – to the time of the Mahabharata, in fact. This is a place for the lover of history, as well as those with a fondness for the epics. Immerse yourself in the commanding architecture, majestic stone doors and secret entrances of the citadel.

Highlights

- **Chitradurga Fort:** A well-maintained and formidable slice of ancient history.
- **Chandravalli Caves:** A significant excavation site from the pre-Christian era.
- **Van Vilas Sagar Dam:** Breezy and picturesque stop over before you reach Chitradurga.

CHITRADURGA FORT

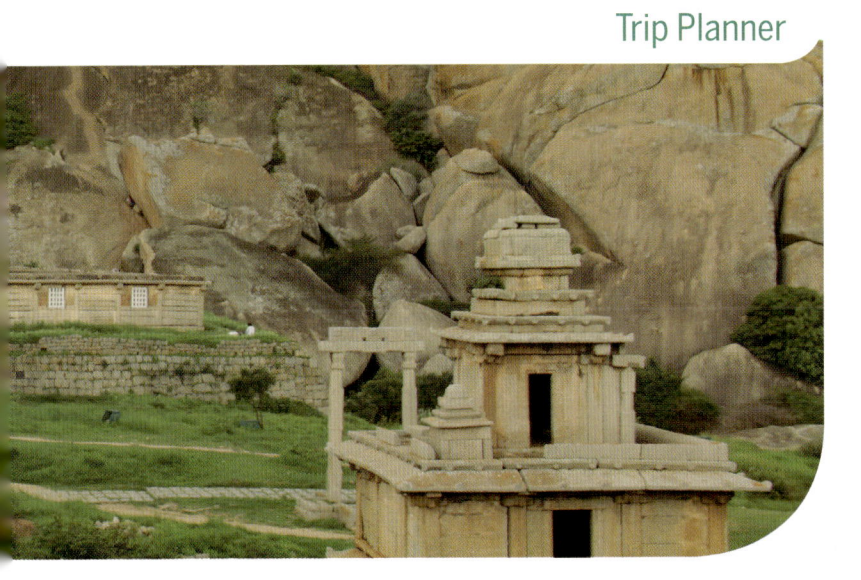

Trip Planner

Getting There — 211km

🚗 **4hr 30min** — NH4

- **Route:** Head out of the city on Tumkur Rd and stay on the well-constructed NH4, till you hit Chitradurga.

🚌 **4hr**

- KSRTC runs buses between Bengaluru and Chitradurga, but the most convenient way to visit is by car, as the bus reaches very early in the morning (₹165 onwards).

Top The sprawling citadel houses many structures
Bottom Chandravalli Caves

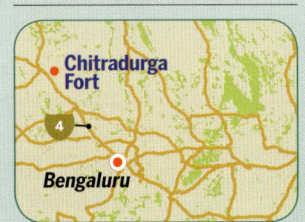

❶ Quick Facts

BEST TIME TO VISIT

J F M A M J J A S **O N D**

GREAT FOR

REST STOP Stop at Kamat Upchar or Café Coffee Day for predictable fare and clean loos; for some tasty idlis, visit the Pavithra Idli Hotel at Kyathsandra Junction.

Fortress with an Epic Past

Highlights
1. Chitradurga Fort
2. Chandravalli Caves
3. Van Vilas Sagar Dam

The earliest reference to the Chitradurga Fort dates back to the time of the *Mahabharata*. It is said that the demon brother-sister duo, Hidimba and Hidimbi, lived on the hill on which the fort is situated. The fort was later attributed to Timmana Nayaka, a military serviceman during the Vijayanagar Empire (16th century). The Nayaka family occupied the fort for over a century, before it fell into the hands of Hyder Ali.

Speckled with boulders, the topography of the region is extremely dramatic and beautiful, especially if one is standing on top of the fort hill. Apart from the fort, one can also visit the ancient Chandravalli Caves. A day trip is sufficient to cover both.

❶ CHITRADURGA FORT

Chitradurga is a fascinating heritage sight, built over the reign of a number of dynasties from the 10th to the 18th centuries If one has a penchant for history, you will love discovering the nooks and corners of this huge stone structure. Towering gates guide one slowly through the fort's meandering path, as interesting sections of the monument appear one by one. The guides at Chitradurga may not be well trained, but they can serve up some fascinating anecdotes about the fort, and draw your attention to interesting parts of the edifice. The sights inside include an elephant memorial, a Ganesha temple, oil tanks, an ancient gym, a humongous 32ft swing and, finally, the more elaborate mandapas (outdoor pavilions).

₹5; 6am–6pm.

✓ Top Tip: *Single female traveller*

After a recent incident of harassment, people at the ticket counter and guards inside warn you sufficiently if you are travelling alone (they might stop you altogether). Be cautious of people trailing you or striking up unwanted conversation. It is best to take a guide, both for protection and information.

CHITRADURGA FORT

❷ CHANDRAVALLI CAVES

Situated 4km from Chitradurga, the pre-Christian era Chandravalli Caves look dry and unimpressive from the outside, but are a storehouse of history; statues, a Shiv Linga and many other daily-use objects were found here during excavation. There is an 80ft drop which you can walk down to, but it is recommended to go down only a few steps as the pitch-dark caves can get a little claustrophobic. An Ankali Mutt temple stands below a huge rock just outside the caves.

6am–6pm

The Van Vilas Sagar Dam offers scenic views

❸ VAN VILAS SAGAR DAM

Take a short detour from Hiriyur (32km before Chitradurga), 20km off the main road, for a fantastic drive through windmill-flanked mountains, to reach the magnificent Van Vilas Sagar Dam. Also known as the Mari Kanive, the dam is a picturesque spot. A drive through rustic countryside takes you to the top of the dam, from where one can get a spectacular view of the waters below.

🍴 Eating

Hotel Emperor Palms Multi-Cuisine ₹₹
☏ 9986601742; 10/6 Kirubanakallu, Kanive, Holalkere; 12pm–11.30pm

With a lack of options to eat in the vicinity, Hotel Emperor Palms is the best bet for a hearty Indian lunch, though the dishes prepared here are rather predictable. This place also serves Kingfisher beer.

🏃 Activities

Rock Climbing

One can climb Chitradurga Fort's highest tower, but only if you have the agility and expertise for unsupported rock-climbing. There are practically no steps, though one does see a few locals climbing. One such wonder, Kothi Raj, is often seen showing off his climbing prowess near the first few gates.

Tirupati

Why go?

On any given day the holy hill of Tirumala is filled with tens of thousands of devotees, many of whom have endured long journeys to see Lord Venkateswara at his home. Absorb yourself in the chants of 'Govinda', as you line up with pilgrims to visit one of the world's most famous temples. For more insight into temple architecture and rituals, take a tour of the shrines of Tirumala and Tirupati at the bottom of the hill.

Highlights

- **Tirumala:** A place of pilgrimage, and one of the most revered shrines in India.
- **Sri Kalyana Venkateswara Swami Temple, Narayanavanam:** Visit for its peaceful ambience and historical relevance.
- **Sri Kalahasti Temple:** Huge and high-ceilinged, this is the area's only Shiva temple.
- **Chandragiri Fort:** Impressively-maintained 11th century fort outside Tirupati.

TIRUPATI 121

Trip Planner

Getting There   250km

🚗 5hr   NH4, NH18, NH205

- **Route:** Take the Kanakapura Rd and head towards Kolar on the NH4. From Chittoor take a left towards Chandragiri. From here, Tirupati is 15km.

🚌 7hr

- KSRTC has multiple classes of buses that ply from Mysore and Shantinagar bus stands. Catch a bus that arrives early, so that you can start heading up to Tirumala at the earliest.

Top Sri Venkateswara temple complex

ⓘ Quick Facts

BEST TIME TO VISIT

J F M A M J J A S O N D

GREAT FOR

REST STOP Kamat Upchar (6am–12am) at Byrasandra and Café Coffee Day (5am–12am) at Dabapet on your way to Tirupati; on the way back, visit Woodys (6am–10.30pm).

The World of Vishnu

Highlights
1. Sri Venkateswara Swamy Temple, Tirumala
2. Papavinasanam, Tirumala
3. Japali Hanuman Temple, Tirumala
4. Shila Thoranam, Tirumala
5. Sri Varahaswami Temple, Tirumala
6. Sri Padmavati Devi Alayam (Alamelu Mangapuram), Tirupati
7. Sri Govinda Raja Swami Temple, Tirupati
8. Sri Kalahasti
9. Sri Kalyana Venkateswara Swami Temple, Narayanavanam
10. Temple Museum, Tirumala

Astounding statistics have always preceded the grand reputation of the Venkateswara Temple at Tirumala, in Chittoor district of Andhra Pradesh. The temple is said to receive over 1 lakh pilgrims daily and gains an income of ₹60 lakh every day through hair sold from tonsured heads. It is also one of the world's richest religious bodies, earning ₹22.5 lakh daily in cash offerings.

The temple's prosperity is represented in the well-organised, self-sufficient city that has been built around it on the hill town of Tirumala, which stands amidst seven peaks, looking down at the town of Tirupati. The Tirumala Tirupati Devasthanams (TTD, www.ttdsevaonline.com) trust does an excellent job of convening all operations related to the pilgrimage centre.

Base yourself in Tirupati, the service town, and visit the many ancient shrines here, sprinkled over a 40km radius, all with a considerable fervent following. Free and frequently scheduled buses ply between temples (there are also free food halls and locker facilities).

Snapshot: Bald and beautiful

Donate your entire treasure of tresses, or just three locks, at Tirumala's free tonsuring service centres. This traditional offering commemorates the sacrifice made by a princess, Neela Devi, when she offered her locks to Lord Vishnu to fill up a small bald patch on his head. It's not odd to witness a sea of bald heads in the two towns. The practice is very common, and even women unflinchingly donate all their hair.

① SRI VENKATESWARA SWAMY TEMPLE, TIRUMALA

If you are staying in Tirupati, leave early to cover the 18km stretch to Tirumala by road. Intensive checking at the toll is essential to proceed.

After inching through a shoulder-rubbing queue for at least three hours, you get a glimpse of the black statue of Lord Balaji (Vishnu), which lies in the sanctum of the temple. The experience is overwhelming, amidst constant chanting – and getting forcefully pushed by professional ushers to accommodate the thousands that visit here each day. End your spiritual tryst with the sumptuous big ladoo (copyrighted by the TTD).

₹300 (Seeghra Darshan)/₹50 (normal); Darshan timings are different through the week (Mon 7am–5pm, Tue 8am–2pm, Wed 9am–2pm, Thur 9am–5pm, Fri 9.30am–9pm, Sat 7am–9pm, Sun 7am–9pm)

> The towering temple spire can be seen from afar

② PAPAVINASANAM, TIRUMALA

Located 5km from the main Tirumala shrine, Papavinasanam is a holy bathing site of 10 channelised outlets of a river, monitored by a dam. Pilgrims throng here to cleanse themselves of their sins.

7am–5pm

Sea of bald heads in Tirumala

③ JAPALI HANUMAN TEMPLE, TIRUMALA

A 500m-long path of easy steps from the main road leads to a cool forested area, which houses an Anjaneya (Hanuman) temple. The legend goes that Lord Ram and his wife Sita visited this spot. A natural pond (known as the Rama Kund) in front of the temple adds to the beauty of the verdant landscape. Make sure that you plan well so as to avoid landing up at the lunch break, when temple closes.
₹2; 8am–1.30pm, 3pm–8pm

④ SHILA THORANAM, TIRUMALA

A quick stop is enough to witness the geological wonder, Shila Thoranam, which lies in a park close to Tirumala Temple. This rock formation is fantastic enough but other than that, there is nothing spectacular about the park (it is often swarming with tourists).
6am–5pm

⑤ SRI VARAHASWAMI TEMPLE, TIRUMALA

This temple, dedicated to Sri Adi Varaha Swami, is situated in the same complex as the Lord Venkateswara Temple. Varaha is the boar-faced Vishnu avatar. It is said that one must come here first before visiting the Tirumala Temple, as this was originally Varaha's abode before Lord Vishnu arrived. He had to seek permission from Varahaswami to take residence here.

⑥ SRI PADMAVATI DEVI ALAYAM (ALAMELU MANGAPURAM), TIRUPATI

This temple, 4km from Tirupati town, is dedicated to Lord Vishnu's spouse, Sri Padmavathi Devi. Expect meandering lines in metal barricades, and a short glimpse of the deity.
5am–5pm

✓ *Top Tip: Queuing*

All devotees have to keep to a well-constructed narrow path, lined by metal guards so that no-one jumps over into the line. Free milk is served to pilgrims; many come without eating, to pay homage, so this refreshment is a relief during the tiring wait. There are also clean loos built along the line.

✓ *Top Tip: Book ahead*

To avoid the slow, snaking lines, book online in advance (at least a week). Reserve a spot on www.ttdsevaonline.com to reach a 'waiting lounge' directly, as per your designated darshan timing. From here, one joins the common line to the sanctum but the time taken is less than an hour.

❼ SRI GOVINDA RAJA SWAMI TEMPLE, TIRUPATI

Situated in the middle of the bustling market street of Tirupati, the Govinda Raja Swami Temple is famous for the impressive statue of a reclining Vishnu. Like the others around here, it is a busy temple with slow-moving queues of hundreds of devotees.

4.15am–9.30pm

❽ SRI KALAHASTI

The only Shiva temple in the region, it's worth the 34km drive from Tirupati. The name is derived from Sri (spider), Kala (snake) and Hasti (elephant), animals that worshipped Shiva to gain salvation. Besides housing impressive statues, the thick, sturdy walls bear testimony to centuries of history. A deep, narrow-creviced temple meets you as you enter. Steps lead down to a dingy prayer area for Ganesha; these steps are narrow but are taken by people of all ages. Don't forget to see the 'Vaayu Linga', a lamp that burns inside the innermost sanctum without any air; there are no doors or windows, but the lamp flickers relentlessly.

www.srikalahastitemple.com; 6am–9.30pm

❾ SRI KALYANA VENKATESWARA SWAMI TEMPLE, NARAYANAVANAM

If you have time, a trip to this temple (37km from Tirupati) is worth your while. It is said that Lord Vishnu got married here to Padmavathi Devi. The peaceful environs of the shrine are a pleasant relief from the frenzied pace of the other temples close to Tirupati town. One will often see

✓ *Top Tip: Must read*

Hindu mythology can seem extremely complicated but Dr Devdutt Patnaik's book, *Seven Secrets of Vishnu*, simplifies the symbols, stories, rituals and perspectives in straightforward, storytelling parlance, making your experience in the temple town even more enjoyable.

young, unmarried girls visiting this temple for a special puja.
6am–1pm, 3pm–8pm

⑩ TEMPLE MUSEUM, TIRUMALA
The temple museum in Tirumala is a sparkling-clean building which houses paintings, sculptures and photographs related to the history of the Sri Venkateswara Swamy Temple.
Admission free; 8am–8pm

📷 *Snapshot: Inside the Venkateswara Swamy Temple, Tirumala*

One quickly gets over the exhaustion of getting to the temple, as a number of bewildering experiences and quirky sights keep you engaged inside the shrine. Here, you'll see the glass-encased money-counting section. Peep in to find the amusing sight of sombre-faced, half-naked priests sorting through cash and coins with dexterity. The sheer quantity of money that is offered is astounding. If you are travelling abroad, say a prayer to Lord Vimana, marked with a red arrow on the gold gopuram (gateway). A weighing scale in the temple premises is often seen with people donating rice or wheat (even gold) as much as the weight of a family member. There is also a rough stone where devotees jostle to scribble their wishes with their fingers, in the hope that they come true.

Devotees lining up to see the idol at Sri Venkateswara Temple

Accommodation

If you're looking for lavish accommodation, and proximity to all the temples, it is recommended you stay in Tirupati, though Tirumala does have basic guesthouses.

TIRUPATI

Udayee International   Hotel ₹

📞 0877-2266581; www.udayeeinternational.com; No. 13-6-771/20, opp APSRTC bus terminal; d incl full board from ₹2108-4497; 📶 With all the trappings of a fairly big hotel, Udayee International is an ideal option if you do not want to spend too much. It isn't very plush, but has all the comforts, including flat-screen TVs, running hot water and spacious rooms.

Sindhuri Park   Hotel ₹

📞 0877-2256438; www.hotelsindhuri.com; 14-2-118, 119, TP Area; d incl full board from ₹2631-4159; 📶 Besides guaranteeing a reasonably-priced and comfortable stay, Sindhuri Park provides an excellent view of an old pushkarni (temple pond) and the bustling streets of Tirupati – perfect to get you in the mood for temple hopping. The courteous staff and vantage location make up for the lack of plush furnishings and facilities.

ASR Guest House   Guesthouse ₹

📞 0877-2251501; www.asrguesthouse.blogspot.in; 19-9-4 A1, Old Tiruchanoor Rd, next to electricity revenue office, near Annapoorneshwari Temple; r ₹1360 If you're looking for budget accommodation, ASR fits the bill with its clean and spacious AC rooms. A short drive away from the railway station and bus stand, it's not on the main arterial roads, but any local would be able to guide you. Hot water is available only on request, so don't expect the facility for 24 hours.

Minerva Grand   Hotel ₹₹

📞 0877-6688888; www.minervagrand.com; near railway flyover, Renigunta Rd; d incl full board from ₹3800-11,000; 📶 The latest addition to luxury stay in Tirupati, Minerva Grand pleasantly breaks the clutter by offering a superior experience, with minimalistic white décor and a soothing ambience. Amenities like a multi-cuisine restaurant, gymnasium, coffee shop and laundry combine to make your stay more than comfortable. The well-furnished rooms come with flat-

---

> ✓ **Top Tip: Personal belongings**
>
> Most temples strictly do not allow cell phones or cameras inside their premises. You are thoroughly searched at the gates. It is better to not carry these when visiting the temple. Shoes can be left outside in the manned enclosures, at a small cost.

screen TVs, refrigerator and tea/coffee machines.

Fortune Kences — Hotel ₹₹
0877–2255855; www.fortunehotels.in; opp APSRTC bus terminal; d incl full board from ₹3100–7000; The spacious, wide lobby of this hotel is a welcome relief from the packed streets outside. Fortune has a coffee shop and in-house restaurants, while its comfortable and lavish rooms are fantastic to recover in, after the exhaustion of the temple tour in Tirumala.

TIRUMALA

TTD Guest Houses — Guesthouse ₹
0877–2277777; www.ttdsevaonline.com; d incl full board from ₹100–₹2000 The no-frills TTD-operated guesthouses are ideal if you are willing to rough it out. Book well in advance (90 days). Though dormitories are available, the ₹1000-plus rooms offer more privacy and comfort.

Eating

Greens, Tirupati — Multi-Cuisine ₹₹₹
0877–2255855; www.fortunehotels.in; opp APSRTC bus terminal; 7am–10pm Part of the Fortune Kences hotel, this restaurant offers decent vegetarian food.

Woodside, Tirumala — Multi-Cuisine ₹₹
Ring Rd, near Museum; 6am–10.30pm Great for a quick north/south Indian meal or snacks, after you have completed the temple trail in Tirumala. The place is high on energy, with the typical hectic pace of a tourist destination.

Sandeepa, Tirumala — Multi-Cuisine ₹₹
Ring Rd, near Museum; 5am–midnight Low on ambience but high on taste, Sandeepa meets you with a constant buzz of weary and hungry pilgrims who come here to pack in sumptuous south and north Indian meals and snacks like idlis and dosas.

India Coffee House Tirumala — Coffee House ₹
Lepakshi Rd; 6am–10pm The famous coffee stop of south India has found its way to Tirumala, next to the Lepakshi showroom. Grab a quick, relaxing cup of coffee and snacks in this dingy but clean cafe.

Nightlife
Alcohol is available in Tirupati town but not in Tirumala.

Blue Fox
0877–6688888; www.minervagrand.com; near railway flyover, Renigunta Rd; noon–11pm The in-house bar and restaurant of Minerva Grand has a decent stock, served in snazzy bluish lighting, true to the hotel's contemporary décor.

TIRUPATI | 129

Activities

Walk to Tirumala
Depending on your enthusiasm levels, you can also climb to Tirumala from Tirupati. Start at the Garuda Circle, and take the 3550 steps (11km) to Tirumala. This route is closed between 12am and 3pm. It takes about four hours to complete the climb.

Sri Venkateswara Zoo
0877-2249235; www.svzoo.org; Pudipatla Post; adults/children ₹15/5; car ₹250; camera ₹75 (additional charge of ₹25 for safari inside); 8.30am-5.30pm About 16km from Tirupati, the Sri Venkateswara Zoo is a good stop over if you are traveling with children. The zoo has animals that have been mentioned in the Indian epics – leopards, elephants, tigers, peacocks, and a large variety of birds. It is very well maintained, and you can take your car inside and drive around.

Chandragiri Fort
₹10; photography prohibited; 9am-5pm (closed Fri) Less than 15km from Tirupati, the Chandragiri Fort is an impressive reminder of the kingdom of the Vijayanagar ruler, Krishnadevaraya Raya. The 11th century fort, maintained by the Archeological Survey of India, now serves as a museum. A manicured lawn and a lake add to the beauty of the place.

Shopping

Lepakshi　　　　　　Handicrafts
0877-2277246; www.lepakshihandicrafts.gov.in; Tirumala Hills; 10am-9pm Memorabilia is in plenty here. Balaji-themed curios, jewellery, key chains, statues, wooden toys and more line the congested shop in the town centre of Tirumala. Other than small knick-knacks, one can also pick up elaborate wooden sculptures.

Shilparamam　　　　Handicrafts
Tiruchanoor Rd; ₹10; camera/video ₹100/150; 10am-8.30pm An arts and crafts village, Shilparamam is a good place to pick up some bric-a-brac from handicrafts shops of the region. Aesthetically charming, this establishment, themed with Indian motifs, is also perfect for relaxing.

Souveniers on sale with pop art Venkateswara

Pondicherry

Why go?

Pondicherry, with its quaintly Gallic ambience, promises a laid-back seaside break. It is one of the few places in India that offers a slice of India's French colonial past. Another face of Pondicherry is the Aurobindo Ashram that colours much of the city's personality. Combine heritage and spirituality, with some pleasant hours at the ocean promenade, for a serene break.

Highlights

- **Aurobindo Ashram:** Discover Sri Aurobindo and his teachings at this spiritual haven.
- **Auroville:** Explore this blissed-out world village that grew around the ashram.
- **Cathedral of Our Lady of the Immaculate Conception:** Admire the architecture of one of Pondicherry's most famous churches.

PONDICHERRY

Trip Planner

Getting There — 310km

🚗 **3hr 30min** — **NH7, NH32**

• **Route:** Exit Bengaluru from Hosur and take the NH7 through Chengam, Tiruvannamalai, Gingee and Tindivanam. Take a right onto NH32 and, finally, another right to Pondicherry. The drive is very lush and scenic.

🚌 **9hr**

• KSRTC buses (₹590) leave in the night from Shanthi Nagar bus stand in Bengaluru and arrive in Pondicherry pretty early. Book ahead to get a seat in the morning. There are plenty of private operators that also ply buses on this route.

🚆 **10hr**

• The Puducherry Express (12255) starts from Yesvantpur station in Bengaluru at 11.15pm, and reaches Pondicherry by 8.50am. There is no service on Sundays.

Top The rocky beachfront
Bottom The cathedral facade

❶ Quick Facts

BEST TIME TO VISIT

J F M A M J J A S **O N D**

GREAT FOR

Spa · 🍴 · 🔒 · 🚶 · ❤️ · 👥

REST STOP Stop at 2B Ghar Dhabha for a decent meal and reasonably clean loos. (6am–12am).

Un Weekend Paresseux (A Lazy Weekend)

Highlights
1. Sri Aurobindo Ashram
2. Promenade Walk on Goubert Avenue
3. Monument Avenue
4. Churches of Pondicherry
5. Manakkula Vinayagar Koil
6. The Government Museum
7. Bharathi Park
8. Chunnambar Boat House

The characteristic cobble-stoned streets, criss-crossing through the French quarter, are still the most feet-and cycle-friendly in India. One will often find tourists, map in hand, tracing their way through different 'rues' (roads). The familiar circular area on the map clearly shows the arterial canal which divides the city into Tamil (Black Town) and French (White Town) quarters. Stay in the French Quarter for an atmospheric break.

Previously governed by the Dutch and then French colonists, Pondicherry (now Puducherry) is the largest district of the four enclaves that make up the union territory (Karaikal, Yanam and Mahe being the other three). The French influence has been fairly strong here, and one can see this in the high walls, sparse aesthetics and clean lines of the architecture. This Gallic touch merges interestingly with the essential 'kolam' (religious floor designs) seen outside both French and Tamil houses.

The Gandhi statue on the promenade

Detour: *Arikamedu*

Arikamedu is a 1940s excavation site just outside Pondicherry. Having created active interest among renowned historians, Arikamedu threw up evidence of being a major port in the Chola Kingdom, which traded with the Romans. It is said to have been in existence since before the 1st century. Today, the site lies in ruins with no signages or information for visitors. The Pondicherry Museum has a few exhibits related to Arikamedu.

❶ SRI AUROBINDO ASHRAM

Immerse yourself in the serene atmosphere of the Aurobindo Ashram, where the flower-covered samadhis of Sri Aurobindo and the Mother are the central attraction for devotees and tourists. A walking path is chalked out for order, while spots are taken by regulars to meditate for a longer time. Founded in 1926, this is where the two spiritual gurus lived. Books on the philosophy of the Ashram are available on sale in international and regional languages.

📞 0413–2233604; Francois Martin Str-Manakkula Vinayagar Koil Str; 8am–12pm, 2pm–6pm; children under 3 not allowed; no photography

❷ PROMENADE WALK ON GOUBERT AVENUE

Pondicherry offers a different coastal experience. Instead of shacks serving beer and snacks, you'll come across a long promenade along the rocky edge of the sea, with an old jetty in sight. Evenings are alive on Goubert Avenue (Beach Road), with locals and tourists nibbling on local snacks and enjoying the vibrant atmosphere. Benches line the footpath for weary legs, and there is a pleasant break from traffic on this street between 6pm and 7.30am every day.

❸ MONUMENT AVENUE

Pondicherry's landmark monuments are located in short intervals on Goubert Avenue, with a statue of Gandhi at one end and one of Marquis Joseph Francois Dupleix (governor of Pondicherry between 1742 and 1754) at the other. In between are the French War Memorial, the Old Lighthouse, a statue of Joan of Arc, the Old Customs House, a statue of Jawaharlal Nehru, and a newly-built memorial for BR Ambedkar. All of these can be seen on the right of the street.

❹ CHURCHES OF PONDICHERRY

There are three important churches in Pondicherry. Follow a short trail from the Eglise de Notre Dame des Anges (better known as the 'French Church' amongst locals), located on Dumas Street, to the Cathedral of Our Lady of the Immaculate Conception on Cathedral Street, and finally to the Church of the Sacred Heart of Jesus on Subbaiah Salai. All of them are known for their masonry and beautiful facades.

❺ MANAKKULA VINAYAGAR KOIL

This Ganesha Temple is more than 300 years old but it's largely been made famous by Lakshmi the elephant (she was on sick leave when we were there), whose blessings are sought by the many who come to visit her. Manoeuvre your way through a lively crowd of devotees, who arrive from across India to pay homage to the depiction of the countless incarnations of this friendly lord.

Manakkula Vinayagar Koil Street; shoes ₹1; 5.45am–12.30pm, 4pm–9.30pm

❻ GOVERNMENT MUSEUM

Housed in a restored century-old villa of a French tradesman (Carvalho), the Government Museum describes a disjointed trajectory of Pondicherry's history. This is the only place

---

✓ *Top Tip: Walk, pedal or ride*

The best way to explore this pleasant town is by grabbing a map from the friendly bunch at Puducherry Tourism Department Corporation (PTDC; Goubert Avenue: 9am–5pm); they will speedily mark out the important places with rehearsed skill.

The streets of Pondicherry are friendly to walkers, cyclists and motorbike riders, making it a simple town to explore. One can rent two-wheelers and cycles on a per-day basis – or longer – from a line of shops on Mission Street. You need to leave an original photo id with the owner (this is common practice, so do not be alarmed). Recommended: J Praja (📞9894121133, No 106-B Mission Street; cycle/Activa/bike ₹50/200/150 per day).

where you can get a glimpse of the famous Arikamedu excavations. You can also see some artefacts from the Pallava and Chola dynasties, bizzarely juxtaposed with Dupleix's own bed.
₹10, free entry for children; no cameras allowed; 10am–1pm, 2pm–5pm

> Bharathi Park is named after the poet

❼ BHARATHI PARK
Located in the heart of Pondicherry, this welcome patch of green is used by many as a resting spot from the intense sun. It houses a bright white monument, the Aayi Mandapam, built during the time of Napoleon III.
Victor Simonel Street; 6am–9pm

❽ CHUNNAMBAR BOAT HOUSE
Visit this PTDC-run establishment only if you like boat rides. Avoid the dowdy-looking children's rides and the coffee shop, and head straight to the boarding point. One can take boat rides to the nearby Paradise Island or the backwaters. The experience has a slight package-holiday feel to it, but is recommended to entertain the kids.
Adults/children ₹50/25; camera ₹300; 1.30pm–6pm; 7km from Pondicherry

Detour: Auroville

Auroville has often been a source of puzzlement, and many travellers are unsure of what to expect here. It was the brainchild of Mirra Alfassa, known as the Mother, who wanted to build a township promoting harmonious living and unity. The 2200-plus people from 45 countries who inhabit the place are responsible for projects on art, culture, small enterprise and health, in tandem with the locals. There are quite a few restaurants offering eclectic cuisine here.

The most famous structure here is the **Matrimandir**, which gets hundreds of visitors each day. It embodies the teachings of the Mother and Sri Aurobindo. In the centre of the amphitheatre adjacent to the golden-domed shrine, a marble structure shaped like a lotus bud stores soil from 124 countries and 23 Indian states, a symbolic gesture of Aurovillean unity. Watch a video (22 minutes) on Auroville and obtain a free pass before setting out; meditation passes are given out a day in advance upon a personal visit. The walking route to Matrimandir from the information centre has an open exhibition, herbal garden, coffee shop and pavilions.

The golden dome of the Matrimandir Meditation Centre

Auroville can be accessed from Pondicherry via a rented two-wheeler, or an auto-rickshaw (₹200). One can roam freely here; visit the reception centre, where volunteers will guide you further. You can also drop in at the Solar Kitchen for an organic meal.

☎ 0413–2622239; www.auroville.org; Auroville Visitors Centre; 9.30am–4pm Mon–Sat, 9.30am–12.30pm Sun; 14km from Pondicherry

Accommodation

L'Escale   Guesthouse ₹
☏ 0413–2222562; www.lescalepondicherry.com; No 31 Dumas Street; d from ₹1600–2500; 📶 Narrow and steep steps from the street open out into a bright lounge and breakfast area on the rooftop, decidedly the most charming part of this warmly-run guesthouse. Immaculately furnished rooms (with bright curtains and Indian artefacts), framed photographs of Pondicherry's history, bikes on hire, and the welcoming hosts, all go a long way towards making your stay here a wonderful one.

Mango Hill   Hotel ₹
☏ 9597891966; www.hotel-mangohill-pondicherry.com; Old Auroville Rd, Bommayapalayam; d from ₹2500–3800; 📶🏊 Mango Hill is ideal for those seeking a relaxing place away from Pondicherry town. It has a pool, Ayurvedic spa (though not highly recommended) and a restaurant. Suitable for families and large groups. The place gets busy on weekends, and lone travellers and couples may not appreciate the high-activity environment. The Italian and French cheeses (stored in a cellar), are worth sampling.

Les Hibiscus   Guesthouse ₹
☏ 0413–2227480; www.leshibiscus.in; 49 Rue Suffren; d incl full board ₹2500; 📶 Tanjore paintings, incense-doused Ganeshas and other Indian artefacts fit perfectly into this old colonial house in the middle of the White Town. With just four rooms, the owners, Bascarane and Gladys, ensure that the property maintains its quiet and hospitable charm.

Maison Perumal   Heritage Hotel ₹₹
☏ 4843011711 (central reservation); No 44 (old No 58) Perumal Street; d incl full board from ₹4730; 📶 Built in 1900, this Indo–French heritage hotel, a former Tamil home, has 10 intimate rooms. The central courtyard and verandah in front exhibit the building's Hindu lineage, while the high roofs and minimalistic wooden doors have a French feel to them. Large earthen pots with plants, stained-glass arches and ethnic furnishings give the Maison Perumal a warm and friendly air.

La Closerie   Hotel ₹₹
☏ 0413–4200573; www.lacloseriepondichery.com; 32 Dumas Street; d incl full board from ₹3000–4000; 🏊📶 Plush but reasonably priced, this home-run hotel on Dumas Street has five attractively-furnished rooms. With plenty of refurbished old wooden furniture, a sun-drenched lush garden and a narrow natural pool in the centre, you are going to love your peaceful weekend here.

Ajantha Sea View Hotel   Hotel ₹₹
☏ 0413–2349032; www.ajanthaseaviewhotel.com; 50

Goubert Avenue, Beach Road; d incl full board from ₹3500–4000; 🛜 Ajantha boasts Pondicherry's most prestigious address – a sea-facing view on Goubert Street. However, issues over the ownership of the building have left the hotel with only four rooms, besides a bar, ice cream shop and restaurant. Don't expect the ambience and aesthetics of the town's other hotels here.

La Maison Tamoule Heritage Hotel ₹₹
☎ 0413–2223738; la-maison-tamoule.neemranahotels.com; New No 44 (old No 36), Vysial Street; d incl breakfast from ₹4000–5000 (one ground-floor room is handicap-friendly); 🛜 La Maison Tamoule is located in the middle of the Tamil Quarter. Recently acquired by the Neemrana Group, the decently-priced rooms have gorgeous bright cottons, old wooden switchboards, copper-bath tubs and hefty wooden furniture. Little light comes through to the central courtyard, so it's recommended to take a room on the second floor for access to a sunny roof.

The Richmond Hotel ₹₹
☎ 0413–2346363; www.therichmond-pondicherry.com; 12, Labourdonnais Street; d incl breakfast from ₹4296–6445; 🛜 The Richmond offers economical rooms and plenty of package deals, including complimentary nights, discount on Ayurvedic massages and free ironing. This hotel, which lies at the edge of the White Town, also has a restaurant and bar.

Hotel De L'Orient Heritage Hotel ₹₹
☎ 0413–2343067; www.neemranahotels.com; 17 Rue Romain Rolland; r incl breakfast from ₹3500–7500; 🛜 This 1760s renovated mansion presents a plush stay in typical Neemrana style – a small number of rooms with lush furnishings, and a historic hook. The rooms overlook a courtyard restaurant which comes alive in the evenings. All 16 rooms are named after French territories, and are well equipped with large sitting areas, day beds – and plenty of art.

The Promenade Hotel ₹₹
☎ 0413–2227750; www.sarovarhotels.com; 23 Goubert Avenue; d incl full board from ₹5000–8000; 🛜 🏊 This sea-facing hotel on Goubert Avenue is perfect for families as it has all the amenities of a large hotel. Two restaurants, a 24-hour cafe and a large buffet spread invite a steady stream of guests (which may not be appreciated by those who are looking for privacy). Room numbers 16, 17, 20 and 21 are recommended for families as they are spacious.

Villa Shanti Hotel ₹₹₹
☎ 0413–4200028; www.lavillashanti.com; 14 Rue Suffren; d incl full board from ₹7000–11,000;

📶 With its high ceilings, white walls and simple wooden furniture, the minimalist furnishings of this recently-launched luxury hotel echo the architecture of the French buildings here. The staff is pleasant and professional. Ideal for those who want a private stay, and are not looking to interact much locally.

🍴 Eating

Madame Shanthes   **Multi-Cuisine ₹₹**
📞 0413-2222022; 40-A, Rue Romain Rolland; 12pm–10pm Rooftop cafe and restaurant, Madame Shanthes is centrally located on Romain Rolland street. Evenings are breezy and relaxed with English retro music playing in the background, as the speedy and polite waiters flit around serving great continental dishes. The seafood here is particularly popular. The alcohol choice is limited.

Rendezvous Café Restaurant   **Multi-Cuisine ₹₹₹**
📞 0413-2339132; No 30 Rue Suffren; 12pm–3pm, 6.30pm–10pm, Tue closed This popular establishment now stands in its new avatar, minus the rooftop that many loved. Despite the structural change, Rendezvous still dishes out great seafood. The fish/chicken/mutton and rice combinations are scrumptious and reasonably priced too.

Le Café   **Cafe ₹₹**
Goubert Avenue; 24 hours A historic address on Goubert Avenue, this used to be the old port of Pondicherry. The great view of the sea, beach and promenade makes up for the slow and disinterested service of this government-run establishment. The chocolate cake and fries here are exceptional.

Le Vietnam   **Vietnamese & French ₹₹₹**
📞 0413-2340111; No 6 Bussy Street; 11pm–11pm The novel blend of Vietnamese and French cuisine is far from peculiar (strains of Vietnamese and French music alternate through the day). The ambience is predominantly Vietnamese, with paintings from the East adorning the walls and chopsticks placed on the table, ready for digging into typical preparations like Pho Bo and Chaiyo.

La Terrasse   **Continental ₹₹**
📞 0413-2220809; No 3 Subbiah Salai; 8.30am–10pm Visit the green and airy La Terrasse for an impressive choice of salads and a continental spread, served in a space resembling a covered garden. The restaurant also has a good selection of fresh juices through the day.

Surguru Spot   **Indian ₹₹**
📞 0413-4308084; No 12 Jawaharlal Nehru Street; 6.30am–10.30pm The Surguru chain is hugely popular with both Indians and foreigners. Here, you'll get value for money, prompt service and a delicious Indian spread.

Visit Surguru for a delightful South Indian breakfast. A busy, no-frills outlet of the same name is located on Mission Street.

Nightlife

Le Club — Restaurant/Bar ₹₹₹
📞 0413-2227409; 38 Dumas Street; 8.30am–11pm One of the most famous restaurants in Pondicherry, Le Club is needlessly over priced when it comes to food, but boasts great ambience for a few drinks. With more than plenty brands to select from, enjoy this breezy garden set-up on Dumas Street.

Asian House — Club ₹₹₹
📞 0413-2226139; 7 Beach Boulevard (South), next to Park Guest House, entry with cover charge single/couple ₹700/1000 If you want to shake a leg in Pondicherry, there is no better place than Asian House. Loud and thumping electronica and dance music and hysterical outbursts can be heard in unison on Saturday nights up to 11pm. The club also invites stags, so be cautious. Hanging around with familiar groups is highly recommended.

Activities

Scuba Diving
📞 9789197227; www.templeadventures.com; Colas Nagar; 9am–6.30pm Ron from Temple Adventures has put together an impressive scuba-diving school here. The best season to experience underwater delights is from May to June, and from September to October. An introduction to scuba diving can be done over a weekend, though four days would be ideal.

Surf Lessons at Kallialay
📞 9442992874; www.surfschoolindia.com; Bodhi Beach Cafe; 10am–6.00pm Take beginner to advanced-level surfing lessons on Bodhi beach (near a small fishing village called Tandryankupam), from the enthusiastic duo of brothers, Juan and Samai. On-beach classes are followed by personal or group instruction at the shallow end of the sea. The teaching is very hands-on and entertaining. Fee (₹800 onwards) includes rash vest and surfboard. It's essential to know how to swim. Bring your own towel and sunscreen.

INTACH (Indian National Trust for Art and Cultural Heritage) Pondicherry Walks
📞 0413-2225991; www.intachpondicherry.org; 62 Rue Aurobindo Street; 9.30am–1pm, 2pm–6.30pm Sat closed Working towards heritage awareness and conservation since 1984, Intach organises guided walks through different pockets of this coastal town. The walks help orient you to the town, and also help one understand the nuances of the architecture and

the social fabric of Pondicherry, a fascinating blend of Tamilians, French, Christians and Muslims. Prior booking is advised.

Kerala Ayurveda — Spa
☏ 0413-6453434; No 27 Muthumariamman Koil Street; 9am–7pm Though not an elaborate luxury establishment, one can get reasonably-priced massages (₹1000 onwards), ideal for weary travellers. Abhyangam, Shirodhana and head-and-shoulders massage are the non-clinical, short-duration treatments that you can choose from here.

🛍 Shopping

Auroboutique — Handicrafts
☏ 0413-2233705; 12-AJ Nehru Street; 9.30am–1pm, 4pm–7.30pm, Tues closed Handmade paper products, candles, incense, soaps and perfumes, crafted by the small-scale industries run by the Aurobindo Ashram, are displayed in this small boutique shop. Highly recommended for reasonably-priced memorabilia and gifts.

Nirvana Boutique
☏ 0413-4209610; 28 Rue Dumas; 10am–1pm, 2pm–7pm, Sun closed Amongst many kitsch product shops, this one offers unique Royal Enfield T-shirts and fridge magnets. Colourful bags, cushions and other bric-a-bracs are in plenty.

Via Pondicherry — Boutique
☏ 0413-2223319; 22 Romain Rolland Street; 9am–1pm, 3pm–8pm, Sun closed Designer Vasanty Manet's creations (mostly bags, scarves and clothes) sit cosily at Via Pondicherry on Romain Rolland. The staff here is helpful and offers constructive guidance while you shop.

Sri Aurobindo — Handmade Paper
☏ 0413-2334763; 50 SV Patel Salai; 9am–5.30pm Mon–Sat, 10am–1pm Sun; no photography allowed One of the small-scale industries that have flourished under the Aurobindo Ashram, this handmade paper unit employs many locals. The workshop is open for visitors and also has an elaborate shop from where one can pick up beautiful – and moderately-priced – paper products.

Take a crash course in surfing

Hampi

Why go?

The magnificent capital of the Vijayanagar Empire, is an architecture buff's dream. Declared a Unesco World Heritage Site, the ruins of over 20 elaborate temples, and many other smaller structures, bear testimony to a flourishing empire in the medieval era. In addition, the boulder-strewn topography, dissected by the Tungabhadra River, provides a stunning backdrop to your experience.

Highlights

- **Virupaksha Temple:** Most iconic of the 83 marked monuments in Hampi.
- **Matanga Paravath:** Climb this hill for some fantastic views of the vast temple-scape.
- **Lotus Mahal & Elephant Stables:** This splendid structure incorporates facets of Hindu and Muslim architecture.
- **Anjanadri Hill, Anegundi:** Believed to be the birthplace of Lord Hanuman.

Trip Planner

Getting There 365km

Tumkur Rd, Bellary-Hiriyur Rd

🚗 7hr

- **Route:** Exit through Tumkur Rd and follow the Bellary-Hiriyur Rd. Before you hit Bellary, take the left and head towards Daroji-Kamlapura Rd. From here Hampi is about 20km. The road is not in great condition; overnight driving is not recommended.

🚌 7hr

- Hampi is well connected by KSRTC buses (AC and non-AC). Buses leave 9.45pm onwards and reach Hospet by 5am. However, you may arrive too early, much before the guesthouses open.

🚆 9hr Hospet

- The Hampi Express (16592) departs at 10pm and reaches Hospet at 7.42am. Autos ply in abundance (₹150) from Hospet, which is 13km from Hampi.

Top The Virupaksha Temple rises above Hampi's landscape

❶ Quick Facts

BEST TIME TO VISIT

J F M A M J J A S O N D

GREAT FOR

[REST STOP] Kamat Upchar is one the better restaurants on this road; it has relatively decent loos, for a highway. Another option is Cafe Coffee Day at Dobbespet.

Stories in Stone

Highlights
1. Virupaksha Temple
2. Matanga Paravath
3. Mahanavami Dibba
4. Lotus Mahal & Elephant Stables
5. Queens' Bath
6. Vijaya Vittala Temple
7. Achyutaraya Temple

Hampi and its neighbouring areas find mention in the Hindu epic *Ramayana* as Kishkinda, the realm of the monkey gods. In 1336, Telugu prince Harihararaya chose Hampi as the site for his new capital Vijayanagar, which – over the next couple of centuries – grew into one of the largest Hindu empires in Indian history.

Hampi, today, has three themes running parallel to each other: a strong religious attachment to Lord Hanuman; the historical perspective of the ruins of an ancient kingdom; and a Bohemian and hippie-like vibe (thanks to the influence of the many backpackers from the West who converge here).

1 VIRUPAKSHA TEMPLE
This Shiva temple is synonymous with the image of Hampi – the town is practically spread around it. A long 'bazaar' street stretches out in front of the shrine, ending in a large monolithic Nandi Bull facing it. Virupaksha is an active temple with plenty of devotees coming here to worship. After manoeuvring through a monkey-infested path, admire the intricate ceiling paintings, and look out for an interesting pin-hole camera image of the tower inside the complex.
Hampi Bazaar; ₹2; 6am–8pm

The hammam or Queens' Bath

2 MATANGA PARAVATH
The Matanga Paravath stands directly opposite the Virupaksha Temple at the far end of the street. Irregular steps lead up to the top, from where you can get an incredible view of the shrine, the bazaar, the Achyuthara Temple in

Quick Facts: Hampi lowdown

The three key points to explore, and experience, here are the main street leading from Virupaksha Temple; the Virupapur Gaddi; and the village of Anegundi. Hampi Bazaar and the village of Kamalapuram are the two main points of entry to the ruins.

The ruins are divided into two areas: the Sacred Centre, around Hampi Bazaar; and the Royal Centre, towards Kamalapuram. To the northeast across the Tungabhadra River is the Virupapur Gaddi, and the historic village of Anegundi further beyond.

front, and other ruins. On the hilltop is the small and simple Veerabhuvneshwara Temple. The trek up takes about 30 minutes. The sunrise view is highly recommended (for that you will have to stay this side of the river, closer to the spot).

❸ MAHANAVAMI DIBBA

For relief from the temple trails, visit the Mahanavami Dibba, which was a monument built to commemorate King Krishnadevaraya's victory over the Kingdom of Kalinga. The 22ft-tall plateau has a 1600sqft-wide platform on top. The walls are embellished with carvings of hunting scenes and elephant processions. The complex also has a geometrically-designed 'kalyani' (bathing pool).

8am–5.30pm

A stone chariot outside Vittala Temple

An arched pavilion in the Lotus Mahal

④ LOTUS MAHAL & ELEPHANT STABLES
The distinctive look of this monument is apparent in its blend of Hindu and Muslim architectural styles. The Lotus Mahal is flanked by lush and well-maintained gardens; it was probably a rest house for royalty. Further on from the gate stand eleven dome-shaped stables; these were constructed for the royal elephants.
Hampi Bazaar; ₹10; 6am–8pm

⑤ QUEENS' BATH
One of the more detailed structures here, there is no doubt that the bath or hammam, with its special aesthetics, was built for the many queens that Krishnadevaraya married. Beautiful windows hang over a central bathing pool, more than hinting at a life of extravagance.
8am–5.30pm

⑥ VIJAYA VITTALA TEMPLE
Built in 1513, this temple is dedicated to Lord Vishnu and is considered an architectural marvel for its musical pillars and extraordinary workmanship. However, due to heavy wear and tear, the Archeological Survey of India (ASI) has

ⓘ Detour: *Daroji Sloth Bear Sanctuary*

Just 17km from Hampi, the immaculately clean and well maintained Daroji Bear Sanctuary is home to (amongst other animals) 120 sloth bears; they can be seen roaming a wide gorge from a watch tower. The bears are given their food at 2pm, so it's best to get here an hour later, when you can watch them from relatively closer. You can drive up to the watch tower.

Kamlapura; adults/children ₹50/25; camera ₹300; 1.30pm–6pm

now banned guides from showing visitors how the pillars sounded when struck. The iconic chariot, inspired by the one in Konark, was functional till it was cemented in by the authorities. The long pathway to the temple can now be crossed in battery-operated vehicles (₹20 per ride).
Hampi Bazaar; ₹10; 6am–8pm

❼ ACHYUTARAYA TEMPLE

This important Vishnu temple is marked by its pillared walkway, which can be distinctly seen from the Mathanga Paravath. The pillars have carvings depicting episodes from the *Mahabharata* and *Ramayana* (as do the other large shrines here). It has a wide 'bazaar' street in front, indicating that the Vijayanagar Kingdom had flourishing trade. It also has a kalyana mandapa (marriage hall), like many other temples from that era.
8am–5.30pm

A coracle by the Tungabhadra River

✓ *Top Tip: River crossing*

Hampi street and Virupapur Gaddi are separated by the Tungabhadra River, across which two boats ferry people every day between 7am and 6pm (₹15 per ride). Be aware of the timings, as getting stuck on either side would mean a ride of 40km by auto on a different route.

Accommodation

Hospet (the rail and bus hub closest to Hampi) is situated 13km away, and is a slightly larger town with comfortable hotels offering amenities like pool, in-house restaurants and internet. Since Hampi provides mostly backpacking stay options, this is suitable for those travelling with families. For cheap and clean guesthouses (and better access to food and beer), Virupapur Gaddi is recommended.

HOSPET

Sri Krishna Inn — Hotel ₹₹
8394294300; www.krishnapalacehotel.com; Station Rd, Hospet; d incl breakfast from ₹4770–5500; The first thing that strikes you about this four-year-old establishment is the extremely courteous and accommodating staff. A warm welcome is extended even if you arrive at an ungodly hour. Rooms are clean and well equipped (though slightly musty-smelling). A gym, swimming pool and internet facilities are unanticipated and, therefore, welcome.

Royal Orchid Central — Hotel ₹₹₹
8394300100; www.royalorchidhotels.com; Station Rd, Hospet; d incl breakfast from ₹8359; This is undoubtedly the best luxury option in Hospet but it does not match the chain's other hotels across the country. Though Royal Orchid does have all the expected amenities, they are not in top condition. A swimming pool, spa and gymnasium make up for what is otherwise a modest place to stay.

HAMPI

Shanthi Guest House — Guesthouse ₹
8394325352; www.shanthihampi.com; Virupapur Gaddi, Hampi; d incl full board from ₹800–1500 (depending on season) In terms of aesthetics and amenities, Shanthi has led the way since 1992. It has basic, clean rooms (thatched or concrete), each with a mosquito net and a swing outside. The staff is cheerful, trained and welcoming. Shanthi also has an in-house travel desk, and can arrange for sightseeing with local guides.

Mowgli Guest House — Guesthouse ₹
9448003606; www.mowglihampi.com; Virupapur Gaddi, Hampi; d incl full board from ₹990–1200 (depending on season) The basic rooms at Mowgli either face lush paddy fields or the courtyard. A mosquito net is the only additional necessity provided. The lounge area has Hampi-style floor seating, great food and some lazing farm animals in the vicinity, to add to the ambience of an easy-paced holiday.

Boulders Hotel ₹₹₹
☏9242641551; www.hampisboulders.com; Narayanpet, Bandi Harlapura Munirabad, Koppal District; d incl breakfast and dinner ₹9000–11000; ✱

The only non-backpacking option in Hampi, Boulders is for those seeking a plush holiday. Spacious sit-outs and exclusive rooms promise undisturbed views of the River Tungabhadra, flowing right beside the property. The hotel offers a nature trail where you can view stunning rock formations from a rickety wooden walk-bridge and a vantage deck set up on a cave.

Eating

Mango Tree Multi-Cuisine ₹₹
☏9448765213; Riverside Drive, Hampi; 7.30am–9.30pm An inconspicuous gate into a banana plantation leads you to Hampi's most popular haunt. You are greeted by a dozen cats and dogs, and a stepped, amphitheatre-like area with 'barefoot' seating. Floor mats are perfect for taking in the river view. The egg curry and roti combo, downed with a mango lassi, is the perfect start to a lazy afternoon here.

Activities

Coracle Rides
There are two points in Hampi from where coracles operate; one is near the Kodanda Rama Temple and the other, Talwarkatta in Anegundi. Immensely popular with tourists, apart from the novelty of the ride, it also gives an opportunity to see rock formations on the banks. If you are starting from the Kodanda Rama side, ask to see the thousand lingas and sleeping Vishnu sculptures on the rocks. Depending on the duration of the ride, it can cost you anywhere between ₹150 and ₹250 per head. Bargain well.

Shopping

Clothes & Jewellery
In tune with its Bohemian status, Hampi is sprinkled with small shack-like shops selling clothes and jewellery. You can find flowing harem pants, string tops and such on the other side of the river. These shops were earlier lined adjacent to the Virupaksha Temple in the main Hampi Bazaar, but have now been shifted to Virupapur Gaddi.

Gali Music Shop
☏9449982586; Virupapur Gaddi; 10am–7pm Meet the music wizard, Gali, at his shop on the Virupapur Gaddi. A multitude of Vietnamese and African instruments line his tiny shop; you can learn to play – and buy – some of the instruments. Gali picked up technique from visiting foreigners but now plays regularly at some of the guesthouses in the evenings.

NATURE ESCAPES

- Ramanagaram 152
- Bheemeshwari 156
- Yelagiri Hills 162
- Hogenakkal 170
- Sakleshpur 174
- Chikmagalur 182
- Wayanad 192
- Brahmagiri Trek 202
- Tadiandamol Trek 206
- Kudremukh Trek 212

■ The Irupu Falls at Brahmagiri

Ramanagaram Day Trip

Why go?

Rock-climbing destinations don't come much better, or more popular. In quirky Ramanagaram, you can marvel at some of the world's oldest granite outcrops – or even better, climb them. Film buffs can pay homage to the surrounding landscape, scene of iconic flicks ('Sholay' topping the list); while those with an interest in silk can visit India's biggest cocoon market.

Highlights

- **Rock Climbing:** Try climbing the 'Gabbar Ki Asli Pasand' rock!
- **Ramadevara Betta:** Climb a few hundred steps to reach this famous Rama temple with a breathtaking view.

RAMANAGARAM 153

Trip Planner

Getting There — 50km

🚗 **1hr 30min** — **SH17**

• **Route:** Take the easily navigated Bengaluru-Mysore Rd (SH17) to get to Ramanagram.

🚌 **2hr 30min**

• Most buses going to Mysore/Coorg, from the Satellite bus stand on Mysore Rd, will pass through here.

Top and *Bottom* The granite rocks of Ramanagaram

ℹ️ Quick Facts

BEST TIME TO VISIT

[J F M] A M J J A [S O N D]

GREAT FOR

Spa | 🚫 | 🔒 | 🚶 | ♥ | 🧍

REST STOP Taj Biryani Paradise (short of the township) for meals; petrol pumps for toilet break.

Rocking & Rolling

Highlights
1. **Rock Climbing**
2. **Ramadevara Betta**

If you have watched *Sholay*, the path-breaking film of the 1970s (and who hasn't?), you've been to Ramanagaram without having travelled there. This place is defined by its topography. Gabbar's sinister-looking Ramgarh, surrounded by mammoth rocky outcrops, is today a climbers' paradise.

But Ramanagaram is more than just about rocks and *Sholay*. Named after the Ramgiri Hills, this town is equally popular with nature enthusiasts and birdwatchers. It is home to endangered species like the yellow-throated bulbul and the long-billed vulture. Sloth bears have also been known to make an appearance around here.

The iconic backdrop to some truly iconic movies

📷 *Snapshot: 'Filmy' landscape*

The granite hills of Ramanagaram have appeared as a backdrop in a number of films. Most notably in *Sholay*, the iconic Bollywood blockbuster that had all the elements of a spaghetti western – bandits on horseback, fierce gunfights, train robberies and a rocky terrain.

The rugged landscape also shows up as the echoey Marabar Caves, in David Lean's *A Passage To India*. For the film, the production team had faux cave entrances chiselled into the smooth rock-face; the shallow doorways still exist, and can be spotted some distance away.

> ### ✓ *Top Tip: Guided climbing*
>
> **Mars Adventures** does a typical guided trip that departs from Bengaluru at 6am and reaches Ramanagaram an hour later, after a packed breakfast en route. The next four or five hours are devoted to rock climbing, using ropes and harnesses. Lunch break at one of the eateries on the highway is followed by 'free-hand bouldering'. Tea and snacks are provided before you're ferried back to Bengaluru.
>
> **☏9886664666; www.marsadventures.in; 501 Kamakshi Nilaya, RM Nagar Main Road, Doda Banaswadi Post, Bengaluru; ₹950 per person (including travel, meals, permit, gear)**

The town's traditional occupation, however, is silk-worm farming (Ramanagaram houses India's largest cocoon market). With close to a hundred factories churning out pure silk, it has earned itself the sobriquet of 'silk town'. Most of the silk produced here finds its way into the coveted sarees made in Mysore.

❶ ROCK CLIMBING

Ramanagram's proximity to Bengaluru allows comfortable day excursions. Giant rocks dot the landscape to the right of the Bengaluru–Mysore Highway, and are visible from afar. Once there, look for signs to turn off towards the starting points. Permits costing ₹150 to ₹250 are required from the forest department (Arangya Bhawan, Malleshwaram, Bengaluru). It's advisable to do this activity under professional supervision, and using quality outdoor gear.

❷ RAMADEVARA BETTA

Turn right after Ghousia College; drive on for a couple of kilometres on a narrow winding road and you'll arrive at the base of this temple hillock. The first flight of steps leads you to a Hanuman Temple beside a natural pool, formed by water collecting in a stony crevice. Another rather steep flight, cut into the rock face, reaches skywards to the Rama Temple. It's not for the faint-hearted. The magnificent panorama will take your breath away – if the climb hasn't already done so. Don't forget to bring a cap, water and sunscreen lotion.

Bheemeshwari

Why go?

Immerse yourself in the serenity of nature beside the Kaveri, southern India's most majestic river. Trek through the lush forests of the Basavana Betta; watch birds and spot wildlife. Check out of metro madness for some well-deserved stargazing. Or simply play 'spot the difference' between rocks and crocs.

Highlights

- **Trekking:** Options for the adventurous – and the not-so-adventurous.
- **Rafting:** The Kaveri offers an enjoyable outing for beginners.
- **Wildlife:** A feast for the eyes for animal and bird lovers.

BHEEMESHWARI 157

Trip Planner

Getting There 100km

🚗 **3hr** Kanakapura-Kollegal Highway

- **Route:** Drive 15km past Kanakapura town, turn left at Sathanur and go down Muttathi Rd. The JLR Camp is located 5km past Muttathi.

🚌 **4hr**

- Buses for Kanakapura depart regularly from KR Market. Frequency from Kanakapura to Bheemeshwari is very limited.

Quick Facts

BEST TIME TO VISIT

J F M A M J J A S O N D

GREAT FOR

REST STOP Lookout for petrol stations, for essential facilities.

Top Green as far as the eye can see
Bottom A grizzled squirrel

In the Lap of Nature

Highlights
1. Trekking High & Low
2. River Rafting
3. Animal & Bird Spotting

A former angling paradise, Bheemeshwari is located in Mandya district, between the Barachukki and Gaganachukki falls. The surrounding Kaveri Wildlife Sanctuary, through which the sacred river flows leisurely, is fast becoming a popular spot to encounter the abundant joys of nature. The sanctuary is home to crocodiles, leopards, monkeys, deer and wild boar, while among avian life you are likely to spot cormorants, ibis, kingfishers and herons.

A comfortable ride from Bengaluru, Bheemeshwari has also become a favourite of the corporate set, seeking to unwind from their hectic, office-bound lives. Throw in some kayaking and mountain biking, and you can also experience the adrenaline rush of an adventure break.

1 TREKKING HIGH & LOW
Bheemeshwari has treks of varying durations, for both beginners and professionals. Treks here are categorised as easy, moderate and tough, depending on the distance (from as little as 4km, up to 30km). Snaking trails along the Kaveri, including one from Basavana Betta that winds along Chellure Hill almost parallel to the river, present a panoramic view of the valley below. You can also camp under the stars, in the craggy terrain of the Kaveri Wildlife Sanctuary.

Snapshot: The sacred River Kaveri

Legend has it that Brahma gave his celestial daughter Vishnumaya (or Lopamudra) to Kavera Muni in adoption, as a reward for the latter's long penance. Vishnumaya's adopted father married her to Sage Agasthya before her wish to serve mankind was granted. In order to continue her noble cause, she assumed the form of a river, Kaveri (also called Dakshin Ganga). The entire course she traverses is considered holy ground. The sacred river is worshipped as Goddess Kaveriamma in numerous shrines along the way.

📷 *Snapshot: Mahseer alert!*

The mahseer had established a reputation as a fighter fish, surpassing the likes of trout and salmon. Said to be the biggest – and finest – tropical game fish known to anglers, it's also known as the 'large-headed one'. The waters of the Kaveri are considered a natural habitat of the silver, golden, pink and black mahseer.

Once a serious pastime, mahseer angling is now banned, except for supervised catch and release in some spots (p266).

❷ RIVER RAFTING

The Kaveri is ideal for rafting, especially if you're a novice. One can easily tackle the moderately fast rapids at Bheemeshwari – the 8km run is enjoyable without being too terrifying. This scenic ride passes through verdant forest and beautiful valleys. The monsoon is the best time to indulge in a spot of river rafting.

❸ ANIMAL & BIRD SPOTTING

With a rich ecosystem that supports wildlife, Bheemeshwari is home to over 200 species of birds, including the commonly sighted grey-headed fish eagle and the pied-crested cuckoo. Among the mammals one can spot here are sambar, spotted deer, jackals and elephants, as well as the endangered grizzled giant squirrel.

Waterbirds on the river

Accommodation

Bheemeshwari Adventure and Nature Camp — Camp ₹₹₹

☎8231694248, 9379454317; www.junglelodges.com; Byadarahalli Post, Halgur Hobli, Malavalli Taluk; **₹8000–13,000 (incl lodging, meals, guided treks, coracle rides, forest entry, camera fees, and taxes)** A Jungle Lodges and Resorts property, the camp, looking out over the Kaveri River, embraces the enterprise's well-known eco-tourism philosophy. Equipped with eight log huts and 10 tented cottages that blend with the wooded environs, it is the perfect spot for those looking to connect with nature.

Eating

Gol Ghar — North & South Indian ₹

10am–8pm An open-to-all-sides circular gazebo, Gol Ghar offers a sumptuous buffet of delicious north and south Indian vegetarian and non-vegetarian dishes. All meals, including tea at the crack of dawn, are served at pre-specified times. Do keep a watchful eye out for errant simians.

The accommodation here blends with the natural surroundings

Activities

Jungle Lodges and Resorts organise the following activities exclusively for the guests at the Bheemeshwari Adventure and Nature Camp:

Day Visit

☎8231694248, 9379454317; www.junglelodges.com; **₹1500 per person (incl lunch, tea, coracle ride, guided trek, forest entry, camera fees, and taxes); 10am–5.30pm** A typical excursion will comprise of a welcome drink at check-in, followed by a two-hour trek. A post-lunch coracle ride takes up the afternoon, before evening tea and check-out.

Adventure Package

☎8231694248, 9379454317; www.junglelodges.com; **₹2000 per person (incl meals, entry permits, camera fees, and taxes); 10am–5.30pm** This package includes rope and water-based activities – including 'Burma loop', zip-line and 'parallel walk' – in the first half of the day. Kayaking and a coracle ride in the second half are followed by tea and check-out.

Veer off the Highway

The Mysore Road (SH17) is one of the major exits from Bengaluru, and is the route taken for many destinations out of the city. Head southwest on Mysore Road to reach Coorg, Masinagudi, Bandipur, Ooty, Coonoor and Wayanad. En route, one can stop in places like Channapatna and Kokkare Belur Bird Sanctuary – informative and fun pit-stops if travelling with the family.

- **Channapatna** – The dwindling Persian art form of making wooden toys and lacquer-ware can be seen in this small town (after Ramnagar). The toys are made from the soft wood of the local 'Aale mara' tree, which is cut into blocks, made moisture free and then hand- or machine-chiselled to make attractive toys using vegetable (non-toxic) dyes. To pick up attractive souvenirs, visit the Katerpillar shop at Kadambam restaurant. Contact the owner, Mr Venkatesh (📞080–27253358) in advance if you want to visit his toy-making unit.

- **Kokkare Belur** – A bizarre flock of painted storks and spot-billed pelicans have adopted a small village 21km from Channapatna (13km left off the highway). Visitors meander though the scenic village road to Kokkare Belur to witness this striking spectacle. Most of the trees and roof-tops are packed with these avian friends, who do not venture outside the village limits. The villagers are used to the persistent cacophony from all around, and consider themselves blessed as the chosen spot for the birds.

- **Heritage Winery** – Swing left, just after Channapatna and before Kadambam Hotel, to the Heritage Winery, 1km inside. The bottling plant is set amidst a rustic backdrop; the winery has an open restaurant and a small educational video on wines in India. Book ahead for a guided tour and tasting (45 minutes to an hour); contact Linet Sequeira (📞9741798666) between 10.30am and 5pm.

Pelicans roosting in a tree at Kokkare Belur village

Yelagiri Hills

Why go?

Pretty farmhouses sitting by green fields, fruit orchards and forests and perfect weather in every season sum up the Yelagiri experience. But the area offers more than just natural beauty. There are a number of man-made attractions here – you can go boating on the Punganur Lake, enjoy the expansive gardens of the Nature Park, or even opt for an adventure activity.

Highlights

- **Swami Malai:** The highest point in the hills, offering stunning views all around.

- **Punganur Lake:** A man-made lake rimmed by picnic attractions, popular with families.

- **Jalgam Parai:** A pretty seasonal waterfall on the other side of the hills.

YELAGIRI HILLS

Trip Planner

Getting There   160km

🚗 3hr   NH7, NH48

• **Route:** Take the NH7 to Krishnagiri (follow the road signs carefully). Take the NH48 towards Vaniyambadi and Chennai. Turn right onto Kethandapatti Rd, 2km from the toll gate. Take a left to cross the railway lines and head towards the Tirupattur–Vaniyambadi Rd; turn right, towards Tirupattur. Take a left at Ponneri for Yelagiri Hills.

🚌 4hr

• Buses go regularly to Krishnagiri from Majestic bus terminus. There are also regular buses from Krishnagiri to Tirupattur, and Tirupattur to Yelagiri.

🚆 3hr   Jolarpettai

• The Lalbagh Express (12608) departs from Bengaluru City station at 6.30am for Jolarpettai Junction. Buses and taxis for Yelagiri are available from the station.

Top Colourful mustard fields
Bottom Punganur Lake

❶ Quick Facts

BEST TIME TO VISIT

[J F M] A M J J A S [O N D]

GREAT FOR

Spa · Dining · Privacy · Activities · Romance · Family

REST STOP Freshen up at Krishnagiri before getting onto the highway; Ponneri is the last stop before a steep climb.

Land of Fruit & Honey

Highlights
1. Swami Malai Hill
2. Punganur Lake
3. Nature Park
4. Lord Murugan Temple
5. Jalgam Parai Waterfall

Sleepy and undisturbed, the Yelagiri Hills comprise 14 different hamlets: some touched by the main road that runs through the hills, others only accessible by the dirt roads that fork away in unexpected directions.

When the wind blows from the west, it carries with it the powerful fragrance of eucalyptus trees, but otherwise, during the summer, almost every village is suffused with the aroma of ripening jackfruit, punctuated every now and then by the smell of mangroves. In fact, walking through the villages of Yelagiri, one is struck by the profusion of fruit that grows here, all just an arm's length away.

Even with growing development and tourism, the hills are predominantly agricultural, with private bungalows, missionary schools, temples, churches, forest and farmland dotting the landscape. It is an invitation to visitors – an opportunity to discover a completely different rhythm of living every day.

Swami Malai is the highest hill in Yelagiri

❶ SWAMI MALAI HILL
This is the highest point in the Yelagiri Hills area and, not surprisingly, provides a spectacular view of the surrounding hills as well as the countryside below. It's a stimulating 3km walk from Mangalam village, Swami Malai's base. Depending on the weather, it is advisable to start early to avoid the intensity of the sun.

❷ PUNGANUR LAKE
Located almost in the centre of the hills, the spot offers a panoramic view of the surrounding area. You can make your way to the villages on the other side of the hills just by walking along the promenade that hedges the lake. This is a popular spot for tourists – particularly families – with landscaped gardens, a snacks corner, playground and facilities for boating.

Adult/child ₹10/5; camera ₹5; boating 20min/10min ₹50/25, group of 4 ₹200, discounts for children

❸ NATURE PARK
Situated directly opposite the lane that leads to the Punganur Lake, this park is a delightfully landscaped series of gardens flush with flowering trees, built to attract those who enjoy quieter pleasures. Apart from some minor attractions – like a water cascade, musical fountains and a limited aquarium – the park offers visitors an opportunity to laze about on its manicured lawns and enjoy the weather.

♥ *If You Like: Horticulture*

At the Athanavoor bus stop is the Arun nursery, run by P. Jayachandran. It is deceptively large and contains over 200 kinds of plants: from a variety of flowering and fruit-bearing trees to different kinds of cacti, bamboo and palm trees, including the most coveted (and extremely expensive) Cycus palm. If you have a green thumb of any size, this nursery is for you.

But even if you don't, a short stroll through the nursery can leave one wide-eyed and open-mouthed at the incomprehensible diversity of nature – and all in one place.

The nursery also has a branch in Punganur, selling saplings of many of the plants available at the main nursery. ☏9486335499, 9443967564, 9486081182; Athanavoor bus stop.

Punganur; adult/child ₹15/5; camera/video ₹10/50; 8am–8pm; parking, cars/two-wheelers ₹10/5; musical fountain adult/child ₹25/10, 7pm

❹ LORD MURUGAN TEMPLE

There's no pealing of temple bells here as the wind blows on this small rise above Nilavoor Road. The statue of Lord Murugan stares down from the boulder on which it stands, mace in one hand and a cobra in the other. Fruit trees grow at the base of the temple stairs, where local boys can often be found, picking whatever fruit they can lay their hands on.
Nilavoor Rd

❺ JALGAM PARAI WATERFALL

The waterfall at Jalgam Parai now only flows from around September to January, once the monsoon arrives. The surrounding area is lush, however, and a trek (or taxi ride) to the spot during the drier months is rewarding for the moment's solitude it offers, and the chance to enjoy the idyllic weather of the hills.
5km from Lord Murugan Temple

Custard apple grows in profusion at Yelagiri

✓ Top Tip: Nature's bounty

Yelagiri is home to innumerable fruit orchards – mango, jackfruit, custard apple, starfruit and jamun, to name but a few. And accompanying this profusion of fruit, there is also natural honey to be found in the groves and forests. The locals harvest both fruits and honey, and sell them freely in shops and roadside stalls. Be sure to pick some up.

🛏 Accommodation

A range of self-contained resorts pepper the hillside – from quiet, nature-oriented estates to large resorts offering urbane luxuries.

Zeenath Taj Gardens Hotel ₹
📞4179245231, 4179295445, 4179245376; Kottaiyur village & post; d ₹750; P The most 'homely' of all the hotels and resorts in the area. The cottages, surrounded by gardens and orchards, have simple yet clean and comfortable interiors. You'll get a warm welcome from the staff. Home-cooked meals are served three times a day, with breakfast and lunch served in the open air, under the trees.

Madhura Resort ₹
📞4179245320, 4179295451, 4179295511; www.sterlingholidays.com; 164 Athanavur Main Rd; d ₹2500; P A Sterling Holidays hotel, Madhura lives up to the brand's standard. All rooms are doubles, with refrigerators and large bathrooms. The hotel organises picnics and day trips and often hosts large groups, both private as well as corporate. There is a playground for children, as well as a massage centre.

O Nila Resorts Resort ₹
📞4179245371, 4179245241; www.onilayelagiri.com; Mangalam Rd; cottages/deluxe rooms/standard rooms ₹1500/2000/3500; P 🏊 Possibly the most elaborate hotel in the area – with a swimming pool and multi-gym to boot – O Nila also offers cycles on hire, for travellers looking to explore the hills independently. Cottages are ideal for families, housing up to four people at a time. Evenings spent at an open-air cinema or around a bonfire are arranged at an extra cost.

Hotel Landmark Deluxe Hotel ₹₹
📞4179295410, 4179295411; www.hotellandmarkyelagiri.com; Boat House Rd, Athanavur, opp Murugan Temple; d ₹3500; P Situated between the Punganur Lake and the Murugan Temple, this hotel boasts an impressive number of rooms – and sophisticated facades, with faux-Roman statues adorning its lawns. The rooms are spacious, regularly serviced and (given the layout of the hotel) provide ample privacy. The Hotel Landmark also offers special group packages, making it ideal for large groups.

Peter's Park Cottages ₹₹
📞4179295456; www.petersparkyelagiri.com; 3–510 Manjankollai Pudur; cottages from ₹3500–4500; P Offering exclusive private cottages as accommodation, Peter's Park is the perfect destination for a group getaway, with either family or friends. The smallest of the cottages houses four people, and there are special discounts for children and for

A private cottage at Peter's Park is perfect for a family vacation

groups of 20 people. The rooms are immaculately kept. Food is served at regular mealtimes as well as snacks and tea early in the evening.

Mid Valley Residence　　　Resort ₹₹₹

☏4179245238, 9894156728; www.midvalleyresidence.com; 48/1 Athanavur Rd; villas 2-bedroom/3-bedroom ₹7000/10,000 Particularly protective of its guests' privacy, the Mid Valley Residence is the most exclusive of all the resorts in Yelagiri. The facilities are ultra-modern, with a health club and multi-gym included. The hotel itself is divided into self-contained villas with well-equipped kitchens attached. Bookings are only made online, through the hotel's website.

Eating

Nigress　　　North & South Indian ₹

Kottaiyur; 8am–10pm The only restaurant in the area that also offers open-air seating, Nigress serves 'tiffin' even during hours other than regular mealtimes. The kebabs are undoubtedly the best items on the menu, though they're only available in the evenings. Like all other establishments in these hills, it is a 'non-alcoholic zone', and smoking is also strictly prohibited.

Tandoori Hut　North & South Indian ₹

Punganur; 10am–10pm Located near Punganur Lake, this small restaurant offers decent south Indian breakfasts and boasts of serving the best biryani in the hills. It is perhaps the best option in the area, especially after an invigorating walk or a bout of paddle-boating on the lake.

Activities

Yelagiri Adventure Sports Association (YASA)
☏ 9840593194, 9442357711, 9444449591, 9444033307; www.yasa.co.in; Athanavoor Main Rd The Yelagiri Adventure Sports Association is predominantly active during the months of April and May, the summer holiday season. Offering courses by trained professionals in paragliding, rock climbing and trekking, YASA does its best to attract adventure enthusiasts to the hills.

Subuthi Massage
☏ 4179245320, 8940498660; Kottaiyur Rd This massage parlour is part of the Madhura Hotel and offers traditional Ayurvedic treatments through a variety of methods, from oil massages and aromatherapies to purifying treatments that can last up to seven days. There are only two massage rooms, so one will need to make an appointment before visiting. The staff are friendly and help you choose treatments. Both children and adults can avail of the therapies.

♥ *If You Like: Walking*

Most people choose to drive through the Yelagiri Hills, but for those interested in getting a closer look, there is no better way than on foot.

Yelagiri is not so much a location as a situation that looks a lot like an untidy shoe-string. One road winds its way between the villages of the hills, splitting away every now and then but always winding its way back into a single line.

Pastures, paddy fields, fruit orchards and forestland cover most of the distance between the villages, sloping away from the road in either direction.

The weather is generally refreshing, although the sun can be strong and the rain frequent during its season, so it's best to carry a sunhat and an umbrella. A bottle of water, and a comfortable pair of walking shoes, would not go amiss. And if you intend to pick up any fruit along the way, remember to bring a bag along – one that's easy to carry!

| Yelagiri Hills is a paradise for walkers

Hogenakkal Day Trip

Why go?

Hogenakkal is primarily a place of pilgrimage, being the precise spot where the Kaveri enters Tamil Nadu in a series of waterfalls. Pilgrims and tourists gather under the falls to bathe and coracles take sightseers down the river. A crocodile centre, housing a large number of these dozing beasts, adds to the attractions of an interesting day trip.

Highlights

- **Hogenakkal Falls**: The waterfalls attract hundreds of people every week.
- **Coracle Rides:** Large basket-like boats bear passengers down the river.
- **Crocodile Rehabilitation Centre:** Houses a number of sunbathing crocs.

HOGENAKKAL

Trip Planner

Getting There — 182km

🚗 **3hr** — Hosur Rd/NH7

Route: Take the Hosur Rd down to Krishnagiri. Turn right on NH7 at Krishnagiri and drive south to Dharmapuri. At Dharmapuri, take a right on the first major turning as you enter the town, onto the Dharmapuri–Hogenakkal Rd to the falls.

🚌 **3hr 45min**

• There are direct bus services to Dharmapuri; contact a local travel agent for more details. Reserved bus tickets can cost as much as ₹300.

🚆 **3hr 45min** — Dharmapuri

• The Ernakulam Express (12677), departing at 6.15am, is the only express train to Dharmapuri. Local trains leave regularly from the Yesvantpur station; buses are available to Hogenakkal from Dharmapuri.

Top The many waterfalls
Bottom Coracle-weaving in progress

ⓘ Quick Facts

BEST TIME TO VISIT

J F M A M J **J A** S O N D

GREAT FOR

Spa 🍴 🔒 🚶 ❤ 👪

REST STOP Stop at Krishnagiri for a snack and rest.

For Faith or Fun

Highlights
1. Hogenakkal Falls
2. Coracle Rides
3. Crocodile Rehabilitation Centre
4. River Bathing

Hogenakkal is a small village with a big waterfall attracting both the fun-loving and the faithful. The Kaveri River enters Tamil Nadu precisely at this point, steadily and powerfully making its way across the stones, down to the Stanley Reservoir.

The village and the area around the falls bear witness to a perpetual flow of humanity that arrives to pay its respects to the gods – or simply to enjoy the river and the roar of the waterfalls. Many parts are unpleasant, littered with garbage, but a coracle ride around the falls can certainly revive one's spirits. Hawkers nearby sell all the necessities for bathing in the falls – soaps, shampoo, towels, and even a change of clothes. Nearby, professional masseurs stand ready, and food stalls sell fried fish and marinated chicken.

1 HOGENAKKAL FALLS
You need to cross the river twice – once across a hanging bridge, and again across some slippery rocks – to get a proper look at the main falls. Though the path is well marked, you should be careful as the rocks are uneven and slippery with sand and litter. Once past the stones, however, you'll have the chance to enjoy the unsullied and tranquil natural beauty of the trees and rocks lining the banks of the Kaveri.

2 CORACLE RIDES
A ride down the Kaveri in coracles, large basket-like boats, can be both gentle and thrilling. The boatmen steer the coracles almost directly under the main falls, and one

---

Value for Money: Fresh fish

The food stalls around the waterfalls are good places to get cheap and tasty fried fish. Choose the piece you want; the best shops have at least two varieties of fish on display. A large piece costs ₹20. The stalls are open from 7am to 8pm.

> ### ✓ *Top Tip: Getting in and out*
> Start early from Bengaluru, as the drive is over three hours. Leave Hogenakkal before sundown. Though there are hotels in the area, they are not recommended.

can hardly avoid getting wet. You can even, if you wish, persuade the boatmen to stop at mid-river islands for a break. Although a single ticket costs ₹10 and is to be paid to a government official, the real cost of hiring a coracle depends on the boatman. If reserving a boat (as most people do), charges are negotiated according to the number of persons and the number of hours, costing up to ₹600.

❸ CROCODILE REHABILITATION CENTRE

A very short distance away from the bus stop is the crocodile rehabilitation centre. Some crocodiles are juvenile, barely five feet long, but there are others twice as long from the tip of their noses to the end of their tails. For only ₹1, you can see them sunbathing together in separate enclosures (though there is seldom anyone to collect the fee).

❹ RIVER BATHING

Past the fish market, make your way down to the sandier banks of the Kaveri River, away from the crowds. Here, one can bathe and swim at a quiet spot. It is advised, however, to pay heed to the safety signs, urging swimmers and bathers to stay away from the more turbulent parts of the Kaveri, where the water tends to swirl with undercurrents.

A local boy dives into the river

Sakleshpur

Why go?

A lesser-known coffee destination, under-the-radar Sakleshpur makes for a welcome change from the regular stops on the plantation trail. Nature lovers will surely delight in the estate walks (with ample opportunity for birdwatching), while those with a taste for adventure can look forward to some hiking in the hills of the Western Ghats.

Highlights

- **Plantation Visit:** Experience the fresh, open vistas of the coffee estates.
- **Manjarabad Fort:** Climb up and soak in the stunning views.
- **Bisle Reserve Forest:** Discover the joys of nature in the fringes of the forest.

SAKLESHPUR **175**

Trip Planner

Getting There 226km

🚗 **4hr 30min** NH48

- **Route:** Take the Nelamangala Rd onto NH48 and follow it through Sakleshpur. All resorts and homestays are off the main highway; one needs clear directions from the bus stop.

🚌 **6hr**

- Take any of the KSRTC buses, starting from Kempegowda bus stand, for Mangalore. Get down at the Sakleshpur bus stop (₹535 onwards). An overnight bus would be perfect to optimise time, but ensure that you coordinate a pick-up at Sakleshpur, as the bus reaches at an unearthly hour (there's an old and a new bus stand, so specify which one you'll be alighting at).

🚆 **7hr** **Sakleshpur**

- The overnight Bangalore-Mangalore Express (16515) leaves from Yesvantpur Junction at 7.30am and reaches at 12.40pm.

Top A local tea estate *Bottom* Bisle Forest

ⓘ Quick Facts

BEST TIME TO VISIT

[J] [F] [M] A M J J A S [O] [N] [D]

GREAT FOR

Spa 🍴 🔒 👫 ❤ 👬

REST STOP Get Inn Food Court is the only place for a quick snack, and a decent loo. But this short ride is easily done in one go.

Off the Beaten Coffee Trail

Highlights
1. Manjarabad Fort
2. Manjehalli Falls
3. Plantation Visit
4. Betta Byreshwara
5. Bisle Reserve Forest

Sakleshpur's history goes back to the 6th century, when it was ruled by the ancient Chalukya dynasty; during the medieval period, the Hoysalas held sway here. However, it was the British rulers who recognised its potential as a fertile coffee location, with the pleasant weather adding to its appeal. Colonial touches can still be seen in the plantation life that revolves around old bungalows and the club culture.

Cross the bridge over the Hemavathi River, at the entrance of this small but busy town, and turn into any of the two arterial roads. The dramatically wild and unmanicured landscape, quite typical of coffee plantations, unfolds around you. Home to the second highest peak in Karnataka, Jenukal Gudda, Sakleshpur offers scenic mountain views from everywhere. Unfortunately, trekking to this peak has recently been stopped by the authorities. Bear in mind that the interior roads are difficult to negotiate; a four-wheel drive is recommended, especially during the monsoon, as the roads change very quickly from paved to muddy.

1 MANJARABAD FORT
Trek up a stairway (unfortunately littered with plastic) to this weathered fort, built by Tipu Sultan as a strategic defense location. The effort of dragging yourself up the steep hill is certainly rewarding, for you'll get to experience a wonderful bird's eye view of the surrounding area. The view apart, the fort has little to recommend it; Manjarabad is, in fact, rather

Detour: Belur–Halebidu circuit

Sakleshpur is an excellent base for exploring Belur and Halebidu (p108). At a maximum distance of 55km (an hour's drive), the temple towns can be easily covered in a day, yet you won't stray far from the lush-green plantations.

unimpressive due to a lack of upkeep, while the information provided about the site is inadequate.
Bengaluru-Mangalore Highway, 7km beyond Sakleshpur

The ruins of Manjarabad Fort

❷ MANJEHALLI FALLS
A certain amount of nimbleness is required to reach the 20ft-high falls, as you look to manoeuvre your way down to a good spot near the water. A great place for a picnic close to Sakleshpur, Manjehalli Falls is particularly beautiful after the monsoon.

❸ PLANTATION VISIT
Almost all homestays and hotels are flanked by coffee plantations. A walk through any of these is a leisurely experience, with opportunities to indulge in some birdwatching. Coffee-picking season in December is particularly fun as there is a lot of activity around that time. Coffee beans are picked before being spread and left to dry in almost all courtyards. If you are visiting during March or April, you may chance upon the small window of three days when the coffee flowers are in bloom and entire hillsides turn white.

❹ BETTA BYRESHWARA

This temple, located a short distance from Sakleshpur, is over 600 years old. Not much can be gauged of the history of the structure, but it definitely offers a great view from atop the hill it stands on. Some people opt to climb the steep steps instead of trekking to the top.

❺ BISLE RESERVE FOREST

The rainforest cover that spills onto Sakleshpur, is a joy for nature lovers with its many birds and animals. The drive through the Bisle Ghats is full of verdant views. However permission granted at the entry gate to enter the forest is sporadic.

Snapshot: The Green Route, or Sakleshpur railway trek

Green Route was the name given to a verdant stretch of a non-functional railway track from Sakleshpur to Kukke Subrahmanya, on the Mangalore–Bengaluru sector, many decades ago. Popular on the trekking circuit, people hiked from Donigal to Edkumeri railway station via the Gondiya Pass, crossing tunnels, waterfalls and deep gorges, since the track was closed down in 1996 (to change the gauge from metre to broad). Before passenger trains again started plying on this route in 2008, trekkers could enjoy a long, arduous trek of 56km, crossing 58 tunnels and 109 bridges on foot. For those who have heard fabulous stories about this route, note that the trek is no longer possible. Even though a lot of trekking groups might urge you to join in, locals will suggest that you steer clear of this as its illegal and more importantly, unsafe.

The spectacular Green Route is unfortunately no longer operational

Accommodation

The Planters Bungalow — Plantation Homestay ₹₹
☏ 9481925930; Kadamane Checkpost, Hassan Distt; d incl full board from ₹4851 This century-old, English-styled house comes with typical high ceilings, sprawling verandahs and a marvellous view of tea plantations. Expect some great food, treks on the property, tea tasting and elephant sighting (they are regular visitors to the property). The 7500-acre Kadamane Tea Estate, on which the Planters Bungalow is located, has had illustrious owners like the Earl of Warwick and tea conglomerate Brooke Bond.

Mugilu — Homestay ₹₹
☏ 9845451055; www.mugilu.com; Bugadahalli village, Kyanahalli Post; d incl full board from ₹4200 An exquisitely misty view of the coffee plantation from your wide balcony is reason enough to opt for a personalised, and uninterrupted, holiday at Mugilu. This is a great place to catch up on a good book, or go for a walk in the coffee estate.

Jenkal Homestay — Heritage Bungalow ₹₹
☏ 9448144091; www.jenkal.in; near Devalankere; d incl full board from ₹4000 Thick wooden pillars and an intricately-carved door will likely catch your eye as you enter the Jenkal Homestay. Though now

Mugilu is a homestay in a coffee plantation

refurbished with every modern facility, this century-old house still retains past touches like the narrow lockable columns, right next to the door, which were used to store weapons. Great food and respect for private space will keep you coming back.

Jenukallu Valley Retreat — Resort ₹₹
☏ 9241611610; www.jenukallu.com; Athibeedu, Devaladakere Post, Sakleshpur Taluk, Hassan Distt; d incl full board from ₹6000 The wide expanse of a bare hill dotted with four cottages is a pleasant relief to the eyes after the thick coffee copses. Opt for the cottage right at the edge of the hill for a better view. The common deck area with lounge chairs is a great spot if you don't have a larger group sharing the space.

> **✓ Top Tip: Get clear directions**
>
> Ensure that you're given proper directions to the place you are staying in, as resorts and homestays are far apart and set among scattered villages with very few passers-by. Non-Kannada speakers are bound to find it even more difficult to get directions.

Tusk And Dawn   **Nature Stay ₹₹**
☏ 09845503354; www.tuskanddawn.com; Agani Post, Hanbal; d incl full board from ₹4200 (couple for cottage), ₹1800 (per head for dorm) Enjoy a camp like ambience (without any real roughing out) with three comfortable twin cottages and a log house 8-bedded dormitory. There is an open pavilion for meals, hiking trails off the property and a small water body. Tusk and Dawn puts you in a real outdoors mood with its crackling camp fire at the end of the day.

The Hills   **Resort ₹₹₹**
☏ 080-41158187; www.thehills.in; Kuntahalli village, Devaladakere Post, Sakleshpur Taluk, Hassan Distt; d incl full board from ₹7000-8000 The only luxury option in the area, The Hills is a combination of Indonesian-style wooden cottages and lavish tents. While the rooms are well equipped, the standard of service leaves much to be desired.

🍴 Eating

The Ossoor   **Vegetarian ₹₹**
☏ 08173-318072; BM Rd; 7am-11am
A pleasant option with ample parking space, The Ossoor, just out of town, is an offshoot of the estate by the same name. The restaurant is the best place for a quick vegetarian meal on the highway.

Mythri Restaurant   **Vegetarian ₹₹**
☏ 08173-245244; Puspagiri Comforts, BM Rd; 7am-11am One among the few choices to eat out in Sakleshpur, Mythri is nothing out of the ordinary, but is nonetheless a decent stop for vegetarian food.

Surabhi's Nxt   **North & South Indian ₹₹**
☏ 9008271807; BM Rd; 6am-10am
A branch of the famous Surabhi restaurant in town, this new eatery has more seating, and plenty of parking space. Ask to be seated on the first floor, to enjoy the view of the lush countryside.

🚶 Activities

Jenkal Gudda   **Trekking**
Also known as the 'honey stone mountain', one can see this high peak from many points in the area. An erstwhile favourite with trekkers and camping enthusiasts, to climb Jenkal Gudda you need permission (which is now sporadically given). A medium-

level hike to the windy summit is recommended only if you are in good shape, and are accompanied by locals.

🛍 Shopping

Salish Tea
☏ 08173-319353; BM Rd, Kollahally; 9.30am–10pm The shop stocks locally procured tea, coffee, pepper and honey. Though many small shops dot the main Bengaluru-Mangalore Road, what makes Salish Tea a pleasant choice is its polite staff.

The Bee Keepers Co-operative Society Limited
☏ 08173-344075; near bus stand, Sakleshpur; 10am–5.30pm Sakleshpur is famous for its fresh honey. Though many shops stock similar brands, the Bee Keepers Co-operative is the best place to buy some local honey.

> See quirky driftwood items being made by artisans

Soundarya Handicrafts
☏ 9480249845; BM Rd, Donigal; 10am–5pm Driftwood products are available in five or six shops just off the main road on the way to Manjarabad Fort. Not only can you get some unusual pieces from Soundarya, you can also see them being made in front of you.

✓ *Top Tip: Clubs*

There are three clubs in Sakleshpur which offer good sports facilities: the Planter's Club, the Cosmopolitan Sports Club and the Munzerabad Club. Unfortunately, only members of affiliated clubs from Bengaluru have access. However, if you are putting up in a homestay, there is a chance that the owners can help you get in.

Chikmagalur

Why go?

Besides its historic links with coffee, Chikmagalur is a scenic getaway with a plethora of destinations. For the spiritually inclined there are the Horanadu and Belavadi temples. Nature and adventure lovers have options aplenty, among them Hebbe Falls and rafting on the Bhadra River. Chikmagalur is also home to Mullayangiri, Karnataka's highest peak, and a popular trekking option from Bengaluru.

Highlights

- **Coffee Yatra:** Get an insight on how the humble bean ends up in your cup.
- **Hebbe Falls:** Nature at its very best, with a spectacular view from above.
- **Horanadu Temple:** Experience the spiritual attraction of this important pilgrimage centre.
- **Trekking heaven:** Kudremukh and Mullayangiri are popular spots in what is great hiking country.

Trip Planner

Getting There 245km

🚗 5hr NH48

- **Route:** From Bengaluru, take the Tumkur–Nelamangala Rd on NH48 and follow straight through till Hassan. From here, follow the SH57, then turn left at SH64. After Hassan, you will hit the Thannirhalla Junction; from here, Chikmagalur is 50km towards the right.

🚌 7hr

- A host of private and KSRTC buses run between Bengaluru and Chikmagalur at regular intervals. Opt for an overnight bus (₹345 onwards) to make the most of your time. Most travellers stay on the outskirts for proximity to coffee plantations, so you can safely add another hour to your final destination.

Top Polished soapstone pillars at the Belavadi Temple

Quick Facts

BEST TIME TO VISIT

J F M A M J J A S **O N D**

GREAT FOR

Spa ❌ 🔒 🚶 ❤️ 👥

REST STOP Atithi Hotel, just before the Charoti Naka intersection on the main highway, has ample parking, a restaurant, and toilets.

High on Coffee

Highlights
1. **The Big Mountain Loop**
2. **Kemmanagundi & Hebbe Falls**
3. **Kalhatti Falls**
4. **Coffee Yatra**
5. **Horanadu**
6. **Belavadi**
7. **Ayyanakere**

Imagine the difficulties faced while smuggling coffee beans across borders in the 17th century. India owes its coffee lineage to Baba Budangiri, a Sufi pilgrim who managed to bring in seven beans from his trip to Mecca. He found that Chikmagalur had the perfect altitude for planting this crop.

Many generations on, the plantations continue to flourish. The Katlekhan Estate, now owned by the largest producers of coffee in India (Coffee Day), bears testimony to this wonderful bit of history. Chikmagalur, has evolved into one of the biggest coffee production hubs in the country. You can actually wake up and smell the coffee here!

Chikmagalur is a large area, so it's best to divide your trip into parts, depending on the experience you are looking for. Choose between the big mountain loop of Mullayangiri, Baba Budangiri and Kemmanagundi, or the section that comprises Kudremukh (p202), Horanadu and the Bhadra River.

Be ready to do a lot of exploring on foot as the region demands walking through coffee estates and covering easy hiking trails. Chikmagalur is a popular trekking area. Bhadra Wild life Sanctuary consists of four parts: The Muthodi Forest Reserve, Tanikecoil, Lakkavalli and Hebbe. Entry to the forest is only allowed from the Lakkavalli side via safaris organised by Jungle Lodges and Resorts Ltd (River Tern Lodge). One cannot enter this forest from Chikmagalur town.

1 THE BIG MOUNTAIN LOOP
Go past city traffic towards Kaimara and start in the foothills, heading straight to **Sheethalagiri**, a 1000-year old Mallikarjuna temple. Duck below the low door into this intriguing shrine to receive your share of 'prasadam', a fistful

of water from a natural pool inside. It is better to arrive early in the morning, when the tourist rush is less. Next on the 'loop' is the mist-covered **Baba Budangiri Hill** (or Dattagiri Hill Range). Here, a small temple perched at 6217ft offers breathtaking views of the valley below. The shrine is visited by both Hindus and Muslims, and is an important pilgrimage centre. Finally is **Mullayangiri**, Karnataka's highest peak (6332ft), which affords another great view (it can get windy and cold, so be sure to carry a jacket). If you're lucky, you might catch the Kurinji flower (p66) in bloom. If visiting during the monsoons, do not leave too early as the clouds only clear by late morning to reveal the splendid views.

> ### Detour: Belur–Halebidu circuit
>
> The Hoysala temple circuit is a short detour (less than 45 minutes in car) when visiting Chikmagalur. If you have time to spare, make a quick stop at two of the famous temples, Belur and Halebidu (p108).

❷ KEMMANAGUNDI & HEBBE FALLS

The hill station of Kemmanagundi provides an access point to the picturesque Hebbe Falls. Though hugely popular with tourists, Kemmanagundi itself does not have much to offer apart from an unimpressive rock garden, a government-run children's park and a badly-managed restaurant.

Getting to Hebbe Falls involves an adventurous off-road journey of 13km which can only be covered in a four-wheel vehicle, driven by an experienced driver. Rickety jeeps are

> The temple at Belavadi is a tranquil stop

You're never too far away from coffee in Chikmagalur

available on hire (₹300 per person in a shared vehicle) for a round trip. The falls are reached after a short walk on foot. There are a couple of points where you'll need to hop across a shallow but rocky stream (take off your shoes and wade across the stream). Be wary of leeches in the rainy season. The effort, however, is absolutely worth it for you'll get to see a 551ft drop from below the gushing water.
₹10; parking ₹50; 8am–4pm

❸ KALHATTI FALLS
From Kemmanagundi, the drive to Kalhatti is only 10km but the falls here are not as impressive as those at Hebbe. Kalhatti's only point of interest is the presence of a Lord Veerabhadra (Shiva) temple. The temple gets its share of zealous pilgrims in the months of March and April, for a three-day festival to commemorate the god. Kalhatti Falls are at their prettiest just after the monsoons. If you are driving down from the Kemmanagundi loop, the falls are just off the main road, and make for a very short stop. If you have to choose between the two, Hebbe Falls is a better bet.

❹ COFFEE YATRA
A Coffee Board of India initiative, the Coffee Yatra is a thematic and well thought-out museum display on the origin of coffee (including the different types of coffee) and its subsequent evolution in the country. Expectedly, the touch-screen displays are disappointing as they are perpetually not working, but the rest of the exhibits are informative and creatively showcased. There is also a laboratory where one can see a demonstration of how coffee is processed. Unfortunately, a tasting experience is missing.
Coffee Centre, Behind ZP Office, Kadur Rd; ₹20; 10am–1pm and 2pm–5.30pm, closed on Sat, Sun and general holidays

❺ HORANADU

Horanadu is an important pilgrimage centre in Chikmagalur and is famous for the deity of Annapurneshwari – a goddess who feeds one and all – which was installed by Adi Shankaracharya. Queue up in a long but fast-moving visitors' line to get a quick glimpse of the goddess (and be ushered out by strict priests). Do not miss out on the simple but tasteful prasadam, served every day. Thousands sit in neat rows on the floor while Malnad-style food is served by priests in a hurried but orderly manner. An elaborate menu of the offerings can be obtained at the information counter.
Lunch noon–2.30pm, dinner 8pm–9.45pm

❻ BELAVADI

A pleasant break from the overtly touristy places in Chikmagalur and around, the 13th-century Belavadi Temple is a haven of peace and quiet. More than 100 soapstone pillars greet you in the main hall before your eyes latch on to the three shrines of Lord Vishnu: Narayana, Venugopala and Yoganarsimha. If you are lucky, you'll bump into the temple's young English-speaking priest, who will be only too happy to share details with the trickle of visitors who come here. The temple, dating back to the Hoysala Empire which ruled Karnataka between the 10th and 14th centuries, is also mentioned in the *Mahabharata* as the location where the demon, Bakasura, was slain.
29km from Chikmagalur; dawn to dusk

❼ AYYANAKERE

Located just 26km from Chikmagalur, Ayyanakere is yet another picturesque spot and makes for a good drive. The tank here is said to have been built by Rukmangada Raya, a chieftain of Sakrepatna (a small town in Chikmagalur). Its history can be traced from 1156 AD, after the Hoysala rulers renovated it. The lake, built to provide irrigation to the nearby village fields, is now a picnic spot.
26km from Chikmagalur; dawn to dusk

🛏 Accommodation

Chikmagalur has a burgeoning list of plush guesthouses, hotels and homestays for travellers. Most of these are coffee themed and are reasonably close to the key attractions. Many of the owners are a passionate lot, who strive hard not to over-commercialise the destination and also to protect its natural resources.

Woodway — Homestay ₹₹

📞9663071775; www.woodwayhomestay.com; Jakkanhalli Post; d incl full board from ₹6000

The pioneers of homestays in the region, Sushmita and Shreedev have run Woodway for over 10 years. You can look forward to some great company, knowledgeable plantation walks with Shreedev and delicious local food, preparation of which is supervised by Sushmita. The highlight for most guests is the walk in the coffee plantations led by Browny, the old family dog who steers you through a trail, patiently waiting if you take too long. Woodway is tastefully furnished and very comfortable; there are plenty of places to lounge around in the common areas. Ask for a room with a fireplace for a snug night – in case it gets chilly.

Thotadhahalli — Homestay ₹₹

📞8262320655; www.thotadhahalli.com; Thotadhahalli Estate, Kaimara Post; d incl full board from ₹5000

Proximity to the Mullayangiri circuit, authentic Malnad food and rooms with aesthetic charm make Thotadhahalli a great choice for families. You'll be amazed by the plethora of bonsai plants and antiques, painstakingly collected, in the house. If travelling with kids, choose the mezzanine-floor room, which has a charming flight of steps for the kids to climb up to.

Coffee Village Retreat — Heritage & Luxury Homestay ₹₹

📞8262229599; www.coffeevillageretreat.com; Kimmane Plantation, Billur Post, Mudigere; d incl full board from ₹5000–7000

Choose between a 150-year-old colonial plantation bungalow and a unit that oozes modern luxury at this unique set-up on a 300-acre coffee estate. Though most parts of the modern block overlook the valley, the perfect spot to catch up on a good book is the outdoor seating area next to the dining room. You can also choose from activities like indoor games, cycling, birdwatching, trekking, boating and fishing – or just relax by the bonfire.

Hunkal Woods — Homestay ₹₹

📞9886000788; www.hunkalwoods.com; Thogarihunkal Group Estates; d incl full board from ₹4400

Offering both comfort and a starting point for treks, Hunkal Woods is ideal for family getaways and adventure groups. The Gowda family are veterans in running coffee plantations and have put together some interesting trails, including a graveyard walk and sambar track (and one for birdwatching too). The property itself was built in 1875 and still retains an old-world charm. Wildlife spotting is easy, especially if you walk to the highest part of the plantations.

Shanthi Kunnj — Plantation Stay ₹₹
☏ 0824-2485180; www.shanthikunnj.com.com; Devdhana village, Honnekoppa, Sangameshwarpet, Near Kadabagere; d incl full board from ₹5900–6700 Sitting right at the edge of Bhadra, with coffee plantations between the creatively constructed cottages, Shanthi Kunnj is a perfect pick for nature lovers. Extremely popular with families, there are a host of activities that one can indulge in here, coracle rides and swimming in the river topping the list. Cottages are named after the prime material used in making them – log (cabins), areca, and glass. Though all the cottages face the river, choose the ones (Areca, Glass) that are closest to the water.

The Serai — Resort ₹₹₹
☏ 8262224903; www.theserai.in; KM Rd, Mugthihalli Post; d incl full board from ₹22,000–69,000 ❄ Luxury accommodation was first introduced to the Chikmagalur region by The Serai (a holding of Coffee Day). The folks here arrange visits to the plantations, where you can learn about the processes of coffee making, and also get to taste coffee (only for checked-in guests). The Serai also offers an OMA Spa and personal pool (or Jacuzzi) in every villa. The best part of the property is the wide swimming pool at the end of a palm boulevard.

Flameback Lodges — Boutique Resort ₹₹₹
☏ 8263215170; www.flameback.in; Billur Post, Pattadur village,

| Woodway is one of the oldest homestays at Chikmagalur

Value for Money: Travel with parents & pets

Hunkal Woods (p189) encourages travelling with the family. If you are travelling with family members who are above 60 years, it will cost only ₹1500 per head. Those above 70 years can stay free of cost. And pets are important to the Gowdas too; you can get 70% off on your stay if you bring a pet along (discuss details before booking).

Mudigere Taluk; d incl full board luxury villas/suites ₹15,000, paddy cottages ₹12,000 Private villas, suites, and cottages with wide sunny decks and personal Jacuzzis are the attractions at this exclusive boutique resort. The lodge offers views of a lake, waterfall and paddy fields, making for a welcome break from the coffee topography. Flameback has only eight rooms, ensuring a private holiday. If you are a dog lover, you will love the place even more for the three friendly German Shepherds on the property.

Villa Urvinkhan — Luxury Homestay ₹₹₹

9449651400; www.villaurvinkhan.com; Niduvale, Mudigere; d incl full board from ₹10,000 Perched atop a hill, this luxury homestay with five cottages is located in the middle of a 400-acre coffee estate that has been around since the 1800s. The five cottages, spread across a small area, come with private verandahs and complete privacy. The efforts of Shwetha and Sunil to provide for a lavish stay are backed by an infinity pool, marvellous aesthetics, fireplaces, restored antique furniture and a delicious spread of food. Most guests tend to spend a lot of time in the pool. Breakfast time is abuzz with everyone sharing their travel experiences.

Eating

Town Canteen — South Indian ₹₹
8262222325; RG Rd; 11.30am–2.30pm, 6.30pm–8.30pm Mon–Sun, after 1pm Sat Get your dosa fix at the oldest haunt in the city, the 52-year-old Town Canteen. Though this noted Chikmagalur landmark's unassuming ambience, of weathered wooden benches stuffed in a cosy room, is far from glamorous, the food is definitely something to write home about. A must visit.

Food Palace — Multi-Cuisine ₹₹
8262228116; RG Rd; 7am–9.30pm Quick stop for South Indian snack food or slightly more elaborate Indianised Chinese. The fare here has not much to recommend, but for a high turnaround of customers, the service is efficient.

Activities

Capture – Rafting & Trekking
9845355087; www.capture-earth.

com; 272, 16th Cross, 23rd Main, 5th Phase, JP Nagar, Bengaluru; 10.30am–6.30pm** Besides providing a wonderful backdrop to parts of Chikmagalur, the Bhadra River offers rafting opportunities for adventure tourists. Capture, an outdoor company led by Krishna, is ideal for those seeking a rafting experience and guided treks. It is well known in the region for outdoors training, and stocks decent equipment.

Trek to Kemmanagundi and Mullayangiri

Private groups can trek to the Kemmanagundi and Mullayangiri ranges with local guides. But camping is strictly prohibited in these areas (though it is advertised by many adventure groups in Bengaluru).

Chikmagalur Golf Club
8262656500; PB No 154, MG Rd, Karadihalli; 6.30am–6.30pm This well-maintained nine-hole golf course – which has an impressive clubhouse with rooms, a restaurant and a bar – is a fantastic setting for those looking to play a round or two on their holiday. Members of affiliate clubs like Bangalore Golf Club and the KGA (Bengaluru) are allowed entry. But even if you're not a member, many homestay owners are, and they can get you in as a guest. A caddy (₹70 for nine holes) and golf set (₹200 per hour) are available on hire.

> The Chikmagalur Golf Club has a clubhouse with eating and staying facilities

🔒 Shopping

Hunkal Heights — Coffee
8262230472; KM Rd; 10am–5.30pm Watch how coffee is ground here, and pick up a pack of fresh and authentic Chikmagalur coffee.

Panduranga Coffee Works
8262235345; PB No 150, MG Rd; 9am–9.30pm Though coffee is best consumed fresh, if you must carry a souvenir back, try the well-known Panduranga shop on MG Road, a one-stop shop for locally branded coffee. Not big on service, though.

Kamadhenu Provision Store
8262237823; MG Rd; 8am–10pm MG Road is lined with small traders and you are bound to find options for spices and honey. Among these is the Kamadhenu store, which has a reasonable selection of pepper, cardamom and other local spices.

Wayanad

Why go?

Wayanad's landscape is a symphony of verdant rice paddies, clumps of bamboo, spiky ginger fields and rubber, cardamom and coffee plantations. Tourist infrastructure is beginning to sprout, though it's still fantastically unspoilt (with epic views). Given its lush forest cover, you're almost guaranteed to spot wild elephants along with unique species of birds and reptiles.

Highlights

- **Edakkal Caves:** Containing petroglyphs dating back thousands of years.
- **Thirunelli Temple:** Bustling shrine often called the 'Kashi of the South'.
- **Kuruva Island:** A mini rainforest experience.
- **Muthanga & Tholpetty Wildlife Sanctuaries:** Visit here for your wildlife fix.

Trip Planner

Getting There — 275km

🚗 6hr 30min — SH17, NH766

- **Route:** Take the SH17 till Mysore, then head towards Nanjangud and Gundlupet. From here take a right towards the Muthanga–Sultan Bathery route on NH766.

🚌 8hr

- A few KSRTC buses are available, starting from Shanthi Nagar bus stand (9.05pm/ ₹450). You can also opt for private buses from multiple boarding areas in the city.

Top A dense canopy of green greets you here
Bottom The Thirunelli Temple

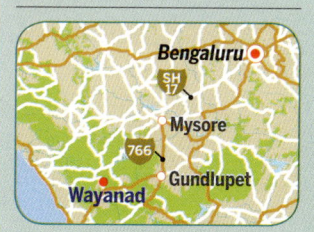

ⓘ Quick Facts

BEST TIME TO VISIT

J F M A M J J A S O N D

GREAT FOR

Spa · 🍽 · 🔒 · 🚶 · ❤ · 👥

REST STOP For a good meal and reasonably clean loos, the Mysore Rd has Kadambam (for breakfast; just after Channapatna), Indradhanush Complex and Kamat.

A Rainforest Retreat

Highlights
1. Edakkal Caves
2. Pookode (Pookot) Lake
3. Kuruva Island (Kuruvadweep)
4. Thirunelli Temple
5. Jain Temple
6. Muthanga Wildlife Sanctuary
7. Tholpetty Wildlife Sanctuary
8. Banasura Sagar Dam
9. Pakshipathalam
10. Waterfalls of Wayanad

An unusual break in Kerala, Wayanad sweeps you into a great outdoors mood with its intensely green cover. Here, all you need is a sturdy, black umbrella and a taste for wildlife.

The district of Wayanad is spread around three main towns – **Mananthavady** in the northwest, **Kalpetta** in the south and **Sultan Bathery** in the east. It's impossible to cover all in a short time, so depending on your interests, plan your holiday around one of these. Sultan Bathery and Kalpetta are better equipped with hotels, but Mananthavady has its own charm, being slightly further away and isolated.

While the wildlife experience is best near Mananthavady, Sultan Bathery is for those who want to indulge in comfortable resorts. The famous Pookot Lake and Banasura Sagar Dam are closer to Kalpetta. For a spiritual trip, Thirunelli Temple can be accessed best from Mananthavady. Wherever you are planning to stay, you will cross the Muthanga Wildlife Sanctuary while entering from Bengaluru, and can make a quick stop here.

❶ EDAKKAL CAVES
Make your way, amongst a swarm of tourists, to the steep spot of Edakkal Caves. The trek is definitely worth the effort, for you'll get to see pictorial carvings dating back to 5000 BC, and jaw-dropping views of Wayanad district.
☏9446052134; adults/children ₹15/5; camera/video ₹20/75; 9am–4pm, Mon closed; 12km from Sultan Bathery

❷ POOKODE (POOKOT) LAKE
A bumpy, untarred road leads you to this natural freshwater lake. Arrive early in the morning to avoid the tourist rush.

The lake is reasonably well kept, with options for boating. One can also pack in a snack at the restaurant or buy souvenirs from the shops in the same enclosure.
04936–255207; adults/children ₹15/5 (boating extra); camera/video ₹20/150; 9am–6pm (boating to 5pm); 15km from Kalpetta

❸ KURUVA ISLAND (KURUVADWEEP)
A raft or fiber-glass boat plies across the water for a 10-minute ride to transport you to this dense rainforest island, which has some unusual species of birds and plants (including rare orchids and herbs). A potentially exotic experience can turn slightly disappointing due to the large crowds, even in off-season. Passes from the Forest Department are necessary to visit this protected island; these are available at the counter.
04936–245180; ₹50; camera/video ₹25/100; 9.30am–3.30pm; 17km from Mananthavady

❹ THIRUNELLI TEMPLE
The scenic drive to the Thirunelli Temple adds to the spiritual experience. A barefoot walk to the Papanasini River behind the temple is an effort, though essential if you are participating in a religious ceremony. Non-Hindus are not allowed in the innermost sanctum area, but for the otherworldly view of the temple's exterior with its pillars and

An inscription about a king who killed tigers, at Edakkal Caves

> ### ✓ Top Tip: *Plan judiciously*
>
> Wayanad is very big and one must plan ahead to optimise time, especially if you are only going for a short break. Choose the places you'd like to see, and the activities that you want to engage in, and then decide on a stay in one of the three regions (Mananthavady, Kalpetta, Sultan Bathery). Handy maps are available online to guide you, on the official Kerala Tourism website. (www.keralatourism.org/wayanad.php)

stone carvings, set against a backdrop of mist-covered peaks, it is worth a visit.

PO Thirunelli Temple; dawn to dusk; 36km from Mananthavady

❺ JAIN TEMPLE

The 13th-century Jain temple in Sultan Bathery has splendid stone carvings and is an important testimony to the region's strong historical Jain presence. You can find a board at the entrance, which gives some information on the monument's history.

8am–12pm, 2pm–6pm; Sultan Bathery

❻ MUTHANGA WILDLIFE SANCTUARY

This sanctuary is easy to visit, as you will cross it on the way from Bengaluru. Here, you'll see elephants and deer (among other wildlife) and a lot of avian life, besides the lush flora of the region. The sanctuary is closest to Sultan Bathery (15km). Jeeps can be hired with drivers who double as guides. Personal heavy vehicles are allowed inside, but at extra cost.

☏04936–271010; ₹60; jeep ₹400; camera/video ₹25/150; 7am–10am, 3pm–5pm

❼ THOLPETTY WILDLIFE SANCTUARY

The flip side of Tholpetty is that the picnickers and noisy groups create an atmosphere not befitting that of a sanctuary. Your only chance is to hope for a silent jeep ride (one hour) through the forest. If one has received the proper clearance, you can also take your own vehicle (only SUVs) into the forest. This sanctuary is doable only if you stay in Mananthavady (24km), otherwise Muthanga is your best bet. Unlike Muthanga, Tholpetty remains closed during the monsoon months.

☏04936–250853; ₹60; jeep ₹400; camera/video ₹25/150; 7am–10am, 3pm–5pm

⑧ BANASURA SAGAR DAM

A visit to the largest earthen dam in India – and the second biggest in Asia – is worth the time and the climb. Ignore the paltry food stalls and the children's park, and focus instead on the view of the catchment area, which is breathtaking. The speed-boat facility here is erratic. The structure, construction of which began in 1979, is part of the Indian Banasurasagar Project, comprising a dam and a canal.

📞04936–273562; adults/children ₹15/10; camera/video ₹25/100; 9am–6pm; 25km from Kalpetta

⑨ PAKSHIPATHALAM

A formation of large boulders deep in the forest makes for an adventurous trek which is best done between October and February, when the rains have subsided. The lush deciduous forest is particularly good for birdwatching. Permits are necessary, and can be arranged at forest offices in south or north Wayanad. Reach the Thirunelli Temple, off Mananthavady, at about 8am, to start the 7km trek (after obtaining permission). The DTPC office in Kalpetta organises trekking guides (₹600 per day), camping equipment (₹250 per person) and transport.

📞04935–210377; Forest Station, Appapara, Thirunelli; ₹1000 (per 5 people); 8am–5pm; 32km from Mananthavady

An Uravu artisan at work using bamboo

⑩ WATERFALLS OF WAYANAD

Plan a monsoon-aligned trip in Wayanad to see the many spectacular waterfalls. Most of these involve some amount of trekking (check with guides). Among those worth seeing are Meenmutty, Karalad and Soochipara.

📞04936–202134; www.dtpcwayanad.com; District Tourism Promotion Council (DTPC), Kalpetta

🛏 Accommodation

In India, Kerala has been a pioneer in developing the homestay culture. If you haven't already experienced it, Wayanad is a great destination to do so. In this sprawling region, a steady supply of warm coffee – and pertinent travel suggestions – are best sourced from local families.

Ente Veedu — Homestay ₹₹
☎04935–220008; www.enteveedu.co.in; PO Kayakkunnu, Pananmara; d incl breakfast ₹3500 Boasting comfortable, multi-levelled rooms with private balconies and a splendid view of paddy fields and plantations, Ente Veedu is the perfect holiday setting. And after sampling the delicious home-made Kerala fare here, you won't feel like leaving. The homestay is central to all three locations, Kalpetta (19km), Mananthavady (15 km) and Sultan Bathery (23 km).

Kliff's View — Homestay ₹₹
☎04936–218452; Vattathuvayal, Vatuvanchal PO; d incl full board from ₹6700 Get a great view of the sunset behind the Nilgiris from a hammock, in the well-manicured lawn of Kliff's View, a relatively new establishment. You can be assured of an enjoyable experience here, and a holiday that combines luxury and privacy. The common lounge area offers a gorgeous vista of plantations. Ideal for a small group looking for an understated holiday.

Rain Country — Resort ₹₹
☎04936–329798; www.raincountryresort.com; Lakkidi; d incl full board from ₹5600–8600 onwards The Kerala-style cottages at this resort, which sits on the Calicut-Wayanad border, are set apart for privacy but can get musty. The open-roofed bathrooms are a charming addition. Take a dip in the bizarre natural pool, with fish for company. A short drive from Rain Country is a spot with a great view of the Ghats.

Fringe Ford — Jungle Lodge ₹₹₹
☎9880086411; www.fringeford.com; Cherrakarra PO, Talapoya Post, Mananthavady; d incl full board ₹7000 (special off season and Christmas rates) An apt tag line, 'Get Lost', follows this faraway jungle resort (closest to Mananthavady). Present

---

✓ Top Tip: *Watch out for leeches*

The downside to Wayanad's verdant surroundings is the leeches. It's a way of life with the locals, so you may not be given extra warnings. Leeches can be quite a menace during the monsoons if you are on nature trails. Carry small packs of salt to put on a leech if you see one on your skin; once in contact with the salt, it will fall off immediately. Try not to yank it out as it tends to dig its teeth into the skin.

♥ If You Like: Treks

Trekking in Wayanad is extremely dependant on the season, with no expeditions during the monsoons. Chembra Peak is often spoken of with awe, as it's the highest in the region (6890ft), but try the ascent only if you are extremely fit. For beginners, many of the estates have thrilling trails where one can encounter plenty of flora and fauna.

yourself with a 'middle of nowhere' holiday, with only birdsong and wildlife for company. The 520-acre forest houses four well-furnished rooms; the knowledgeable staff here will regale you with wonderful stories from the jungle. Spot the regular herd of elephants (and a lone bison) from the lounge area.

Tranquil Plantation Homestay ₹₹₹
☎ 9947588507; www.tranquilresort.com; Aswati Plantations Ltd, Kuppamundi Coffee Estate, Kolagapaa PO, Sultan Bathery; d incl full board from ₹7500; ☎ This luxury homestay in a 400-acre coffee estate is a big departure from the regular lodging options here. The eco-conscious Tranquil has walking trails (with a list of birds) that have been interestingly mapped. There is also the option of a massage.

The Windflower Resorts & Spa Resort ₹₹₹
☎ 9895226611; www.thewindflower.com; VI/108 A, Ammarao, Achooranam village, Pozhuthana PO, Vythiri Taluk; d incl full board from ₹9247–14,796; ☎ It's difficult to go wrong with the Windflower property, with its luxury rooms, a well-equipped spa, and the beautiful backdrop of tea estates. Battery-run vehicles take you from one spot to the other efficiently. With an in-house restaurant, and many activities slated for the day, you will hardly ever have to step out.

Silver Woods Resort ₹₹₹
☎ 0484–2322552; www.wayanadsilverwoods.com; Manjoora (PO), Pozhuthana; d incl full board from ₹12,500–29,750 This distant resort, recently opened, would be an apt pick for those looking for complete isolation in luxury. A monsoon view of the Banasura Dam catchment area can be enjoyed from a Jacuzzi in the sit-out of your lavish suite.

Vythiri Resort ₹₹₹
☎ 0484–4055250; www.vythiriresort.com; Lakkidi; d incl full board from ₹9000–15,000 onwards Nineteen years on and still going strong, the Vythiri is a busy resort which offers a complete experience for the family. Book well ahead if you want to enjoy the spa and Ayurveda facilities. With its popularity, you can

✓ Top Tip: *Karingali water*

Do not be alarmed if you are served warm, pinkish water in restaurants in Wayanad – this means that the water has been sterilised (a practice that's followed across Kerala). The magic ingredient is none other than an Ayurvedic herb, Karingali (it is actually the bark of a tree). This is the best way to prevent any water-borne infection on your travels, and one can safely have non-bottled water. Cumin or coriander seeds are used for a similar sterilising effect.

---

expect consistent service but not an exclusive experience.

🍴 Eating

Mint Flower
Family Restaurant   **South Indian ₹₹**
☎04936–227179; www.hotelmintflower.com; Chungam, Mysore Rd, Sultan Bathery; 8am–9.30pm Even though Mint Flower looks better from the outside, the simple setting inside will not disappoint you. The reasonable Kerala fare here is sufficient for a quick lunch. Opt for the filling 'thaali', which has a large variety of preparations.

Jubilee   **South Indian ₹**
☎04936–220937; Sultan Bathery Market Rd; 7am–10pm Only if you are absolutely famished should you step inside this buzzing restaurant. Lunchtime is particularly packed as the food is tasty, and time taken to grab a quick combo is short.

Century Restaurant   **South Indian ₹**
☎04935–246166; Kozhikode Rd, Mananthavady; 7am–11pm This eatery entertains a large number of locals and tourists. It is high on taste but low on experience. Stick to the standard Kerala dishes.

Green Gates   **Multi-Cuisine ₹**
☎04936–202001; www.greengateshotel.com; TB Rd, Kalpetta North; 6am–11pm The slow service at this Kalpetta restaurant is more than compensated by a delicious and hearty meal. One of the better places in Wayanad for lunch.

The Woodlands   **South Indian ₹₹**
☎04936–202547; www.thewoodlandshotel.com; Main Rd, Kalpetta; 7am–10pm The bright, cheerful interiors of Woodlands are inviting for a good local meal or a small snack. It's best to stick to the south Indian preparations here.

🏃 Activities
AYURVEDA
While many resorts have spas and massage centres, only a few allow non guests to book.

Windflower:
☎9895226611; www.thewindflower.

Bamboo products on display at Uravu

com; VI/108 A, Ammarao, Achooranam village, Pozhuthana PO, Vythiri Taluk; 9am–6pm Luxury facility with award-winning choice of Ayurveda services. One of the few resorts that allows outside guests.

Upvan
☎04936–255272; www.upvanresort.com; Lakkidi; 8.30am–5.30pm A small but clean facility with an appointed doctor. Suitable for short-duration treatments, they are also equipped for long-duration therapies.

Santhigiri Ayurveda & Siddha Hospital
☎04936–347775; www.santhigiriashram.org; 18/213, near Collectorate Bungalow, Madiyoorkuni, Main Rd, Kalpetta; 8am–5pm An authentic Kerala Ayurvedic centre, run by doctors, in association with an extensive ashram of the same name.

Shopping

Uravu
☎04936–231400; www.uravu.net; Thrikkaipetta PO; 11am–5pm; Mon–Sat The bamboo by-products of this non-profit establishment (the name of which translates as 'spring') are the most wonderful souvenirs you can carry back. The workshop is tucked away in Thrikkaipetta village but a visit here is worth the effort – you can see the products being made by the locals. Uravu also provides opportunities for skills training, marketing and eco-tourism. The bamboo blinds, lampshades, paintings and earrings (among other items) are tasteful and value for money. But watch out for the many shops in town that make false claims of stocking Uravu products.

Brahmagiri Trek

Why go?

The wavy ridge of the verdant Brahmagiri Range can be easily seen running through most parts of Coorg. Besides testing climbing ability, these mountains give trekkers an opportunity to explore the area's rich biodiversity (it's a hotspot for snakes and other wildlife). Be challenged by this picturesque trek – and admire the flora and fauna along the way.

Highlights

- **Irupu Falls:** Pleasant waterfall that spans the Karnataka and Kerala borders.
- **Munikal Caves:** Fascinating rock caves which trekkers cross en route.
- **Narimale Peak:** Hike up here to enjoy panoramic views of the valleys.

BRAHMAGIRI TREK

Trip Planner

Getting There — 243km

🚗 5hr — SH17

- **Route:** From Bengaluru, take the SH17 (Mysore Rd) till Hunsur; the 187km can be covered in 3½ hours. After Hunsur, take the diversion to Kutta through the Nagarhole Forest. This scenic stretch (55km), flanked by dense jungle, is closed between 6pm and 6am. It's advisable to leave Bengaluru early and reach Kutta well in time to start your trek, at Irupu Falls (8km from Kutta).

🚌 6hr

- KSRTC buses from Bengaluru are mostly Madikeri bound. Others include stops (Virajpet, Gonikoppa, Kushalnagar). Since these routes are different, ask for a bus heading to Kutta.

Top The Brahmagiri Range
Bottom Trekkers descending

❶ Quick Facts

BEST TIME TO VISIT

[J] [F] [M] A M J J A S O N [D]

GREAT FOR

[REST STOP] Kadambam for breakfast (just after Channapatna); Indradhanush Complex and Kamat for a good meal and relatively clean loos.

Along the Irupu Falls

Highlights
1. Planning
2. Approach
3. Ascent
4. Sights
5. Amenities

The Irupu Falls is at the start of the trek

The Brahmagiri trek is popular for its level of difficulty as well as the chance it affords to get up-close to the region's biodiversity. The trail passes through rich deciduous forests, Shola copses and grasslands. On your way, you're likely to spot macaques, the Indian gaur, wild dogs, elephants, boars, and (if you're lucky) a tiger. The forest is also home to a variety of snakes, including the dreaded king cobra.

The trail starts from Irupu Falls, which is often mistaken by locals to be Talakaveri (the source of the Kaveri River). It straddles the Kerala and Karnataka borders. In fact, there is a trekking route that starts from Kerala, which also ends at the highest point here (5276ft).

1 PLANNING
Apply a week to 15 days in advance for permission at the Range Forest Office in Srimangala. It's best to leave this to the homestays so that when you arrive, you can go directly for the trek. You must be accompanied by a forest guard for the entire stretch.
📞 08274-246331; **Office of the Range Forest Officer, Srimangala; 10.30am–5.30pm; forest entry ₹200 (per head), trekking ₹75 (per head), guide ₹500 (group)**

📷 Snapshot: Cobra Man

'Cobra Man' Bose has been scaling the Brahmagiri Peak, and many more, over the last decade. The ex-army man is also a snake enthusiast (he has caught over 42 king cobras in six years). A popular trekker in the Kutta region, there is no one who knows the slopes of Brahmagiri better than him. Bose does not usually guide trekkers but is happy to help enthusiasts with his vast knowledge of the area. You can call him to take his help in arranging the trek. 📞 08274-246843; **Shop No 3 Padmashree Complex, Srimangala; ₹200 per group for orientation, ₹3000 per head for overnight package (incl food, stay, trek)**

❷ APPROACH

The base camp, at Irupu Falls in Kutta, has an old temple, ticket counter and a shop.

❸ ASCENT

Start the trek at 8am, so that you can cover the distance by 6pm. The first and last kilometres are the toughest; the forests and dry grasslands in between are comparably easier. Usually, trekkers stay overnight at the Narimale Guest House, which can be reached in three hours (5km). Day trekkers take a lunch break here and head out for another 4km to ascend the peak. The summit is windy and cold, so do carry a warm jacket.

❹ SIGHTS

The gurgle of Irupu Falls accompanies you for a long time after the start. Also known as the Lakshmana Tirtha Falls, the water here flows down a stepped height of 170ft. From Narimale, one can take a detour to see the gigantic, and fascinating, Munikal Caves (4km) or hike to the Narimale peak (1.5km), which offers amazing views of the valleys below.

❺ AMENITIES

Carry packed food with you from Srimangala/Kutta. The lone store at Irupu Falls only stocks water and biscuits.

🛈 Quick Facts

- **Difficulty:** Moderate to Difficult
- **Best Season:** October to February
- **Altitude:** 5276ft
- **Base Village:** Irupu Falls
- **Ascent Time:** 8–9 hours
- **Camping Option:** Allowed only in the government-run Narimale Guest House, with prior permission.

🛏 Accommodation

Narimale — Camp ₹

₹1000 per person (extra ₹100 for an extra bed; additional ₹1000 for food and cook) Narimale Guest House, the forest accommodation is the only overnight stop. This solar-powered stay has no water (a stream close by is the only source). The two basic rooms have attached toilets. Despite provision of old beds and mattresses, it's best to take your own sleeping bag. A cook accompanies the group and can dish out decent meals (veg and non-veg). One can put up in homestays in the Kutta (p50) area for close access to Irupu Falls.

Tadiandamol Trek

Why go?

For trekkers, Coorg's highest peak provides the ultimate buzz. Treat yourself to a wonderful view of stacked blue mountains rising from a sea of clouds and deep coffee-clad valleys. This spectacle from Tadiandamol Peak is the reward for braving dense Shola thickets and low grasslands on the steep ascent.

Highlights

- **Nalknad Palace:** Admire the fine paintings in this old Coorgi house.
- **Plantation stay:** Opt for a homestay to experience a dose of Coorgi hospitality.

TADIANDAMOL TREK 207

Trip Planner

Getting There   273km

🚗 **6hr 30min**   SH17, SH88

• **Route:** From Mysore Rd (SH17), turn onto Hunsur Rd (SH88) after the Columbia Asia Hospital. From Hunsur, take the Virajpet Rd till you hit Kaikamba village, just a kilometre from Kakkabe. The stretch from Virajpet to Kakkabe is quite bad, so a lot of travellers come via Madikeri, even though it's slightly longer (291km). If you are taking this route, turn right from Hunsur onto the road to Madikeri and head towards the Talakaveri Rd. Look out for Napoklu, one of the main villages. From here Kakkabe is 11km.

🚌 **7hr**

• KSRTC has one bus (leaves 11.15pm, reaches 6.15am) heading to Bhagamandala, the stop closest to Kakkabe (₹315). From here, take a local bus (under ₹10) to Kaikamba. If going via Madikeri, catch a local bus to Kaikamba (under ₹35).

Top View from the top
Bottom Nalknad Palace

ⓘ *Quick Facts*

BEST TIME TO VISIT

J F M A M J J A S O N D

GREAT FOR

Spa 🚫 🔒 🚶 ❤ 🏛

REST STOP Kadambam for breakfast (just after Channapatna), Indradhanush Complex and Kamat for a good meal and relatively clean loos.

A Walk Among the Clouds

Highlights
1. Planning
2. Approach
3. Ascent
4. Sights
5. Amenities

True to its name (meaning 'broad base' in Malayalam), Karnataka's third-highest peak is a mammoth mountain that overlooks deep valleys of verdant Shola forests and misty mountain ranges. The trail is frequented by experienced trekkers and is very popular with hiking enthusiasts.

Tadiandamol has helped make Kakkabe a credible destination for trekkers and nature lovers. The area is a magnet for outdoor enthusiasts; close by, there are many other adventure activities available (p44).

1 PLANNING
For the trek, ensure that you are equipped with these items: enough water, sunscreen, hat or cap, windcheater, chocolates/dry fruits, rain pants (optional), trekking shoes, salt sachets (to get rid of leeches during the monsoon) and mosquito repellent for the night halt.

The starting point of the trek

2 APPROACH
Tadiandamol lies in southeastern Coorg and is best approached from Kakkabe. Head to Kaikamba village, a kilometre away, from where a tar road leads up to Nalknad Palace (2km). You can start the trek from here or choose to hire a jeep which will drop you right at the end of the tar road (3km). From here, Tadiandamol is 5km.

3 ASCENT
Some people start from Nalknad Palace (8km from Tadiandamol), while others prefer the point where the tar road ends (5km). The trek begins with a reasonably steep path on the edge of

a coffee plantation, which opens up first into a shady forest patch and then a sunny grassland area. You soon hit a big rock, known as Anegundi, from where you can see the peak clearly. Note that there are two mountains in your view; one to the right and Tadiandamol on the left. The way to Tadiandamol is marked by a clear path, which gets steeper as you go up; the path's sheer incline challenges even seasoned trekkers. Stop at the ridge between the two mountains and then head left towards the summit.

> ### Quick Facts
>
> - **Difficulty:** Moderate to difficult
> - **Best Season:** December to May
> - **Altitude:** 5724ft
> - **Base Village:** Nalknad Palace (3km from Kaikamba) or Tar End Rd (5km from Kaikamba)
> - **Ascent Time:** 2–4 hours
> - **Camping Option:** Not allowed

Many trekkers climb Tadiandamol in about two hours and then attempt an ascent of the peak on the right. This is unadvisable, as the latter has no clear path; you have to cling onto the grassy base and find your foothold blindly. It is a more difficult trek than Tadiandamol.

❹ SIGHTS

Visit **Nalknad Palace** for a glimpse of rich Coorgi history. This weathered two-storey structure, built in 1792 by King Dodda Veerarajendra as a hideaway from invading armies, is a key landmark on the trek. Take some time to saunter inside and see the ancient – and beautiful – paintings, spread elaborately on the ceilings and walls. Mr Anand is the designated guard here and he enthusiastically shows you around the wooden-floored palace. Admire the red pillars, a wedding mandapa (hall) and the queen's quarters.
8.30am–7pm

❺ AMENITIES

There are no amenities on the trek route. At the start of the trek is a small shop, though only biscuits are available here. It is advisable to stock up on water and dry food in Kakkabe (which has a few shops), or Madikeri, before reaching Kaikamba. Better still, if you are staying in a homestay, ask for a packed lunch.

🛏 Accommodation

Honey Valley **Nature Resort ₹**
📞 08272–238339; www.honeyvalleyindia.in; PO Yavakapady; d incl no meals ₹1029–1404; guide/transport/campfire ₹400/150/400

Add to your adventure experience by staying at the remote Honey Valley resort, a treat for nature lovers. It's tucked away on a 30-acre coffee plantation, and can only be reached in a four-wheel drive vehicle (ask for a pick-up from Kabinakkad Junction). Accommodation varies from basic rooms (non-attached bathroom) to slightly more elaborate set-ups. From Honey Valley, an exclusive trek to Tadiandamol can be arranged, though this route is much longer (18km, 7 hours), and consists largely of cattle tracks. Book ahead and plan your stay with Mr Chengappa.

Chingaara **Nature Resort ₹**
📞 08272–204488; www.chingaara.com; Yavakapady village Post, Kabinakkad; d incl breakfast and dinner ₹1800–2500 Chingaara is yet another nature-oriented resort, set on a 12-acre plantation which shares a boundary with Honey Valley (it also

| A trekker attempting an ascent of Tadiandamol

✓ Top Tip: Guided trek

One can easily do the trek without a guide, but first-timers may want to be accompanied by a seasoned instructor. Besides providing trekking tips, guides entertain you with anecdotes along the way. **Olive Planet** in Madikeri will help you organise the trek (food/bus/guide ₹650 per head). Ask for Kiran, who has been guiding trekkers for over 12 years now.

requires a four-wheeler drive to reach). The resort has no TVs, so one can hear the sounds of the jungle from the nine cheerful rooms looking down on the valley below. Enjoy the company of dogs, and Lily the donkey, here. If you want privacy, ask for the separate double-roomed unit (not part of the main building).

Palace Estate — Homestay ₹
☎ 08272-238446; www.palaceestate.co.in; Kakkabe, near Nalknad Palace; d incl no meals ₹2000–2500 The bright garden and wooden double-storeyed building of Palace Estate makes for a pleasant break from the shaded coffee-plantation stays of Coorg. Ask for one of the first floor rooms – they have a better view. This is the closest homestay to Tadiandamol, and thus perfect to relax after the trek.

Kings Cottage — Homestay ₹
☎ 9845963883; Kakkabe, Palace Estate, near Nalknad Palace; d from ₹2000 (lunch not included) Budget travellers can opt for this quiet homestay with a spectacular view of the valley. Kings Cottage's USP is its proximity to the start of the trek and Nalknad Palace.

Misty Woods — Family Resort ₹₹
☎ 08272-238561; www.coorgmisty.com; near Nalknad Palace, Kakkabe; d incl full board from ₹7500 Misty Woods is suitable for a family stay, offering 27 comfortable cottages with manicured lawns, play areas, a small waterfall off the approach and a friendly dog named Lee. For trekkers, this is the ideal spot, as it's just behind Nalknad Palace. Though the roofs are old-style (aesthetically so), the look and feel of the resort is modern.

Tamara — Resort ₹₹₹
☎ 8884000040; www.thetamara.com, Kabinakkad Estate, Napoklu Nad, Yavakapadi village; d incl full board luxury cottage/suite ₹18,000/20,000 Tamara is a plush resort perched on top of a hill. After roughing it out on the slopes, you can relax in the super-luxurious wooden cottages here, each with a private deck overlooking rows of coffee bushes on the 174-acre plantation. This place has all the expected trappings of a resort, including uniformed (and courteous) staff, a conference room and in-house restaurant. Tamara's cafe, **The Verandah**, follows a coffee theme and is as informative as it is aesthetically charming.

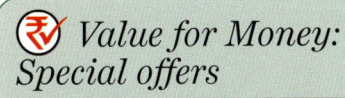

Value for Money: Special offers

Tamara and Misty Woods offer discounts during certain parts of the year. Look out for Tamara's long stay, honeymoon, early bird and introductory offers. Misty Woods gives discounts during the monsoons.

Kudremukh Trek

Why go?

This trip is all about sweat and sinew. The Kudremukh trek in Chikmagalur is a good test of your willpower, agility and physical well-being – perfect, in other words, for a climbing enthusiast. Ascend the second highest peak in Karnataka (6214ft), and watch the topography change dramatically from the thick Shola forests to wide yellow grasslands.

Highlights

- **Lobo House:** Tucked away in a Shola grove, with a green expanse in front.
- **Wildlife spotting:** Enjoy the sight of deer, sambars and wild boar on your trek.

KUDREMUKH TREK

Trip Planner

Getting There 340km

🚗 8hr NH48

- **Route:** Exit Bengaluru through the Nelamangala route on NH48. You may be slowed down by a few sections where the highway is under construction, but largely the road is a long and straight stretch till Hassan. From here, take a right, enter Hassan town and head towards Belur. Next, take the Mudigere Rd, cross Kottigehara and then head towards Kalasa, the base town for the trek.

🚌 9hr

- KSRTC buses from Bengaluru start after 10.20pm and reach Kalasa at about 7am (₹394 onwards). From here, you can take an auto to Kudremukh Forest Office for permissions (20 km, ₹200); if you already have permission, head to Balgal (6km).

Top Green velvet-wrapped hills
Bottom A herd of sambar

ℹ️ Quick Facts

BEST TIME TO VISIT

J F M A M J J A S **O N D**

GREAT FOR

REST STOP Kamat Upachar on NH4 has relatively decent loos (you'll have to take a U-turn at Dobbaspet to reach the eatery); another option is Cafe Coffee Day at Dobbaspet, near Kamat.

Meeting with the Horse-faced Mountain

Highlights
1. **Planning**
2. **Approach**
3. **Ascent**
4. **Sights**
4. **Amenities**

Trekking to the horse-faced mountain (the literal translation of Kudremukh in Kannada) is fun but challenging. The trail is a strenuous one with several stream crossings and steep patches that one has to negotiate; definitely not for the faint-hearted. The landscape here is a study in contrasts, taking in both lush Shola forests teeming with wildlife and sun-baked grasslands – and that's before you even reach the summit; one can spot deer, wild boar, sambars, and even (if you are lucky) packs of bison. The trek is about 9.5km long (one way) and takes a good 8–9 hours to complete. Kudremukh has one main – and popular – route, which is supported by local guides and a reliable travel infrastructure of homestays and a few hotels. Trekking during the monsoons should be avoided as the route is extremely slippery and cold. Even forest guards are unwilling to accompany trekkers at this time of year.

🔴 PLANNING

Get to know key landmarks to make best use of your time; the trek is time consuming for even skilled climbers. Apply in advance for permission from the Forest Department

---

✓ *Top Tip: Permission from Forest Dept*

The Kudremukh trail lies within the Kudremukh National Park, to enter which one needs permission from the office of the Range Forest Officer in the town (📞9480807653, 10.30am–5.30pm; trek/forest entry/guide ₹75/₹200/₹500). If you arrive early, you'll find a guard who, from 6am onwards, grants permission with little delay. This is not difficult to obtain but it does mean that one has to go back 20km to the starting point. Most trekkers sidestep this by asking Mr Rajappa (📞9481179008/08263–249333) to arrange for permission in advance. One can remain in the forest from 6am to 6pm – though this means that you'll miss out on viewing the sunrise or sunset from the hill.

Quick Facts

- **Difficulty:** Moderate to Difficult
- **Best Season:** October to February
- **Altitude:** 6214ft
- **Base Village:** Mullodi
- **Ascent Time:** 4 hours
- **Camping Option:** Not allowed as the trek is inside Kudremukh Forest limits.

(see box p214). For your convenience, it is recommended that you opt for a homestay, and let the owners arrange the permission for you, as well as a packed lunch and a guide.

❷ APPROACH

Kudremukh lies at the far end of Chikmagalur district, 20km from Kalasa town. It towers above its namesake town and adjoining villages. From Kalasa, a key point for trekkers, head to Balgal (9km); take an auto (₹200 one way) or a jeep (₹300 one way), both easily available. The trek's starting point, a place called Mullodi, is 6km from Balgal and can only be reached in four-wheel drive. Here, Mr Rajappa, the area's most well-versed guide, lives with his family. Jeeps are easily available from Balgal (₹600 one way), or from Kalasa (₹1000 one way).

❸ ASCENT

Though the track is well marked, it is advisable to hire a guide. Most guides don't speak English (Kannada or Hindi is predominant) but this does not stop them from feeding you with interesting anecdotes and helping identify significant landmarks on the trail. The sound of the Somavathi River accompanies you for most of the trek, which starts off pretty easy but becomes gradually difficult after the second landmark.

The first landmark is Onte Mara ('lone tree'), a kilometre after Mullodi. The next distinct landmark, Lobo House, comes after crossing five streams; it's a third of the way into the trek. This is at the foot of the ascent and is clearly identifiable. The climb then meanders between copses and grasslands, becoming steeper and more winding. The peak

Hanumangundi Falls makes for a good detour

✓ Top Tip: Packing suggestions

For an enjoyable trek, ensure you are equipped with the following: plenty of water, sunscreen, hat or cap, wind-cheater, chocolates/dry fruits, rain pants (optional), trekking shoes, salt sachets (to get rid of leeches during the monsoon) and mosquito repellent (for the night halt in homestays).

itself is a wide flat expanse of about 50 acres on top, and not a typical crest shape. Apart from the magnificent views, one can also see an old church and a structure built by the Maharaja of Mysore, who often inspected the boundary of his realm from the peak. The climb is strenuous but it's the descent that takes a toll on the knees. Trekkers stop for lunch at the Karikanhalla Waterfall on the way back.

❹ SIGHTS

There are two memorable sights during the trek. The first is a sprawling expanse of grasslands in front of **Lobo House** (tucked away behind a Shola forest grove). The second, **Full Stop**, is a short deviation from the peak. Walk through a thicket and you'll reach a wide, flat rock, known as the 'full stop'. As the name suggests, there is no further path, only a sharp drop to the valley below.

❺ AMENITIES

There are no amenities along the route. Pack a lunch and plenty of water for the long climb. The only place where one can find basic amenities (food, loos) is Mr Rajappa's house at the beginning of the trek.

⟴ Detour: Drive from Kudremukh to SV Road

If you haven't had your fill of the forest during the trek, take the car from Kudremukh to SV Border (20km). Flanked by the Kudremukh Forest, you can drive by the hanging bridge, the Lakya Pollution Control Dam (8.30am–6pm), Kadambi Falls by the road, Gangamoola viewing point (1km off the main road onto a non-motorable trail) and Hanumangundi Falls (₹20; 9.30am–4.30pm), also known as the Soothanabi Falls (descend the 250 steps here for a fine view).

Accommodation

Upasana Retreat   **Resort ₹**
9481651988; www.upasanaretreat.com; Mavina Kombe, Samse; d incl full board from ₹2000 The 14 rooms at Upasana, aesthetically designed and with options of two or three beds, are perfect to relax after the strenuous trek. This retreat can house up to 54 guests but the units are arranged in such a way that privacy isn't intruded upon. The owner, Mr Sukumar, is a yoga teacher with over 30 years' experience – an orientation is recommended if you are staying for a while. The personalised yoga classes (₹100 per hour) are great value; money from the classes goes to the education of girls in the region, via a trust.

KIOCL Guest House, Sahyadri Bhavan   **Guest House ₹**
08263–254148; Sahyadri Bhavan, KIOCL Guest House, Kudremukh; d from ₹400 (2 beds, with TV), ₹350 (3 beds, no TV), ₹600 (5 beds, no TV) The KIOCL guesthouse is often the choice for budget travellers. This place provides no-frills but clean rooms at great value, though the service is a little sleepy and the décor dowdy. For meals, there is an in-house restaurant.

Mullodi House   **Homestay ₹**
9481179008; Mullodi House; r incl full board from ₹600 (incl veg meals), ₹1000 (non-veg) Mr Rajappa has an extremely basic option for budget travellers in his own home. Floor mats and blankets are provided to guests along with all meals. The only advantage of staying here is that one is right at the start of the trek, and can begin early in the morning.

Thangaali   **Homestay ₹₹**
9448657572; www.thangaali.com; Gaaligandi village, near Kalasa; d incl full board from ₹4500 (₹3000 extra for a group of 8, for jeep/trekking facilities; ₹275 forest entry fee per head) This homestay, 12km from Kalasa, comes with four rooms: two Malnad-style cottages and two tents. Enjoy the wonderful view of the valley from a 10-acre coffee plantation, preferably from the cosy spot on the balcony of one of the cottages. The homestay can accommodate both exclusive guests who want their privacy or larger groups. Inform ahead so that trekking arrangements can be made in advance.

✓ Top Tip: Group treks

Bengaluru-based Exotic Expeditions, led by Santosh Nair, is a worthwhile option if you are looking to join a pre-planned group. All arrangements for stay, food, permissions and guides are taken care of.

9986450370; www.exoticexpeditions.org; Flat No 301, Sagar Deepa Building, 4th Main, GM Palya, Bengaluru; rates depend on group size

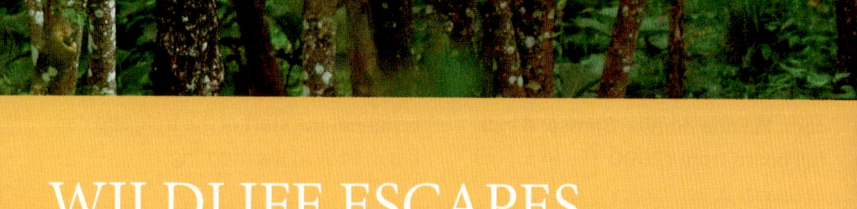

WILDLIFE ESCAPES

- BRT Wildlife Sanctuary **220**
- Bandipur **226**
- Kabini–Nagarhole **232**
- Masinagudi **236**

Elephants are a common sight at Nagarhole

BRT Wildlife Sanctuary

Why go?

Renowned for the abundance and variety of its wildlife – from deer, bison and elephants to sloth bears, leopards and tigers – the Biligiri Rangaswamy Temple (BRT) Wildlife Sanctuary gives you an authentic wilderness holiday. The jungle offers quiet treks, exciting wildlife safaris – and a natural beauty that can be awe-inspiring both in its grandness and its detail.

Highlights

- **Biligiri Rangaswamy Temple:** Situated on the highest peak in the sanctuary, offering stunning views.
- **Dodda Sampige Mara:** Legendary champak tree said to be almost 1500 years old.
- **Jeep Safaris:** Morning and afternoon rides that travel deep into the jungle.

BRT WILDLIFE SANCTUARY

Trip Planner

Getting There — 182km

🚗 3hr 30min — NH209

- **Route:** The only way to reach is by car. Follow the NH209 from the NICE Ring Rd, through Kanakapura, Malavalli and Kollegal, down to Yelandur. Turn left at Yelandur onto the Yelandur-BR Hills Rd, and follow the road signs for the 'K. Gudi Wilderness Camp' to the sanctuary. (Vehicle fee ₹100.)

Top and *Bottom*
BR hills span over Western and Eastern Ghats

Quick Facts

BEST TIME TO VISIT

J F M A M **J J A S O N** D

GREAT FOR

Spa ❌ 🔒 🚶 ❤️ 👥

REST STOP Kanakapura is a good place for a snack, and a toilet break; Yelandur is the last stop before the BR Hills to stretch your legs and stock up on any last-minute supplies.

Bridging the Ghats

Highlights
1. Biligiri Rangaswamy Temple
2. Dodda Sampige Mara
3. Jeep Safaris
4. Jungle Treks

Covering almost 540 sq km of densely forested hills, the BRT Wildlife Sanctuary stretches across the confluence of the Eastern and Western Ghats, showcasing the biodiversity of both the ranges. Famous for its wildlife, the sanctuary is also home to the semi-nomadic Soliga tribe, experts in jungle medicine and preservers of a truly diverse range of plants – from grasslands and deciduous forests to the evergreens higher up – including a gigantic champak.

The sanctuary is filled with birdsong throughout the day and presents birdwatchers an astonishing variety of species. Jungle guides here are knowledgeable and sincere and they must accompany you since BRT has approximately 39 tigers, not to mention herds of elephants and bison. You might find that a day or two isn't enough to do justice to the place.

1 BILIGIRI RANGASWAMY TEMPLE

Although the Soliga tribals are nature worshippers for the most part, they also revere Lord Venkatesh, called 'Biligiri Ranganatha' locally, who gives his name to the land and the hills. The temple is the site of much festivity during early summer, when the annual spring festival takes place. But something to be relished all year round is the view of the dense, green hills, unfolding up to the horizon. An hour's walk away from the camp, the climb up to the temple can be quite steep for some. Carry a bottle of water and something to protect your head from the sun.

A female elephant bathing her calf

❷ DODDA SAMPIGE MARA

Estimated to be almost 1500 years old, the Dodda Sampige Mara – or 'Big Champak Tree' – is truly enormous: over 30.5m tall with a trunk approximately 18m wide. The tree is sacred to the Soliga. Hundreds of stones (meant to be Shivalings) surround the base of a trunk covered in markings and colour. The long trek to the tree from the camp – approximately 80 minutes – has its rewards: at the end, one can refresh oneself in the cold waters of a stream that flows close by.

> ### 🛈 Quick Facts
> - **Area:** 540 sq km
> - **Wildlife:** Deer, bison, elephant, sloth bear, leopard, tiger and an array of birds.
> - **Entry fees:** Free

❸ JEEP SAFARIS

The K Gudi Wilderness Camp (p224) has two jeep safaris everyday: in the morning at 6.30am, and in the afternoon at 4.30pm. Though the morning safari hold higher promise of viewing a tiger in the sanctuary, it is often difficult to sight them. Their droppings are frequently found, however, and guides conduct thorough examinations of the tigers' diets on the spot! Usually, you can spot elephants, herds of deer, and the white-socked bison, but sightings of animals during the rainy season are understandably rare.

❹ JUNGLE TREKS

The sanctuary has a number of well-marked forest trails open to trekkers, though one should be careful not to stray away from these paths. This is a wildlife sanctuary, after all, the natural habitat of a number of fairly territorial animals, tigers and elephants in particular. That said, the sanctuary provides trekkers some extraordinary terrain to walk through, under large, broad-leafed plants and a host of flowering trees.

> ### ✓ Top Tip: Local goodies
> Buy from local shops outside the BRT Wildlife Sanctuary the best examples of what the region has to offer: traditionally-made pickles and natural honey harvested by the locals from the surrounding forests.

Accommodation

K Gudi Wilderness Camp ₹₹
080-25597944, 25584111, 25559261; www.junglelodges.com; Kyathadevara Gudi, Chamrajnagar, Yelandur; log hut/tented cottage/family room ₹5500/4500/4000 (charges include forest entry fees, food and lodging, jeep safaris, nature walk and elephant ride); [P]

This settlement of tents and lodges, surrounded by gulmohar trees, is the only place to stay within the BRT Wildlife Sanctuary. K Gudi Wilderness Camp is a serene and secluded getaway where even the notoriously shy barking deer can be seen on occasion, and monkeys have to be regularly chased off the hammocks. Jungle Lodges and Resorts who run the camp have taken great pains to maintain the presence of the forest within the camp.

The tents, log cabins and rooms are clean and well kept, and in harmony with the camp's natural surroundings, offer the simplest comforts. The camp provides guests with lanterns at night as electricity is in short supply. However, some might consider this a plus, rather than a drawback, since it adds to the experience!

Eating

The food is basic but nourishing, and the staff are happy to cater to the needs of children. The camp also has a bar at the Maharaja's Hunting Lodge, open during the evenings for guests to relax and unwind.

Activities

The camp offers guides for trekking, conducts safaris into the sanctuary, and screens films during the evenings for guests to learn more about the terrain that surrounds them.

✓ Top Tip: Be prepared

The BRT Wildlife Sanctuary is far from shops, restaurants and pharmacies, and one ought to travel prepared. Some items recommended are:

- **Flashlight** for the night, particularly for when there is no electricity.
- **Mosquito repellent cream.**
- **Snacks,** should one get peckish between meals (though beware of the monkeys).
- **First-aid kit,** including band-aids, antiseptic cream and anti-allergens (and prescribed medication for those with pre-existing conditions).
- **Warm clothing,** depending on the season, and for early morning and night.
- **Binoculars** for wildlife watching.

Flora & Fauna of the Nilgiri Biosphere

The triangle-shaped land mass off Bengaluru contains a multiplicity of habitats – rainforests, scrub jungle, lagoons and lakes – sustaining a diversity of life forms. The Western Ghats is a stretch of forest-clothed mountains, one of 18 biodiversity hotspots on earth. The region boasts a bewildering variety of wildlife.

• **Flora** This area's floral wealth includes the iconic Kurinji, which flowers once every 12 years, and rare species of orchids. The Nilgiri Mountains owe their name to this special flower.

• **Wildlife** The region is home to highly endangered creatures like the lion-tailed macaque and the Nilgiri tahr. Major wildlife sanctuaries, including Kalakad-Mundandhurai and Periyar Tiger Reserves, are part of the Western Ghats, as are Mudumalai, Bandipur (p216), Wayanad (p232) and Nagarhole (p222) sanctuaries. They harbour the tiger, elephant and gaur, the great three of the south Indian wilderness. Add to this the Eastern Ghats, with the Shervarayan and Kalrayan hills, and you have an astonishing variety of life forms, many of them endemic, such as the slender loris and Malabar trogon.

• **Bird life** Along the coast, the estuaries and backwaters attract flamingos and sandpipers, and a host of other migratory birds.

• **Acquatic species** The Kaveri and Tungabhadra, mighty rivers that meander across the region, give rise to unique ecosystems which sustain the mahseer fish and also muggers (crocodiles) and turtles, in addition to creatures of the riverine forests like the giant grizzled squirrel. The Gulf of Mannar Marine National Park harbours the rare and shy dugong, a marine mammal, along with dolphins. Sea turtles come ashore to lay eggs in winter in many spots along the coast.

By **Theodore Baskaran** *a trustee of WWF India and a well-known naturalist based in Bengaluru.*

Lion-tailed macaques are among the threatened species in the rainforests

Bandipur

Why go?

Bandipur offers a fascinating experience for wildlife enthusiasts within its approximately 880 sq km expanse of deciduous forest. Look out for the Indian bison, Asiatic elephant (highest population in the country), tigers, deer, boar, dhole (wild dog) and – if you're lucky – the elusive leopard. It is a paradise for birdwatchers too.

Highlights

- **Jeep Safari:** Hop into a jeep and explore the forest's wildlife.

- **Village Walk:** Learn about tribal life and culture in Mangala village.

- **Himavad Gopalaswamy Betta:** Ascend this hill for an unmatched view of the forest.

BANDIPUR 227

Trip Planner

Getting There 235km

🚗 **4hr 30min** SH17

- **Route:** The route trails the SH17 with Channapatna, Mandya, Mysore and Nanjangud on the way. Take the Mysore Rd from Bengaluru and follow it straight with no diversions.

🚌 **6hr**

- There are multiple KSRTC buses from Kempegowda bus stand to Ooty. Get down at the forest checkpost and ask for a pick-up from your resort. The forest part of the highway (Bandipur) is closed between 9pm and 5am. However, you can opt for the 10.15pm or 10.45pm bus (deluxe and luxury ₹349 onwards) which have special permission to travel at night. Its most convenient, however, to leave early morning and arrive by noon.

Top A herd of chital in the forest
Bottom Cattle return home to Mangala village

ⓘ *Quick Facts*

BEST TIME TO VISIT

[J] [F] M [A] [M] J J A S [O] [N] [D]

GREAT FOR

[Spa] [🚫] [🔒] [🚶] [❤] [👥]

REST STOP For a good meal and clean loos, Mysore Rd has Kadambam (for breakfast), Indradhanush Complex and Kamat.

The Wonderful Wild

Highlights
1. Jungle Jeep Safari
2. Mangala Village Walk
3. Himavad Gopalaswamy Betta
4. Birdwatching

The closest spot to Bengaluru for a wildlife fix, Bandipur contributes to nearly a quarter of the Nilgiris Biosphere, and shares its borders with the other zones of Nagarhole National Park, Mudumalai Sanctuary and Wayanad Wildlife Sanctuary. It was one of the first reserve forests chosen under 'Project Tiger' in 1974.

In Bandipur, one is greeted by forest guards diligently stopping every vehicle to forewarn against blowing horns and littering. Elephants, deer and wild boar are often seen crossing the road. Deeper into the forest, Bandipur has an extensive list of inhabitants – Asiatic elephants, tigers (of which there's a stable population), leopards, gaurs (Indian bison), hyenas and sloth bears. Amongst birds, the Indian silver bill, scaly breasted munia, purple-rumped sunbird and the jungle babbler are easily spotted.

1 JUNGLE JEEP SAFARI
With less strict rules than bordering Mudumalai Sanctuary, one can take jeep safaris into Kabini. These are operated solely by the government enterprise Jungle Lodges and Resorts. Only 22 vehicles can enter the forest per day and routes have been limited; this is a boon for the animals, but a disappointment for tourists. Groups are packed in a large

You may suddenly be surprised on a safari by these magnificent beasts

vehicle, and little can be done to control the combined din.

☎0821–2480902; Bandipur Forest Information Centre; ₹300 (45min), ₹1250 (2½ hr); video camera ₹1000; to book with your resort, prepare to pay a convenience charge of ₹250; 6am–9am, 4pm–6pm

❷ MANGALA VILLAGE WALK

The Bandipur region was the home of the Kuruba shepherd tribe, who were also honey collectors. Tourism and outside influences, however, led to the slow decimation of the fragile habitat. Mangala village is now home to a set of resorts, and some remaining households of the Kurubas. Take a walk with a local guide and get to know more about their lifestyle. This activity is included in the package in most resorts.

❸ HIMAVAD GOPALASWAMY BETTA

Get a stunning bird's-eye view of the forest from the hilltop Krishna temple. At 4774ft, this is the highest point in the Bandipur hills. It is a 21km drive from the Bandipur checkpost on your way back from the sanctuary. Take a left from Hangala village.
8.30am–4pm

❹ BIRDWATCHING

Most of the properties in Bandipur are spread over acres of uncultivated land where you can spot many birds. Take guidance from the resident naturalist at your resort. You can enjoy some great birdwatching within the sanctuary too.

> ## ❶ *Quick Facts*
>
> - **Area:** 880 sq km
> - **Wildlife:** Indian bison, Asiatic elephant, tiger, deer, boar, dhole (wild dog), leopard and a variety of bird species.
> - **Entry fees:** Jeep Safari ₹300 (45min), ₹1250 (2½ hr)
> - **Park timings:** 6am–9am, 4pm–6pm

✓ *Top Tip: Exclusive safari*

The monopoly on jeep safaris lies with Jungle Lodges and Resorts. Contact them prior to your visit if you are looking to hire a smaller vehicle for a group. This facility is available to those who are putting up at JLR properties. (☎08229–233001, 9449599754).

Accommodation

Dhole's Den   Luxury Homestay ₹₹₹
08229-236062; www.dholesden.com; Kaniyinapura village, Bandipur National Park, Gundlupet Taluk, Chamrajnagar Distt; d incl full board from ₹10,000; A set of luxury units with wide airy balconies, which accommodate not more than 16 at a time in the entire homestay, come alive with bright animal-themed art and lively furnishings. The food spread is elaborate, yet simple and delicious. And with its rainwater harvesting, and electricity generated through wind turbines, this is a homestay that cares for the environment. Warm and resourceful staff ensures that your experience is memorable.

The Windflower Tusker Trails   Resort ₹₹₹
08229-236055; www.thewindflower.com; 125 Mangala village, Chamrajnagar Distt; studio rooms/ste incl full board ₹8400/10,500; Though the façade of the erstwhile Tusker Trails is intact, the refurbished studio rooms and suites, camouflaged by a dense grove, come with all the features associated with a high-end resort. But this unfenced, rustic property also advocates cutting oneself off from TV, internet and phone. Guests especially enjoy the pool overlooking the forest, and a massage at the Emerge spa.

The Serai Bandipur   Resort ₹₹₹
08229-236075; www.theserai.in; Kaniyanapura village, Chamrajnagar Distt; d incl full board from ₹17,915–₹25,000 (check season/weekend packages); This recently opened (May 2012) 36-acre property provides a lavish stay in rustic environs. The courtyard, cabin and residence cottages have white walls and thatched roofs, and have been built using traditional stonework. To blend in with the surroundings, 17 acres have been left uncultivated. The resort includes a spa, indoor games, gym and an extensive restaurant.

Bandipur Safari Lodge   Resort ₹₹₹
08229-233001; www.junglelodges.com; Mysore–Ooty

| Enjoy the disconnect from the city at Windflower Tusker Trails

♥ *If You Like: Documentary films*

If you want to get a perspective on the original inhabitants of the region, watch the '*The Bee, the Bear and the Kuruba*'. This well-researched documentary by Vinod Raja takes you through the travails of the bee collectors and shepherds of the region – the Jenu and Betta Kuruba tribes. If you cannot find it, you will most likely catch it at one of the resorts in Bandipur.

Rd, Melukamanahalli, Angala Post, Gundlupet Taluk, Chamrajnagar Distt; cottages incl full board from ₹10,000 The landmark Jungle Lodges and Resorts property houses 22 adequately furnished 'value for money' cottages amidst 9.5 acres of unspectacular landscape. The only visual standouts are wildlife artist Sunita Dhairyam's paintings on the walls of five of the rooms. The Gol Ghar (common gazebo) restaurant and the bonfire area teem with families, leaving little privacy. The spa here is very basic.

✖ Eating

Pugmark Restaurant Multi-Cuisine ₹
Bandipur Safari Lodge
☏ 08229–233001; www.junglelodges.com; Mysore–Ooty Rd, Melukamanahalli, Angala Post, Gundlupet Taluk, Chamrajnagar Distt; 1.30pm–3.30pm, 7pm–8.30pm Most of the resorts in Bandipur have their own restaurants and do not allow guests who aren't checked in. Pugmark is the only decent eatery open to the public. Largely a one-man show, the service here is slow, and it can whip up only the most basic of Indian and some Chinese dishes.

🔒 Shopping
The Souvenir Shop
☏ 9449818796 (Indra Kumar); www.templetreedesigns.com; Mariamma Temple Rd, Mangala village, Gundlupet Taluk, Chamrajnagar District; 7am–7pm Bandipur is evidently no shopping hotspot but a few souvenirs here are worth picking up: tees, coasters etc, are available in wildlife themes. It's run under the patronage of Temple Tree Designs – the brainchild of Sunita Dhairyam, who has gotten the locals involved in the shop – and the Mariamma charitable trust, which runs health and education programmes.

🏃 Activities
Film Screenings
Wildlife documentaries are screened in the evenings at most resorts. The practice is standard at Dhole's Den, where it is taken seriously by most guests. All the resorts also have wildlife literature in common areas, for guests to scan through.

Kabini–Nagarhole

Why go?

Kabini's lure is its stunning landscape of beautiful backwaters and lush forestland, home to an amazing variety of wildlife. It's perfect for those seeking solitude and tranquillity, as you awaken to the chirping of birds, and are lulled to sleep by the gentle lapping of the Kabini River. Wildlife enthusiasts can marvel at the herds of elephant and deer, and hope for a lucky tiger or leopard spotting in the jungle.

Highlights

- **Kabini Dam:** You can spot herds of Asiatic elephants here.
- **Nagarhole National Park:** This is the place for tiger and leopard sightings and home to over 250 species of bird life.

KABINI–NAGARHOLE

Trip Planner

Getting There — 240km

🚗 **5hr** — SH17/SH33

- **Route:** Follow the well-marked SH17, the main artery from Bengaluru to Mysore, via Ramanagaram, Maddur and Srirangapatna. At Mysore, take the SH33 for Mananthavady and follow the road signage to reach Kabini.

🚌 **6hr**

- A KSRTC super deluxe bus departs from the Central bus stand at 7.30am daily, returning at 1.30pm from Kabini.

Top A herd of deer on the banks of the Kabini reservoir
Bottom A tiger resting on the banks of the Kabini River

ℹ Quick Facts

BEST TIME TO VISIT

J F M A M J J A S O N D

GREAT FOR

REST STOP Indradhanush Complex near Maddur while on SH17; once on the Mysore-Mananthavady Rd, petrol pumps are your best bet.

A River Runs Through It

Highlights
1. Kabini Dam
2. Nagarhole National Park

About 70km south of Mysore lies the Kabini Lake, a giant forest-lined reservoir formed by the damming of the Kabini River. The area has gradually grown to become one of Bengaluru's best wildlife getaways.

The Kabini River snakes its way from Wayanad in Kerala to join the Kaveri in Karnataka. Along the way, it separates the rich tropical forests of the Bandipur Tiger Reserve from those of the Rajiv Gandhi National Park at Nagarhole. Once the exclusive hunting ground of the erstwhile maharajas of Mysore, Nagarhole is today counted as one of India's best wildlife parks.

Safaris are organised in open jeeps

1. KABINI DAM
Following the construction of the Kabini Dam in 1974, the bamboo-rich fringes have become fantastic wildlife sighting spots, especially for herds of Asiatic elephants. This unspoilt wilderness is also home to predators like tigers, leopards and hyenas. Wild dogs and sloth bears can also be regularly spotted. Access is via HD Kote town, 14km from the dam.
Between Beechanahalli and Biddarahalli villages, Mysore-Manathavady Rd

2. NAGARHOLE NATIONAL PARK
The gentle slopes and shallow valleys of Nagarhole are home to the spotted deer, barking deer, sambar, wild boar and the gaur. The deciduous forest cover is also an ideal

✓ Top Tip: Photography
Kabini's many moods are a shutterbug's delight. Incredible sunsets, exquisite moonrises, tranquil backwaters, a habitat teeming with animals and sundry forest life – all just a click and a frame away. Do carry all equipment and spares.

KABINI–NAGARHOLE

habitat for avian life, with over 250 species including woodland birds and water fowl. You can experience the wildlife in and around Nagarhole with Karnataka Tourism's exclusively managed 'Jeep & Boat Safaris'. Though private vehicles are permitted inside the reserve during specified hours, it would be advisable to sign up for the professionally-managed excursions. Most resorts at Kabini have been allocated a limited number of seats in the safaris. Confirm your ride early as the twice-daily sorties tend to fill out quickly. **6am–6pm (park timings), 6am–9am, 3pm–5pm (safari timings)**

Quick Facts

- **Area:** Nagarhole National Park 643 sq km
- **Wildlife:** Asiatic elephants, tiger and leopard, spotted deer, barking deer, sambar, wild boar the gaur and over 250 species of birds.
- **Entry fees:** ₹50
- **Park timings:** 6am–6pm
- **Safari timings:** 6am–9am, 3pm–5pm

Accommodation

Waterwoods Eco-Lodge ₹₹₹
8228264421; www.waterwoods.in; 19 Karapura, N Belthur Post Office, HD Kote Taluk, Mysore Distt; d full board ₹7000–13,500 (activities extra); ❄ ☼ P This boutique eco-lodge is located on the Kabini river front, affording one an uninterrupted slide show of nature's beauty. The five well-appointed rooms in the converted country home are ideal for small groups seeking privacy.

The Serai Luxury Resort ₹₹₹
8228264444, 9731396221; www.theserai.in; Karapura village, Mysore Distt; d incl full board ₹17,500–25,000 (activities extra); ❄ ☼ P Stretched along the river bank, every suite and plush villa at this luxury resort boasts spectacular views of the landscape – come sunrise or sunset. A row of hammocks out front, under coconut palms, can quickly become your favourite spot here. You can also indulge in a spa treatment.

Orange County
Luxury Resort Luxury Resort ₹₹₹
8228269100; www.orangecounty.in; Bheeramballi village & Post, HD Kote Taluk, Mysore Distt; d incl full board ₹26,000–33,000 (includes coracle ride and guided nature walk); ❄ ☼ P Do not be taken in by the tribal look and feel of the place; this resort is the very embodiment of luxe. The cottages, the scenic coffee and reading lounge, Ayurvedic spa and infinity pool, have been designed to provide guests with a holistic experience in the wild.

Also see Kabini River Lodge (p280).

Masinagudi

Why go?

It may not have the cachet of Bandipur, but Masinagudi offers a wildlife experience as authentic as any. Though the jungle safaris have been restricted due to a court notice, the resorts and homestays in the area give one a chance to unwind in the vicinity of wildlife. The lush and peaceful forests are home to (among other creatures) elephants, deer and leopards.

Highlights

- **Road safari:** Hop onto a jeep for a resort-organised trip; look out for visitors from the forest.
- **Birdwatching:** Masinagudi is a birdwatcher's paradise; expect to spot a variety of species.

MASINAGUDI

Trip Planner

Getting There 250km

🚗 **5hr** **SH17, NH181**

- **Route:** Follow the well-marked SH17 to Mysore. After crossing Mysore, head towards Nanjangud and Bandipur. From Bandipur, follow the forest road for another 20km till you hit Masinagudi.

🚌 **7hr**

- Take a KSRTC bus from Kempegowda heading towards Ooty. Get off at Theppakadu and ask for a pick-up from your stay. Else take a jeep-taxi (bargain down the price). The forest part of the highway is closed from 9pm –5am. However, you can opt for the 10.15pm or 10.45pm bus (deluxe and luxury, ₹349 onwards) which have special permission to travel at night. But its more convenient to leave by an early morning bus, which arrives by noon.

Top A view of Vibudhi Hills
Bottom A brightly coloured male Malabar trogon

ℹ️ Quick Facts

BEST TIME TO VISIT

J F M A M J J A S **O N D**

GREAT FOR

REST STOP For a good meal and reasonably clean loos, the Mysore Rd has Kadambam (for breakfast; just after Channapatna), Indradhanush Complex and Kamat.

On the Edge of the Forest

Highlights
1. Road Safari by the Resorts
2. Birdwatching
3. Nature Trails

Often overlooked as a weekend getaway, Masinagudi actually offers a more complete experience than any other wildlife destination in the vicinity of Bengaluru. Here, in the backdrop of the Mudumalai Forest, you can enjoy the company of wildlife veterans who run a number of resorts and homestays in the area – though properties in the elephant corridor face the threat of closure by a government diktat.

Private safaris are banned, but you are likely to spot elephants, bison, gaur, sambar and deer at the side of the highway. Leopards are also sighted; they're frequent visitors to many of the properties here. And the moist deciduous forest is home to a variety of smaller wildlife.

Masinagudi itself consists of one main street, with paltry options for entertainment. Move along to Bokkapuram, where most of the resorts are situated. Soak in the lovely countryside in comfortable stays, furnished with rustic authenticity to blend in with the jungle.

Green slopes around Kallatti near Masinagudi

Forests as far as the eye can see

❶ ROAD SAFARI BY THE RESORTS
Ever since private safaris were stopped by the Karnataka government, resorts and homestays have introduced jeep rides on the highway. There are fair chances of spotting wildlife on these trips, as animals tend to come out up to the fringes of the forest.
This activity is included in the package in most resorts.

❷ BIRDWATCHING
Fortunately this is one activity that remains personalised since naturalists at resorts can take you on permissible birding trails around the properties. In this region you can spot the rare black and orange flycatcher, Malabar trogon, rufous-bellied hawk eagle, and more. There are over 320 species in the region.
This activity is included in the package in most resorts.

❸ NATURE TRAILS
Again, the forest limits are out of bounds but properties on large areas organise nature trails with naturalists. If one has an enthusiasm for this activity, the walks are quite educational and give you a good perspective on the flora of the region.
This activity is included in the package in most resorts.

Accommodation

Wild Haven — Nature Stay ₹
☏0423–2526490; www.wildhaven.in; Chadapatti village, Mavanalla Post; d incl breakfast ₹2500–3000
Nature lovers are sure to be lured by this neighbour of the jungle. Wild Haven is extremely popular in the wildlife circuit for its offbeat location in the middle of the forest. Lose yourself in the green cover as you bask in the comfort of aesthetically-styled rooms. They also have rooms with 3–4 beds that are ideal for groups.

Jungle Retreat — Family-Run Resort ₹₹
☏0423–2526469; www.jungleretreat.com; Nilgiri Distt; d incl full board from ₹5939–15,940;
One of the oldest family-run resorts in the area, Jungle Retreat is also one of the best. Owner Rohan Mathias and his knowledgeable team offer a host of nature based – and casual – activities, for ecologically-conscious leisure travellers, wildlife enthusiasts and groups. You might end up spending much of your time around the pool.

Forest Hills — Family-Run Resort ₹₹
☏0423–2526216; www.foresthillsindia.com; Bokkapuram, Nilgiri Distt; d incl full board from ₹3890–5240
Forest Hills lies at the end of the Bokkapuram Rd, with a vantage point next to the jungle limits. With its well-spaced-out cottages, Forest Hills is ideal for groups both large and small; opt for the 'Machan' for an exclusive view. Multi-cuisine veg and non-veg food is served in a common area as per buffet timings.

| Forest Hills resort is back-dropped by low hills

Bamboo Banks — Family-Run Resort ₹₹
☏9443373201; www.bamboobanks.in; Nilgiri Distt; d incl full board from ₹6140; ☲ Almost four decades old, Bamboo Bank is the veteran among resorts in the area. Soak in the hunting stories of Mr Kothavala, the owner, and admire his collection of memorabilia (it was, incidentally, he that devised the inventive gate-opening contraption). A garden pool and the Parsi food at the multi-cuisine restaurant will make your stay worthwhile.

The Wilds at Northern Hay — Family-Run Resort ₹₹
☏9843149490; www.serendipityo.com; Singara Post, Nilgiri Distt; d incl full board from ₹5835–6547 This century-old, luxuriously-furnished bungalow blends perfectly with the coffee plantation and forest area around it. The 98-acre expanse allows one to enjoy a more personalised sighting experience. And even when safely ensconced in your cottage, you'll hear sounds coming from the jungle, providing the soundtrack to your stay here.

Jungle Hut — Family-Run Resort ₹₹₹
☏0423–2526240; www.junglehut.in; Bokkapuram, Nilgiri Distt; d incl full board from ₹6900; ☲ A combination of luxury tents, enclosed camping site and deluxe rooms, the Jungle Hut is suitable for large and small groups alike. If you are not admiring the regular pack of deer in the courtyard area, you will find yourself lounging by the swimming pool. The best part of the property is a gushing mini-waterfall, fed by an enormous pipe.

> ❤ **If You Like: Knick knacks**
>
> Masinagudi is far from being a shopping destination. But at this shop, you will find herbs and oils to take back as souvenirs. **Casa Deep Woods** ☏0423–2526335; www.zestbreaks.com; Bokkapuram village, Nilgiri Distt

---

✖ Eating

Casa Deep Woods — Multi-Cuisine ₹₹₹
☏0423–2526335; www.zestbreaks.com; Bokkapuram village, Nilgiri Distt; breakfast 8am–10am, lunch 1pm–3pm, dinner 8pm–10pm Casa Deep Woods is the only resort in Masinagudi which allows non checked-in guests for a la carte and buffet meals. A reasonable spread is served here, but you are unlikely to visit if you are staying in one of the resorts.

Popeye's Chicken — Multi-Cuisine ₹₹
☏9886261454; 8/70 Ooty-Mysore Rd, Masinagudi, Nilgiri Distt; 9.15am–10pm A clean and cheerful option for western snacks and meals in Masinagudi town, Popeye serves delicious chicken delights. For visitors, this is the only reasonable restaurant in town.

ESCAPE TO A RESORT

- Angana – The Country Inn 244
- Soukya 250
- AyurvedaGram 256
- Shreyas Yoga Retreat 260
- Galibore Fishing & Nature Camp 266
- Georgia Sunshine Village 270
- Gorukana, BR Hills 274
- Kabini River Lodge 280
- Amanvana Spa 286
- Orange County 290
- The Windflower Resort & Spa 294
- River Tern Lodge 300
- Destiny 306
- Oland Plantation 312

▌ A villa with a private pool at Orange County

Angana – The Country Inn

Why go?

Angana gives you the opportunity to connect with your roots, and familiarise yourself again with those long-forgotten objects and memories, of your childhood – copper vessels, a spacious courtyard and a swimming pool in the style of a kalyani (stepwell). Just an hour's drive from Bengaluru, the down-to-earth vibe of Angana promises an experience with the difference.

Highlights

- **Panchavati:** Fresh produce from the resort's own orchard and vegetable garden.
- **Art of Living International Centre:** World-famous ashram that offers a generous slice of spirituality.
- **Old world charm:** From four poster beds, lanterns, copper vessels to a swimming pool built in the style of a step well, everything here gives an earthy feel.

Trip Planner

Getting There 25km

🚗 **1hr 30min** Bengaluru–Kanakapura Rd

• **Route:** Cross the Art of Living Ashram on Kanakapura Rd and keep a look out for a small right at Kaggalipura. A board will guide you further inside, via a village road, till you see the brown-brick walls of Angana on the right. One can also avoid traffic and get onto the NICE Rd from the direction of Electronic City.

🚌 **2hr**

• Take a BIG 10 bus from Corporation Circle till Kaggalipura (₹15; 6.20am onwards). Get dropped at the Kaggalipura bus stop; make sure you ask for a pick-up from here beforehand.

Top The resort has been built entirely of recycled material

❶ *Quick Facts*

BEST TIME TO VISIT

J F M A M J J A S O N D

GREAT FOR

Spa

REST STOP The drive is short so no stop is required. But the Art of Living Ashram is good for a healthy glass of juice and clean loos.

ESCAPE TO A RESORT

Connecting with Tradition

Highlights
1. Pyramid Valley International
2. Art of Living International Centre
3. Panchavati
4. Treks to Somanahalli

Angana was started in 2000 by Shashidhar and Sandhya as an extension of their hospitality, to accommodate a steady stream of friends at their farmhouse. The building material was recycled from a broken down labour colony school; low wooden doors, windows and concrete slabs have been used creatively in making this house, employing construction techniques from across India.

With Indian motifs on the walls – as well as lanterns, sculptures, an old sewing machine and four-poster beds – the house aspires to let visitors experience life in an earthy ambience, surrounded by traditional themes.

Most guests arrive with a reference, or are repeat visitors. Minimal marketing has allowed Angana to retain its exclusivity, ensuring there is no intrusion on personal space. The manager connects with all prospective guests personally, to gauge their compatibility with the experience the house offers. And all the staff here are pleasantly discreet, adding to the place's tranquillity.

The gardens are a peaceful retreat

Quick Facts

- ☎ 080-28432888
- **Website:** www.anganacountryinn.com
- **Address:** No 55 Pattareddy Palya, Kaggalipura, Kanakapura Rd, Bengaluru
- **Tariff:** d/cottage incl full board ₹6500/8500
- **Meals:** Breakfast, lunch, tea and dinner included in tariff.
- **Other Facilities:** 🛏

❶ PYRAMID VALLEY INTERNATIONAL

A cathartic meditation experience at the Maitreya Buddha Pyramid (Pyramid Valley) is only 12km away from Angana. The spiritual science centre, started by Brahmarishi Patriji, houses a colossal pyramid for high-energy meditation. Patriji's mission has been to create awareness through meditation since 1979. Pyramid Valley is sprawled across 28 acres of partially cultivated land. There's a cafe on the premises, and one can also avail of an introduction to meditation. The centre's full-moon meditation is very popular. Please note that children are strictly not permitted in the meditation hall.

☎ 080-32723143; www.pyramidvalley.org; Kebbedoddi, Harohalli Hobli, Kanakapura Rd, Bengaluru; 4am–10pm; lunch (free) 12.30pm–1.30pm

❷ ART OF LIVING INTERNATIONAL CENTRE

Another stopover on your spiritual break. At the Sri Sri Ravi Shankar Art of Living Ashram, 4km out from Angana, visitors can take part in a satsang (community prayer), or roam around in the home-like campus and see the Goshala (cow shelter), Yagnashala (place for fire ceremony), Krishna Kutir – The Ayurvedic Spa, or the Sumeru Matap (an

An aesthetic use of stone can be seen everywhere

ESCAPE TO A RESORT

> ### ✓ *Snapshot: Alugulimane at Angana*
>
> Befitting the aesthetics and experience of Angana, do try your hand at 'Alugulimane', a local Kannadiga board game. The game calls for expertise in counting and analysing the number of beads (these can be replaced by seeds and shells) that need to go into a wooden, foldable board which resembles an egg crate. It can be played by children above 5 years, and requires some amount of hand–eye coordination. The game is available in the common area and is a good way to spend the evenings.

auditorium shaped like a lotus). Even if you're not inclined to join any of the courses here, it is recommended that you visit this world-famous ashram just to experience its meticulous operations.

☎ 080–67262626; www.artofliving.org; Ved Vignan Maha Vidya Peeth, 21st KM Kanakapura Rd, Bengaluru; 9am–7pm, Satsang 6.30pm–8pm

❸ PANCHAVATI

Less than a kilometre from Angana, Panchavati is an orchard of fruit and vegetables that belongs to the property. It provides a great opportunity to engage the children in guided farming activities.

❹ TREKS TO SOMANAHALLI

The arid, boulder-clad hills of Somanahalli, only 3km beyond Angana, are a favourite with climbers. If you are not looking at an intensive schedule, opt for a more leisurely ascent amongst the many rocky hills here. Guided day treks are organised by Angana.

The traditional pillared courtyard at Angana

ANGANA – THE COUNTRY INN

The breezy pavilion where guests gather for meals

Accommodation

Six standard rooms and two private cottages are tastefully furnished with four-poster beds, weathered wooden windows and racks, to maintain the old-fashioned look and feel. And to further enhance the traditional experience, the cosy rooms do not have any ACs or TVs. Bathrooms, though modern, have copper vessels for bathing.

Eating

A home-like spread of Indian food, available in vegetarian and non-vegetarian options, is served in a large and airy pavilion overlooking the garden. The vegetables are sourced locally from nearby. With a focus on healthy food, Angana serves nourishing local dishes like kadlebele usli (chickpea salad), bendekai palya (sautéed okra) and mint rice. Non-vegetarians will enjoy the home-made chicken curry, but it is recommended that one sticks to the vegetarian preparations for there is more variety. There is no room service.

Activities

Spa

A small menu of Ayurveda massages is available at an extra cost. A few staff members have been trained professionally. Do not expect elaborate spa facilities. The reasonably-priced massages include: Sarvanga Abhyanga (full body massage, ₹850), Pada Abhyanga (foot massage, ₹350), Shiro Abhyanga (head, neck and shoulder massage, ₹350), Prishta Abhyanga (back massage, ₹350), Sarvanga Swedana (full body steam, ₹200), Sthanika Swedana (local steam, ₹50).

Soukya

Why go?

Soukya offers an ideal blend of traditional and modern treatments which its Indian and international clientele (from over 70 countries) vouch for. This first-of-its-kind centre uses complementary therapies with Ayurveda, yoga and naturopathy, to rejuvenate and de-stress. Wellness doesn't come any more authentic at Dr Issac Mathai's brainchild.

Highlights

- **Tailored therapies:** All wellness packages are tailored to your needs.
- **Yoga:** Start your day with a yoga session under an expert teacher.
- **Organic Farm:** Learn how organic veggies and medicinal herbs are grown.

SOUKYA

Trip Planner

Getting There — 25km

🚗 **1hr** — Whitefield Rd

- **Route:** The most convenient way of getting to Soukya is by car. Reach the Hope Farm Junction (Whitefield) either by the Old Madras Rd or the Old Airport Rd. If coming by Old Madras Rd, after Hope Farm take a left from the tri junction of Thirumalashettyhalli bus stop; the Soukya gate is 200m ahead on your left. If taking the Old Airport road, head to Marathahalli. Keep going straight until you hit Varthur Lake. Here, the road turns left. Look out for Hope Farm Junction, from where you take a right on seeing the Soukya board.

🚌 **1hr 30min**

- From Kempegowda bus stand, take the 304H/304 to Whitefield. Ask the resort for a pick-up.

Top Indulge in some light reading in the common area
Bottom Natural ingredients for massage

🛈 Quick Facts

Soukya • Bengaluru • Marathahalli • Whitefield

BEST TIME TO VISIT

J F M A M J J A S O N D

GREAT FOR

Spa

Well Being of Mind, Body & Soul

Highlights
1. **Treatments & Therapies**
2. **Yoga**
3. **Workshop Visit**
4. **Organic Farm**

Cobbled pathways in Soukya's gardens are ideal for strolls

Spread over 30 acres, Soukya transports you to a harmonious state of mind the moment you arrive. This facility, owned by Dr Issac Mathai, is focused on wellness of the mind and body, through complementary treatments like Ayurveda and modern medicine, for serious illnesses as well as for basic rejuvenation.

The large expanse here has lush-green gardens, and single-storeyed structures built from simple materials, all locally procured. Soukya's distinct ambience is created by the use of India-themed handmade tiles for walls, thatched roofs, small water bodies, and patches of organic vegetables interspersed with small seating areas all around. A large bell is particularly fascinating, as it sits in the middle of a thicket, and is rung every morning. A small prayer starts the day for everyone, followed by an essential yoga session.

1 TREATMENTS & THERAPIES
Though Soukya focuses on long-duration therapies and treatments (lasting at least a week), its integrated system is also used by guests who come to experience the rejuvenation and de-stress packages for shorter durations. Each of these treatments is first evaluated for the individual and then customised accordingly. Any visit is first met with an in-depth consultation with experts, after which a special routine is chalked out. The therapy wing consists of spotless massage rooms, innovative water-therapy apparatus, and a silence room. For ease of operations, the centre is divided by gender.

The short-duration packages consist of:
Shakthi for Rejuvenation: This includes Ayurvedic cleansing and revitalising sessions – including reflexology, acupressure, and the use of mud packs – with experts. The exact number of hours in a day will depend on post-consultation analysis.

Sukha for De-stress: This treatment will include the signature Ayurvedic hot-stone massages, special de-stressing Ayurvedic and naturopathic treatments, yoga, meditation, mud packs, reflexology, acupressure and hydro baths.

A combination of the above two packages can also be worked out for guests. Price available only after personal discussion.

> ### Quick Facts
> - 8028017000
> - **Website:** www.soukya.com
> - **Address:** Samethanahalli, Whitefield
> - **Tariff:** d incl full board from ₹8762–2,94,882 (therapy additional)
> - **Meals:** Breakfast, lunch, tea and dinner included in tariff.
> - **Other Facilities:**

❷ YOGA
Yoga is an essential part of the routine here. Every morning, a large, airy but covered pavilion becomes the venue for supervised classes in yoga for the guests. Depending on the treatment one is receiving, you can also enroll for exclusive extra classes.

❸ WORKSHOP VISIT
Few holistic health centres manufacture their own oils and soaps. But most of the oils and soaps used for treatment at Soukya are made here, and also supplied internationally. A workshop, basic but immaculately clean, is located at the edge of the organic farm. You can visit the workshop to understand how these are prepared.

❹ ORGANIC FARM
Patches of organically-grown vegetables and fruits can be seen across Soukya. You can choose to help out, and learn about how these are grown and cared for. Most of the veggies make it to the kitchen, and the herbs are used for medicinal purposes – for making oils or for use in the therapies.

🛏 Accommodation

There are four categories of rooms at Soukya – deluxe, super deluxe, super deluxe special and suites. Every room or suite has a personal garden, aesthetically-furnished interiors and features like tea maker and writing table, as well as personal-care products in the bathrooms. There are only 25 rooms here, to ensure that the average number of guests at any one time is kept to a minimum. The rooms are set apart to maintain privacy. The suites have a large garden on two sides, and also a small natural pool with bamboo walls for seclusion. Airy verandahs, a common lounge, kitchenette and three rooms are enough to accommodate an entire family. However, the deluxe rooms are equally comfortable and well furnished (and also reasonably priced). There is no room for any opulence at unassuming Soukya, which makes one's stay even more comfortable, and even more of an experience.

🍴 Eating

Meals at Soukya are strictly timed. Breakfast, lunch and dinner are served in a breezy and spacious semi-outdoor area. Since there is no room service, mealtimes are also ideal to meet others in the facility, as much of the time here is taken up by treatments. Since food is integral to the treatments, and an essential element in the cleansing of the body, the meals here (needless to say) are health-oriented and organic. You'll be served ovo-vegetarian Indian food – and a small menu of Western preparations – with a focus on nutritious veggies, juices and satvik dishes. The food is low on spices and oil. Many guests are also given meals specially assigned by the nutritionist.

The traditional mud-walled yoga and meditation hall

📷 *Snapshot: Environmental consciousness*

Not only does Soukya aim at wellness of mind and body, it also concentrates on wellness of the environment. The establishment here is dedicatedly eco-conscious. The property has its own compost waste-management section, solar heaters, and drip-irrigation and rainwater harvesting systems.

🛍 Shopping

Soukya Boutique
A small boutique is located near the reception, from where guests can buy herbal oils, soaps, and special medicinal herbs that can be incorporated into daily life. A special blend, which can be boiled with water, is especially popular; all staff and guests consume this potion here.

🏃 Activities

Walking Track
A paved walking path, almost 2km long, winds through the property, flanked by manicured gardens.

Library & TV Area
A small, cosy library is available for guests to access in the common area of the consultation wing. India-themed books, biographies – and literature on many other topics – make for a diverse selection. One can get access to TVs and the internet in the common lounge and library (there are no TVs in the rooms); the TV is switched on between 5pm and 9.30pm.

Swimming
A swimming pool provides a much-needed break from the treatment schedule. Hay-thatched pagodas are constructed on the edge of the pool, and there are also sun-bathing chairs to relax in.

Indoor Games
A host of indoor games like billiards, board games and table-tennis, are available for guests to play, near the dining area.

Music Concerts
The soothing experience at Soukya is further enhanced by music concerts for guests in the evenings. The artistes perform in the in-house pavilion. Classical Indian music is both relaxing and enriching, at the end of a hard day's regime.

Indian classical music is performed every night

AyurvedaGram

Why go?

A short distance yet a world away from Bengaluru's hustle and bustle sits AyurvedaGram Heritage Wellness Centre – a harbour of healing, and a place of recreation and relaxation. Apart from undergoing the various therapies, just the simple aesthetic of the place – set amidst medicinal trees, fruits and flowers – promises to rejuvenate mind, body and spirit.

Highlights

- **Yogavedagram Kalithattu:** The yoga and meditation centre forms the central hub.
- **Health Centre:** A century-old structure translocated from Kerala.
- **Herbal Garden:** An extensive space containing a variety of medicinal plants.

AYURVEDAGRAM 257

Trip Planner

Getting There 28km
🚗 1hr NH207

- **Route:** Follow the Channasandra Main Rd from Hope Farm Circle in Whitefield, past the MVJ College of Engineering, to the end of the road where it meets NH207. Turn right onto NH207 and drive for about 3km to the village of Bodanahosahalli. Where the main road turns left, keep an eye out for a small lane, and the AyurvedaGram sign directing you to the centre.

❶ Quick Facts

BEST TIME TO VISIT

J F M A M J J A S O N D

GREAT FOR

Spa · 🍴 · 🔒 · 👪 · ♥ · 👨‍👦

Top Traditional architecture and sculptures add to the character of the place *Bottom* The recreation room

Wellness – Within & Without

Highlights
1. Yogavedagram Kalithattu
2. Health Centre
3. Sumukhi
4. Herbal Garden
5. Yogavedagram Recreation Building

The silence in AyurvedaGram is one seemingly borne of serenity and grace. From the carved wooden pillars and cornices, the plastered white walls and red-oxide flooring, to the expansive gardens marked by stone pathways and punctuated by idols and artefacts – all recall a older world, and a less complicated existence.

The centre offers yoga and meditation, Ayurvedic oil and powder massages, satvic diets and detoxifying purges – addressing a wide range of ailments. The busiest time is between October and December, when guests arrive from all over the world.

A guest receives Shirodhara therapy

❶ YOGAVEDAGRAM KALITHATTU
Also known as Kuroor Mana, this vast hall doubles both as a place for cultural performances as well as the yoga and meditation centre. Exquisitely made – with smooth red-oxide floors, and a high ceiling roofed with brick tiles – the hall is suffused with energy both calming and rejuvenating.

❷ HEALTH CENTRE
This 100-year-old building, known as Pulimkunnu Mana, was transplanted from Kerala a little over a decade ago. It houses the health centre; the facilities within are quite modern but in accordance with the aesthetics of AyurvedaGram.

❸ SUMUKHI
Sumukhi is an indulgent herbal beauty parlour housed within the Health Centre. Here you can avail of the application of herbal ointments, massages with oils, steam baths and many more traditional treatments – all entirely bespoke.

❹ HERBAL GARDEN
This lush garden contains over 200 varieties of neatly labelled medicinal plants. Guest cottages surround the garden, and a stone jogging track runs through and around it. Most of these plants contribute to the treatments and medicines.

❺ YOGAVEDAGRAM RECREATION BUILDING
This is the space set aside for recreation. The building looks somewhat like a massive white doorway, leading to the herbal garden and the residences of the Yogavedagram beyond. It houses the multi-gym and the carom and table-tennis tables on the ground floor, and an eclectic library above, with a few darkwood chairs and tables for reading and reflection.

🛈 *Quick Facts*

- ☎ 080–28945430, 65651090, 9845071990
- **Website:** www.ayurvedagram.com
- **Address:** Hemmandanahalli, Samethanahalli Post, Whitefield, Bengaluru
- **Tariff:** Classic/classic deluxe/heritage/heritage deluxe cottage ₹7420/7920/8420/8920
- **Meals:** All meals part of the package.

🛏 Accommodation
All categories of rooms provide similar modern comforts such as TVs and hot-water, but differ with respect to space and privacy. Rooms and cottages are similar in their architecture, in that they follow the aesthetic of the Centre. Classic and classic deluxe rooms are a part of the yoga and meditation centre, with a long communal verandah. Heritage and heritage deluxe cottages line the herbal garden.

🍴 Eating
Suruchi
The beautifully furnished restaurant is open on all sides. Only buffet meals are served; the food is vegetarian and mostly traditional Kerala fare, but dishes from the rest of South India are also available. Most particularly, however, Suruchi serves satvic food, adding just another dimension to the 'wellness' theme that permeates AyurvedaGram .

Shreyas Yoga Retreat

Why go?

Shreyas offers a lavish wellness break with authentic Ayurveda, Yoga and meditation. Though set in the backdrop of a village, this getaway has all the ambience of an international retreat. Stay for at least a night here to experience the impeccable standards, the warm, personalised service and the carefully-tailored programmes.

Highlights

- **Yoga:** Start your day with yoga classes by an expert instructor.
- **Wellness for the Soul:** A comprehensive package for meditation.
- **Ayurvedic Rejuvenation:** Feel refreshed with intensive or light massage therapies.

SHREYAS YOGA RETREAT 261

Trip Planner

Getting There   35km

🚗 1hr 30min   NH4

- **Route:** Follow the NH4 and take a right before Nelamangala at the commercial tax check post. The road goes through a village and, finally, into a rustic, banyan-lined boulevard, the only scenic stretch off the crowded and dusty highway. Follow the boards to Shreyas on your left.

Top The resort pool *Bottom* The treatment room

ℹ️ Quick Facts

Shreyas Yoga Retreat
Nelamangala
Bengaluru

BEST TIME TO VISIT

J F M A M J J A S O N D

GREAT FOR

Spa ✕ 🔒 🏃 ❤️ 👪

REST STOP Stop at Get Inn Food Court for a quick bite; it's on your left, just before you exit the highway onto the right towards Shreyas.

A Journey of Self-discovery

Highlights
1. Yoga
2. Wellness for the Soul
3. Ayurvedic Rejuvenation
4. Silent Retreat
5. Weight Management

Your trip to Shreyas can well be called a spiritual odyssey, one created with meticulous planning by well-trained professionals. The founder's initiative, to offer the timeless spiritual traditions of yoga and Vedanta, is reflected in every aspect of the retreat. All staff members practice yoga daily. Moreover, the need for – and importance of – rejuvenation means that not more than 25 people are accommodated here at one time. Children and pets are not encouraged. Meanwhile, roomy poolside cottages and garden tents guarantee plenty of private space.

The slightly stiff, and overwhelming, welcome – including a straight-out-of-the-refrigerator garland and an Indian 'teeka' – is more in tune with the international palate. But the warm and unassuming staff soon ensures that everyone feels comfortable. The attention to detail is remarkable in the service; one can't help but appreciate the little things that are taken care of at Shreyas.

One of the meditation spots at the retreat

❶ YOGA

The yoga schedule is an important part of the day. Mornings are dedicated to yoga, with an instructor-led session in a wide gazebo. If opting for a Yoga Retreat, you have almost six hours of yoga planned for the day, in which time there would be common sessions and four personalised sittings. This follows an intensive meeting with the yoga teacher, to ensure that your needs are understood clearly.

❷ WELLNESS FOR THE SOUL

Each package is designed differently, depending on the guest's requirement. Meditation is the focus of this particular package. Covert spots have been created in the garden and through the property, so that one can find isolation to practice meditation, both with the instructor and also alone. The meals are planned as per the package chosen.

❸ AYURVEDIC REJUVENATION

At the onset, an Ayurveda doctor gets to learn about your body type over an hour-long discussion, and only then recommends the necessary treatments. Intensive therapy sessions are planned through the stay, with special attention given to diet.

❹ SILENT RETREAT

Guests who opt for the Silent Retreat are monitored every half-hour by the staff. A board is put outside their room and periodically checked for any personal need.

❺ WEIGHT MANAGEMENT

An exhaustive plan is laid out for those who opt for the weight-management therapy. Along with yoga and an exercise regime, their diet needs are taken care of attentively.

> ### 🛈 *Quick Facts*
> - ☏ 080-27737102/3
> - **Website:** www.shreyasretreat.com
> - **Address:** Santoshima Farm, Gollahalli Gate, Nelamangala, Bengaluru
> - **Tariff:** Poolside cottages/garden tents incl full board ₹17,906
> - **Meals:** Breakfast, lunch, tea and dinner included in tariff.
> - **Other Facilities:** 🏊

🛏 Accommodation

The property has a combination of poolside cottages and garden tents, all tastefully furnished, uncluttered and earthy. You might prefer the luxury tents, which come with plenty of space, a roofless shower, and also an adorable verandah to sit out in. A delicate petal or a flower meets you with every object you touch (doormat, wash basin, towel). Yoga mats are available in each room.

The poolside cottages are slightly more elaborate in furnishings, with a couch in each room. The no-TV policy is applicable to these too. If you're seeking extra privacy, it is recommended to stay in the tented rooms, as the poolside cottages are too close to the common areas.

🍽 Eating

Breakfast 8am–9am, lunch 1pm–2pm, dinner 7pm–8pm Only vegetarian and vegan meals are served at Shreyas, in the dining area or a common gazebo, at designated hours. Expect a simple yet delicious range of fresh garden produce served on a flower-strewn table. Your attendant takes care to explain every dish in detail. Though one might be familiar with the Indian dishes, you will be surprised at the unique flavouring and presentation of these preparations. The ginger-spiked watermelon juice is to die for, and is offered to you through the day. Room service is charged on the bill. Specify your vegan needs in advance so the kitchen staff can prepare your meals accordingly.

🏃 Activities

If you feel the need – after a packed schedule of rejuvenation – to indulge

The cottages at Shreyas are well furnished and spacious

A lily pond in the vast compound

in an activity or two, Shreyas offers plenty of choice:

- Cricket nets, equipped with an automated bowling machine, are provided.
- A home-theatre lounge can be booked, and you can watch from a wide collection of movies.
- A jogging track, 2.5km long, meanders through the entire property.
- An open Jacuzzi and swimming pool can be used at any time.
- The greenhouse and cowshed are at the far end of the Shreyas property. Feel free to ask any of the attendants to take you through the indigenous plants, which have been painstakingly chosen for the retreat.
- The library in the reception area has an adequate collection of India-themed books. Biographies and yoga-related literature is in plenty. Most other coffee-table books are in tune with international readers' eagerness to know more about India.
- Culinary classes are conducted in a new-age, well-equipped and plush kitchen. These are popular with international guests keen to learn about the Indian style of cooking.

♥ If You Like: The joy of giving

Shreyas Yoga Retreat is closely associated with an orphanage in a nearby village. Over the years, thanks to the patronage of the guests, the orphanage has been provided a new building and computer facilities, as well as better living conditions. For those who are interested, a community-service option is available; you can spend time at the orphanage, local schools and the village.

Galibore Fishing & Nature Camp

Why go?

Secluded Galibore Fishing and Nature Camp has everything the nature lover could possibly ask for. For the reflective traveller, there's angling and birdwatching – highly recommended when visiting these parts. But if you're seeking a dose or two of adventure, activities like rafting, trekking and kayaking will fit your bill perfectly. This is the ultimate outdoor experience.

Highlights

- **Angling:** Catch and release the largest freshwater game fish – the mahseer.
- **Birdwatching:** A plethora of feathered species to look out for.
- **Adventure Fix:** There's no better option for the adrenaline junkie than the guided activities at Galibore.

GALIBORE FISHING & NATURE CAMP

Trip Planner

Getting There 100km

🚗 2hr   Bengaluru–Kanakapura Rd

- **Route:** Galibore is off the main Kanakapura Highway. Take a left from Kanakapura Junction towards Sangam. At Sangam, look out for an inconspicuous Galibore board. From here, it's a relatively comfortable off-road drive of 9km.

Top The scenic drive
Bottom One of the spots for angling

ℹ️ Quick Facts

BEST TIME TO VISIT

J F M A M J J A S **O N D**

GREAT FOR

REST STOP It's a short drive. You may stop at the Art of Living Ashram for a break.

Kaveri's Secret

Highlights
1. Angling
2. River Rafting
3. Mountain Biking
4. Kayaking
5. Birdwatching
6. Hiking

Galibore is pleasantly hidden between the Kaveri River and the thick forest of the Kaveri Wildlife Sanctuary. The campsite here makes for an outdoors experience as authentic as any, with simple accommodation in tents, strict meal timings and the rigour of outdoor activity. It's run by Jungle Lodges and Resorts Ltd, a government enterprise.

A team of trained naturalists and instructors guide you through a set of activities, among them trekking, angling, joy fishing (fishing for beginners), rafting and coracle rides. Switch off your phone (there is no signal here), internet and TV for a weekend of solitude. The only time your tranquility might be disrupted is when there is a large, noisy group sharing the camp space with you.

1 ANGLING
All fishing activities are on shore, and the 'catch and release' procedure is strictly followed. The 'gillies', or fishing guides, are there to assist you; you're also given a detailed angling instruction card. Since a large number of people come to fish for mahseer, the camp authorities are vigilant about time spent with the catch, and methods of photography, before the fish is released back into the water.
All months except June to September

A quirky signpost to the camp

2 RIVER RAFTING
Don your life jacket and enjoy the exhilarating experience of rafting. Manoeuvre through Type 2 rapids of medium difficulty over a distance of 10–12km. The best time

for rafting is during the monsoons.
Mid June to September

❸ MOUNTAIN BIKING
If you're keen to explore the forest on a two-wheeled machine, bikes are available for hire all year round. You must, however, keep to the accepted tourist track inside the forest.

❹ KAYAKING
A kayak ride can be arranged in the calmer parts of the Kaveri River, with the help of an instructor. Both single and double kayaks are available for hire.
Through the year except June to September

❺ BIRDWATCHING
More than 200 species of birds have been spotted around the camp. If you are a birding enthusiast, make sure to carry your binoculars. You're likely to spot regulars like the grey-headed fishing eagle, tawny eagle, darter and pied-crested cuckoo.

❻ HIKING
Easy hiking trails that snake into the forest have been formed over the years behind the Galibore Camp. And you can choose from a number of guided hikes.

ℹ️ *Quick Facts*
- 📞 080-40554055
- **Website:** www.junglelodges.com
- **Address:** No 49 West Wing Ground Floor, Khanija Bhavan, Race Course Rd, Bengaluru
- **Tariff:** cottages incl full board from ₹8000
- **Meals:** Breakfast, lunch, tea and dinner included in tariff.

🛏️ Accommodation
There are 12 thatch-roofed tented cottages, each furnished with a double bed, clothes rack, table fan and a dresser. The slightly cheerless olive-green canvas is for blending in with the jungle. The bathrooms are attached to the tent, but with a separate entrance. If you have a choice, pick tent Nos 1 or 12 for maximum privacy.

🍴 Eating
Breakfast 8am–9pm, lunch 1.30pm–2.30pm, dinner 7pm–8pm
At Galibore, there's a fixed menu of vegetarian and non-vegetarian meals, available in the common gazebo at designated timings. Guests can expect basic but healthy south Indian food served buffet style.

Georgia Sunshine Village

Why go?

A pet lovers' retreat, Georgia Sunshine is very conveniently located from Bengaluru and certainly not a stressful drive for your four-legged one. Cheerful and homely, the 'Village' has plenty of space for your pet to play (and mingle with nine other dogs). Here, you can hone your fishing skills, or visit nearby Gaganachukki Falls for sightseeing and hiking.

Highlights

- **Hiking:** Explore the relatively easy hiking trails nearby.
- **Fishing:** Spend patient afternoons by the local water body, testing your fishing skills.
- **Waterfalls:** Nearby Gaganachukki and Bharachukki are great for picnics.

GEORGIA SUNSHINE VILLAGE 271

Trip Planner

Getting There 120km

🚗 **3hr 30min** Bangalore–Kanakapura Rd

• **Route:** Take the Kanakapura Rd. After Kanakapura, turn left at the T-junction on NH209. When you hit Shimshapura Junction, take a left towards Hebbani village and follow the signboards. to Georgia Sunshine.

Top and *Bottom* 'Cheerful and homely' sum up this place

ⓘ Quick Facts

BEST TIME TO VISIT

J F M A M J J A S O N D

GREAT FOR

Spa · · · · · ·

REST STOP The drive is short so no stop is required. But the Art of Living Ashram is good for a healthy glass of juice and clean loos.

Bask in Sunny Hospitality

Highlights
1. Fishing
2. Birdwatching
3. Short Hikes
4. Gaganachukki & Bharachukki Falls

After a drive through arid and dusty terrain, you are greeted by an oasis of green. This 10-acre garden boasts plenty of trees, and also has small water bodies. But you might end up spending a lot of time lazing on garden chairs in the breezy common lounge area.

If you're a dog lover, prepare to be trailed like the Pied Piper by Georgia Sunshine's nine canine occupants. They are friendly and used to having frequent visitors around. For Leonard and Georgia, the owners, your pet's comfort is important.

The 'Village' is especially engaging for kids, who will be fascinated by the menagerie of dogs, geese, pigeons and rabbits. There's also a 'recreation room' with a host of indoor games to choose from, plenty of outdoor space for a game of badminton or volleyball, and a bonfire on those chilly evenings. But if you're looking for more than just a lazy getaway, do pack your hiking boots and a fishing rod.

1 FISHING

If you have always wanted to try your hand at fishing, there is no better place to indulge yourself than the water bodies at Georgia Sunshine (you will be provided with a bamboo rod,

A sunshine yellow cottage at the 'Village'

hook and line). A guide can be arranged to accompany you.

❷ BIRDWATCHING
The Shivanasamudra Lake nearby attracts a diversity of avian life. This is a great place both for beginners and avid birdwatchers. In fact, an impressive variety of birdlife can be found on the property itself.

❸ SHORT HIKES
Georgia Sunshine has access to two prominent hiking trails, one to Gaganachukki, and the other to Kundoorbetta Hill, neither of them too demanding.

❹ GAGANACHUKKI & BHARACHUKKI FALLS
The waterfalls at Gaganachukki and Bharachukki are a short drive away from Georgia Sunshine Village. They come alive only after the monsoons, and make for a fun picnic spot. Coracle rides are available near Bharachukki but service is sporadic.

> ### 🛈 *Quick Facts*
> - ☎ 8231247646
> - **Website:** www.georgiasunshine.com
> - **Address:** PO Box 5, Malavalli Taluk, Mandya Distt
> - **Tariff:** standard rooms/ family rooms/ deluxe rooms/ deluxe suite incl full board ₹5500/ 6250/6500/7500)
> - **Meals:** Breakfast, lunch, tea and dinner included in tariff.
> - **Other Facilities:** 🏊

🛏 Accommodation

One is rather spoilt for choice with the 10 spacious – and brightly painted – rooms here (two deluxe suites, three deluxe and four standard rooms, and a family room). They are spread out in small clusters, yet have plenty of privacy. The rooms are not lavish but are comfortably furnished and well equipped. They're also deliberately without TV and internet; one can enjoy nothing but birdsong and the rustling of leaves. Georgia and Leonard are such warm hosts that you'll find your visit worth every rupee you've spent.

🍴 Eating

Meals at Georgia Sunshine are worth reminiscing about long after you have left; much effort, and great attention to detail, goes into preparing them. Georgia personally supervises and cooks a range of cuisines. The food is very tasty, and has a homely touch; her basa fish and chana bhatura are particularly popular. Meals are served in a common dining area in buffet style, and at strict timings, as there is little staff to help (there is no room service). The property stocks limited alcohol (guests can bring their own).

Gorukana, BR Hills

Why go?

Nestled at the base of Biligiriranga Hills (commonly known as BR Hills), Gorukana started as a venture committed to sustainable living for the region's Soliga tribals. Here, you can choose to relax in luxury cottages amidst silver oak stands, or have an activity-packed break with wildlife spotting, nature walks, organic gardening and community work.

Highlights

- **Nature Walk:** Learn about the life and culture of the Soliga tribals.

- **Ayurvedic Massage:** Whatever treatment you're looking for, you'll come away satisfied.

- **Birdwatching:** A definite treat for lovers of avian life.

GORUKANA, BR HILLS

Trip Planner

Getting There — 182km

🚗 **3hr 30min** — **NH209**

- **Route:** Stay close to NH209 on Kanakapura Rd as you head towards Kollegal. From here, cross the forest check post on your left (closed between 6pm and 6am) and follow the signage till the resort. This route is preferable over the alternative, the heavily-congested Mysore Rd, unless you want to stop over at other places on the latter route.

🚌 **5hr**

- There are no luxury buses plying between Bengaluru and BR Hills. At best, one can take a Volvo till Mysore and then hire a cab (₹1500) to Gorukana. This mode is not recommended as it wastes a lot of time on a weekend alone.

Top Tree house at the resort
Bottom The organic garden

ℹ️ Quick Facts

BEST TIME TO VISIT

J F M **A M J** J A S **O N D**

GREAT FOR

Spa | 🍴 | 🔒 | 🚶 | ❤️ | 👨‍👩‍👧

REST STOP The drive is short so no stop is needed. But the Art of Living Ashram is good for a healthy glass of juice and clean loos; on Mysore Rd, break at Kadambam restaurant.

Retreat with a Conscience

Highlights
1. Ayurvedic Massage
2. Birdwatching
3. Nature Walk
4. Wildlife Spotting
5. Tribal Resource Centre

Gorukana is supported by the Vivekananda Girijana Kalyana Kendra (VGKK) Trust, which has been involved in the region's development for over three decades. Here, one can experience responsible tourism, otherwise difficult to find in India. You can't help but feel good about the contribution that your holiday makes to the lives and welfare of the locals. Employment at and revenue from the resort are a source of livelihood for many in the nearby villages.

Though safaris are no longer allowed in the area, you can often spot animals like deer, elephants and gaurs in the vicinity. Ten luxury cottages, a tree house and tent overlook the lush surroundings and a small water body, providing an ideal setting for a peaceful break from the city.

❶ AYURVEDIC MASSAGE
This Ayurvedic centre is well equipped and has well-trained staff, ensuring a satisfying experience. Opt for the full-body massage (₹1500), which is easier on the pocket than the other treatments. Small rituals, like a short prayer and an orientation to the massage, are endearing and set the ambience perfectly. A long, indulgent treatment,

A brown fishing owl at Gorukana

with soothing music in the background, is followed by steam and a copper-vessel bath. ₹1150–6000

❷ BIRDWATCHING

Given that the eight-acre property is replete with over 100 species of birds, it is not difficult to spot some interesting ones right from your deck in the cottage. Wake up early to scan the property for regulars like woodpeckers, eagles, kingfishers, owls, scarlet minivets, and more.

❸ NATURE WALK

Camouflage-clad naturalist, Krishna, makes a sprightly appearance to start your day with a nature walk. Though not spectacular, this is a good educational option for kids. The walk comprises an easy hike through the fringes of the forest and the nearby villages (known as podus). It can take up to two or three hours, depending on how interested you might be to learn about the culture, lifestyle and means of livelihood of the Soliga tribals.

❹ WILDLIFE SPOTTING

BR Hills boasts of a robust population of leopards, elephants, birds, and also tigers. Even though safaris have recently been disallowed due to a government diktat, one can drive on the fringes of the forest and likely spot a few animals. A white board in the lobby lists all the sightings in the area. Elephants and small animals seem to surface regularly in the non-core zones of the forest, making chances of spotting high.

❺ TRIBAL RESOURCE CENTRE

A small museum has been established to showcase the instruments, artefacts, objects of daily use and historical information about the Soliga tribals. One can get a good insight into their customs and traditions. Since this is maintained by Gorukana, the timings are flexible; there are no entry charges.

> **Quick Facts**
> - 08226-244035
> - **Website:** www.gorukana.org
> - **Address:** BR Hills, Chamrajnagar
> - **Tariff:** Tree house/ cottage/ tent house incl full board ₹8000/6900/6000
> - **Meals:** All meals are part of the tariff.

🛏 Accommodation

A row of 10 luxury cottages with a wildlife theme make for a refreshing break from the run-of-the-mill luxury options elsewhere. Each cottage is distinctly denoted by hoof imprints leading to a metal-framed animal on the top edge outside. Local names like kothi (monkey) are given to the cottages. Stones, and silver-oak wood panels interspersed with wide glass panels, give the property an earthy look that blends in well with the surroundings. Inside, subtle but sophisticated furnishings are used. The only special element is a photograph above the bed, taken by renowned wildlife photographer, Kalyan Verma.

A small mezzanine deck with two additional beds is perfect to fit a whole family in one cottage. Balconies in each cottage open out to an unmanicured green patch, and a water body (the small lake dries out during the summers). The tree house and tented accommodation are similar inside, except that the cottages are more spacious. There is purposely no TV and internet in the rooms, so that one can better enjoy the tranquil surroundings.

The warm interiors of a cottage

🍴 Eating

Gorukana **Multi-Cuisine**

Largely Indian buffet meals are served at specified timings in an open pavilion overlooking the water body in front. A wide and delicious spread of South and North Indian food is served at lunch and dinner. There are ample options for both vegetarian and non-vegetarian guests; vegetarian delights like eggplant and mushroom are just as great as the chicken preparations. If you stay for two nights, one of the meals served to you will be as per the local preparation. This includes cuisine from Karnataka, like ragi balls and sambar. Most of the vegetables

✓ Top Tip: The 10pm curfew

It is advisable to stay indoors after 10pm, as the area is replete with wildlife. The proximity of Gorukana to the forest allows for some drifters (leopards, bison, elephants and other small animals) to visit the property.

Snapshot: Vivekananda Girijana Kalyana Kendra

Founded in 1981 by Dr H Sudarshan, the VGKK Trust has made an exceptional contribution towards the lives and the environment of the Soliga tribals in the BR Hills region, and has done excellent work in helping villages in the vicinity. The NGO has set up a block with a school, hospital and small-scale industries, close to the Gorukana property. A trip to the campus will be worth your while. The part-residential school is suitably equipped with a library, museum and well-constructed classrooms. The 50-bed hospital is free for all villagers, and can be easily compared to any facility in the city. The foundation is also strongly focused on conservation and community organisation. It is open to volunteers.

---

are grown in the organic garden of the property, and the rest sourced locally from the village. If, however, you are not comfortable eating Indian food, you can order Chinese and Continental, as long as you intimate your preference in advance.

Shopping

Boutique

7am–9pm A small boutique at the reception stores local products like honey, pickles, juices. Also on sale are stools made from the Lantana weed by the Soliga tribals. Wicker craft is popular in the region, and wicker products make for memorable souvenirs to take back home.

Entertainment

Documentaries

Documentaries on the Soliga tribals, the Vivekananda Girijana Kalyana Kendra NGO, and wildlife, are screened each evening.

Activities

Organic Gardening

If one is interested, the staff will be more than happy to give you a quick introduction to organic gardening at the property itself. There are two green patches where vegetables are grown, and also utilised for the property itself.

Cultural Programme

If there are many guests in the resort, a short cultural programme is organised at the charming, three-stepped amphitheatre. A local Kannada-speaking Soliga group performs an unassuming, non-rehearsed song-and-dance routine. This is translated into broken but understandable English by one of the staff members. A short introduction is followed by a performance, where guests are asked to join in a simple dance around a bonfire.

Kabini River Lodge

Why go?

Escape the city, and embrace life in the wilderness next door to the River Kabini and Nagarhole Forest. Visit the former hunting grounds of erstwhile royalty in the very heart of nature, and experience the old-world charm of a lodge stay. Take a ride down the river, or watch for animals and birds. At Kabini River Lodge, hospitality comes amidst natural beauty.

Highlights

- **Wildlife Safaris:** Discover the local fauna – on land or on water.
- **Coracle Ride:** Cruise down the river in this traditional boat.
- **Birdwatching:** Kabini and surrounds offer much for the lover of birdlife.

KABINI RIVER LODGE

Trip Planner

Getting There   220km

🚗 5hr   SH17

- **Route:** Follow the well-marked SH17, the main artery from Bengaluru to Mysore, via Ramanagaram, Maddur and Srirangapatna. At Mysore, take the SH33 for Mananthavady; 5km past Hand Post, turn right at Beechanahalli Circle (you know you've missed the turn if you find yourself at the Kabini Dam). Be warned: the last stretch to the Lodge (12km) is over a non-existent road, and is likely to take 45 minutes.

🚌 6hr

- A KSRTC super deluxe bus departs from the Central bus stand at 7.30am daily, returning at 1.30pm from Kabini.

Top Huts at the Lodge
Bottom A launch ride down the river

ⓘ Quick Facts

BEST TIME TO VISIT

J F M A M J J A S O N D

GREAT FOR

Spa 🍴 🔒 🏃 ❤️ 👥

REST STOP Halt at Indradhanush Complex near Maddur, on SH17. The petrol pumps would be your best bet on the Mysore-Mananthavady Rd.

An Old-world Experience

Highlights
1. Wildlife Safaris
2. Nature Trail Walk
3. Coracle Ride
4. Birdwatching

The Kabini River Lodge is the former hunting lodge of the erstwhile Maharaja of Mysore. A lover of the outdoors, he built this property on the banks of the Kabini River, the largest river draining the Nagarhole Forest, which was once his exclusive hunting ground.

What makes this Jungle Lodges and Resorts (JLR) property special is that it has managed to retain most of its imperial character, allowing visitors to experience the nostalgia of a bygone era. The Maharaja Cottage, adjacent to the reception cluster, retains much of its original furniture. As does the Viceroy Lodge, at the top end of the sprawling grounds, built to host and entertain the ruler's colonial guests. Today, it houses a well-stocked bar, a lounge and screening room (showing films on wildlife).

1 WILDLIFE SAFARIS
Join JLR's early morning and afternoon group safaris for your share of wildlife sightings. They are conducted in

Encounter with an elephant family

KABINI RIVER LODGE

open-to-side jeeps and locally-engineered boats, especially designed for visitors eager not to miss the chance of spotting a tiger, or the other residents of Nagarhole – leopards, deer, wild dogs, different species of monkeys, tuskers, wild boar, Indian bison. With skilled professionals proffering information and guidance, visitors are encouraged to experience safaris on land and on water.

6.30am & 4pm

> ### Quick Facts
> - 8228264402/3, 9449599755, 9449599769
> - **Website:** www.junglelodges.com
> - **Address:** Karapura, Nissana Beltur Post, HD Kote Taluk, Mysore
> - **Tariff:** d ₹10,000–15,000
> - **Other facilities:** P

❷ NATURE TRAIL WALK

Take a leisurely walk around the spotless, litter-free property on earmarked trails; spot the different types of trees and grasses – and chase butterflies. Acquaint yourself with the effective waste-management and recycling methods here. Visit the grave of Colonel Wakefield – affectionately called Papa John – whose philosophy influenced that of JLR. Make sure you have a naturalist with you at all times as wild boars have been known to make sudden appearances.

❸ CORACLE RIDE

Treat yourself to a short ride on a traditional boat. Circular in shape, the coracle is made of coir and hide, and is still in use by local folk. The boatmen will help you spot resident birds even as they skilfully steer the coracle along the river bank. Check with staff for timings, and wait for your turn at the jetty beyond the Gol Ghar.

❹ BIRDWATCHING

Along with a plethora of plants and animals, the lodge and its surrounds are a veritable delight for birdwatching enthusiasts. An educative handbook, provided at check-in, has been designed to make this activity more pleasurable. Replete with pictures of resident birds and insects, a naturalist will help you identify these creatures and tick them off the checklist.

Accommodation

There are 14 spacious double rooms, 10 river-facing cottages with twin beds and private sit-outs, and six tented cottages – all spread out across well-maintained and sylvan acreage. The accommodation is basic, yet very comfortable, and comes with all modern amenities (though you won't find any TVs here – a deliberate omission on the part of JLR). The package includes boarding, lodging, activities, forest-entry fees and taxes.

Eating

The JLR package includes all meals, served at the Gol Ghar, a large circular pavilion overlooking the river. An excellent buffet, comprising a home-style spread of north and south Indian veg and non-veg dishes, is served at pre-specified timings. Room service is available – except that you don't sign up for the indoors in Kabini!

Nightlife

11am–12noon, 6.30pm–9.30pm
Check out the well-equipped bar in the Viceroy Lodge; bond with other guests over a relaxing drink or two.

Entertainment

Wildlife Film Show

8pm–9pm, Viceroy Lodge A 60-minute film about the many moods of (and life in) the Nagarhole National Park, is screened daily. One of the staff will come by to remind you; do watch. Dubbed by Art Malik, it is a bit scratchy and dated, but will provide you with incredible insight, and delightful visuals not easy to come by.

Activities

Ayurveda Wellness Therapies

Do not expect elaborate spa facilities here. The basic menu includes Abhyanga (general body massage, ₹1250; with steam ₹1500); Udvartanam (medicated massage, ₹1500); and Shirodhara (oil massage, ₹2000). There are also a number of special packages (each ₹2000).

Shopping

Souvenirs available at the reception.

Snapshot: Environment first

Recognising potential in the lush, unspoilt forest around the serene Kabini River, Jungle Lodges and Resorts (a Government of Karnataka undertaking) turned this place into a community-based eco-tourism and wildlife destination. Managed, since 1980, by professionals subscribing to an environment-friendly approach, the Kabini River Lodge is JLR's flagship property. Visitors will be pleasantly surprised by the friendly and thoughtful staff at the lodge, from the top down. Most of the staff – naturalists included – are well-trained, professional, and eager to lend a helping hand.

📷 *Snapshot: Legend of Kabini*

The quietest corner of the Kabini River Lodge is marked by a simple grave with the legend 'Papa John' etched across its headstone. Meet Colonel John Felix Wakefield, brand ambassador of Jungle Lodges and Resorts, and the man who introduced the concept of eco-tourism to Karnataka. Father figure to the forest rangers, guides and volunteers who worked at the resort (a majority of them being locals), no-one quite remembers when he became 'Papa' to everyone.

Following a long stint in the Army, this hunter-turned-conservationist took up a career in wildlife tourism in 1967 and became associated with the Tiger Tops Jungle Lodge, headquartered in Nepal. He came to Karnataka as a representative of TTJL, at the behest of the state government, to set up a wildlife resort at Nagarhole. As resident director of the property (which he became in 1984), his boundless energy and prescience helped make Kabini River Lodge amongst the best wildlife experiences in the world.

Said to share an unusual rapport with wild animals – more specifically tuskers. Papa John also showed a protective love for the people he worked with. This fifth generation Englishman was born in Gaya in 1916 and died in Kabini, his beloved home, in 2010, at the ripe old age of 94. An ardent lover of the wild, and raconteur extraordinaire, he will always be synonymous with Kabini. His room, adjacent to the bar in the Viceroy Cottage, is a wildlife museum for some. For others, it's a shrine.

Papa John pioneered eco-tourism in Karnataka

Amanvana Spa

Why go?

At Amanvana, unwind in the midst of lush, undisturbed greenery on the banks of the Kaveri River. Experience alternative healing, and indulge yourself by checking out the quirky spa therapies here. Throw in a visit to a plantation to get your fix of coffee. This is a break that promises a healthy dose of serenity.

Highlights

- **Spa Therapies:** Experience the delight of liquor or chocolate-based treatments.

- **Nature Walk:** A blissful ramble amidst the Kaveri River.

- **Plantation Visit:** Let your senses come alive with the sweet aroma of coffee.

AMANVANA SPA 287

Trip Planner

Getting There 220km

🚗 4hr SH17

- **Route:** It's location on the highway makes Amanvana hard to miss. It will fall to your left near Kushalnagar, on the Mysore–Madikeri Rd.

Top The poolside restaurant
Bottom The Kaveri flows past the resort

❶ Quick Facts

BEST TIME TO VISIT

[J] [F] [M] [A] [M] [J] J A S [O] [N] [D]

GREAT FOR

Spa · 🍴 · 🔒 · 🏃 · ❤ · 👥

REST STOP Indradhanush Complex near Maddur for toilet break and meals; Cafe Coorg on Hunsur Bypass.

A Healthy Dose of Serenity

Highlights
1. Spa Therapies
2. Nature Walk
3. Plantation Visit
4. Movies

Sandwiched between the busy Mysore–Madikeri Highway and the River Kaveri, this riverside property opens a door to reveal a tranquil, green world. The setting and ambience lend credence to the resort's philosophy – to return to the essentials, and to heighten the senses.

Surrounded by rich greenery (courtesy the ubiquitous Kaveri), the Amanvana is ideal for a relaxing and rejuvenating vacation. The aesthetically-designed cottages, with lily ponds in their courtyards, are set amidst a variety of indigenous plants and trees that attract a number of birds.

Large manicured lawns surround the spa and the wicker-furnished poolside restaurant. A much sought-after space is the thatched coffee hut that overlooks the river – and the barbecue pits below. Accessed by a plant-bordered wooden stairway, this latter level is completely washed away during the monsoon but resurrected every year.

Water adds to the calming ambience of Amanvana

1 SPA THERAPIES
The main reason for your visit to Amanvana. The spa, open from 8am to 8pm (except between 1.30pm and 2.30pm), provides a number of irresistible full-body massages, body scrubs, facial therapies, baths, soaks and reflexology. Their signature body therapies and treatments use quirky ingredients like wine, liquor, herbs and chocolates; they last from anywhere between 45 minutes to 3½ hours, and range in cost from ₹1500 to ₹9000. Remember to book ahead (extension 300) for your preferred time.

❷ NATURE WALK

Guests are taken on a guided walk to the eight islet-like bodies in the Kaveri; this activity includes wading through placid river waters. The walk is discontinued during the heavy monsoon (which lasts through the months of June, July and August, easing up a notch in September and October) which the region experiences. The 1½ hour trek is conducted post lunch.

❸ PLANTATION VISIT

A visit to a privately-owned coffee plantation is also part of the package. Located a short drive away (6km) towards Mysore, do take this short walk for a memorable experience of plantation life; enjoy that one last cuppa, of authentic Coorg coffee you just can't get enough of, while learning to tell a Robusta from an Arabica. It is advisable to exercise this option post check-out, in order to avoid doubling back.

❹ MOVIES

A popular feature, or animation film, is screened daily at 7pm, outside the activity centre.

> ### ❶ *Quick Facts*
>
> - ✆ 8276279353/55, 9480696070/1
> - **Website:** www.amanvanaspa.com
> - **Address:** Post Box No 21, Guddehosur, Kushalnagar
> - **Tariff:** d incl full board for `16,000
> - **Meals:** Breakfast, lunch, tea, snacks and dinner included in tariff.
> - **Other facilities:** ❄ P ≋

🛏 Accommodation

The resort accommodation comprises 18 spacious and tastefully-furnished cottages, each with a patio, living area and bedroom. Engulfed in green, they exude a feel of nature amidst the luxury. They even come in shades of natural elements (red, yellow, green). Walking barefoot on the bespoke tiles in your cottage reportedly lowers your blood pressure.

🍴 Eating

The package includes all meals, served as a multi-cuisine buffet at the poolside restaurant. Room service is also available, while the a la carte option is usually exercised during periods of low occupancy. It is prudent to stick with local preparations; where other cuisines are concerned, the kitchen alternates between good days and bad days.

ESCAPE TO A RESORT

Orange County

Why go?

Step into a bygone world of the privileged gentleman planter, and cocoon yourself in the comforts of a lush plantation. Breathe in the subtle aromas of coffee and spices; unravel the secrets of the misty mountains of Coorg, and the virginal forestland bordered by the Kaveri. Not least, experience the many moods of a working plantation.

Highlights

- **Plantation Tour:** Rediscover the lost world of gentleman planters.

- **Nature Walk:** Bond with nature at her glorious best.

- **Birdwatching:** Experience the stunning diversity of birdlife here.

ORANGE COUNTY 291

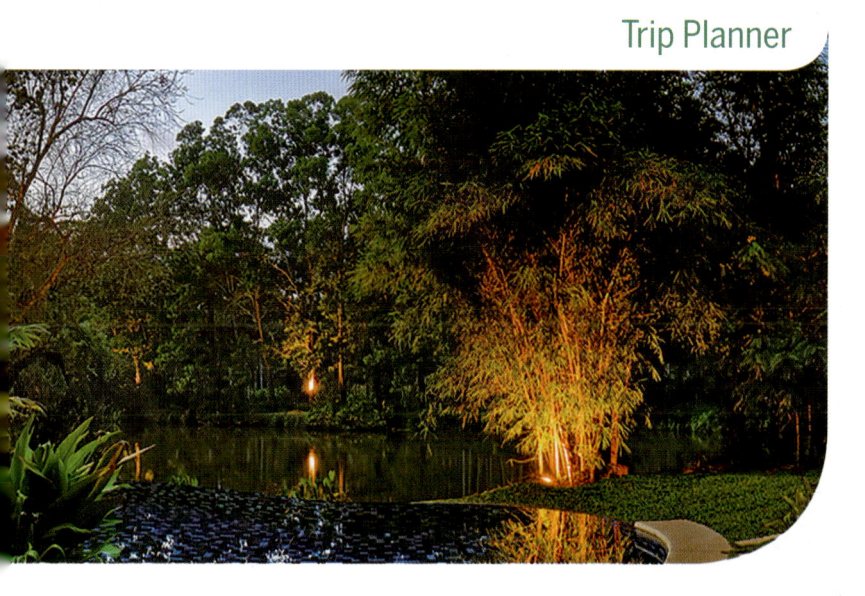

Trip Planner

Getting There 235km

🚗 5hr SH17

• **Route:** Take the SH17 through Ramanagaram, Maddur, Mandya and Srirangapatna before turning right towards Elivala, 4km from Srirangapatna. Continue down Hunsur Rd; 500m after Piriyapatna town, take a left towards Siddapura town. The turn to Orange County is to your right 3km short of Siddapura.

Quick Facts

BEST TIME TO VISIT

[J F M A M J] J A S [O N D]

GREAT FOR

Spa | 🍴 | 🔒 | 👨‍👦 | ❤️ | 🧍

REST STOP Indradhanush Complex near Maddur for toilet break and meals; Cafe Coorg on Hunsur Bypass.

Top The infinity pool
Bottom Coracle ride down the river

Tales from the Plantations

Highlights
1. Plantation Tour
2. Nature Walk
3. Birdwatching

The Orange County Resort in Siddapur lies nestled in the Western Ghats at a height of 2625ft. Located on the fringes of the Dubare Forest Reserve, it is hemmed in by the Kaveri River on the other side. The resort is part of the Chikanhalli Estate, amongst the oldest in the region. Developed by an Englishman in 1850, it was sold to the present owners in 1926.

This getaway is set amidst hundreds of acres of aromatic coffee and spice plantations, and promises exclusivity, tranquility and seclusion. The sinfully luxurious cottages, and pool villas against a cool green backdrop, offer a glimpse into the privileged lives of gentlemen planters, of which bygone era Coorg is possibly one of the last bastions standing.

The excellent food at Orange County's lakeside 'culinary temples', the exclusive infinity pool, and the oh-so-romantic coffee lounge and library, have all been designed to effortlessly divest you (however temporarily) of the world you left behind. Mind you, you will be a more-than-willing victim!

A verdant coffee plantation

1 PLANTATION TOUR
Be regaled with anecdotes from history and folklore even as your guide takes you on a botanical journey through the spice-lined and spice-scented pathways of one of the oldest estates in Kodagu. Learn to tell the difference between the beans that go into creating this globally feted brew. No prior booking is required for this tour.
4pm–6.30pm

❷ NATURE WALK

This two-hour guided walk leads you into the vastness of the moist deciduous forest of the neighbouring Dubare Reserve, alive with ancient trees, insects, birds and wildlife. Remember to sign up in advance; else you may have to wait for your next visit to marvel at the magnificence of the Terminulas Arjuna (aka Mathi) tree; this tree's ability to store water in its bark accords it life-saving status, especially for those that have wandered away from natural sources.
10.30am–12.30pm

> ## 🛈 *Quick Facts*
>
> - ☏ 08274-258481/4
> - **Website:** www.orangecounty.in
> - **Address:** Karadigodu Post, Siddapur
> - **Tariff:** d incl full board from `19,000–37,000
> - **Meals:** Breakfast, lunch, tea and dinner included in tariff
> - **Other Facilities:** P ⛱

❸ BIRDWATCHING

You are likely to be roused by a convincing bird call from your spirited guide for this early-morning activity. The forested character of the resort draws hundreds of birds to its green canopy, the ringing birdsong being a testimony to their presence in large numbers. Orange County's vast avian population includes Indian robins, woodpeckers, bulbuls, hill mynas, grey hornbills and the very noisy jungle babblers.
6.30am–8.00am

🛏 Accommodation

This lush 300-acre plantation includes clusters of plush, plantation-style cottages, and villas with private pools – the latter inspired by ethnic Kodava architecture. Here, you're guaranteed the finest in lodging and furnishing. Endorsing responsible tourism at every step, and keeping energy consumption in mind, the pools and Jacuzzis come without heating.

🍴 Eating

The package here includes all meals; guests are welcome to dine at any one of the three excellent in-house restaurants. **Granary**, adjacent to the reception, offers multi-cuisine buffet meals; the lakeside **Peppercorn**, a multi-course meal of kebabs and grills for lunch and dinner; and **Plantain Leaf** serves vegetarian south Indian food for breakfast, lunch and dinner.

The Windflower Resort & Spa

Why go?

This quiet private retreat in Coorg is tucked away in the midst of a sprawling plantation, nestled in a wooded valley of teakwood and rosewood trees. The slopes – gentle, misty and green – will cloak you in the subtly intoxicating aromas of coffee and spice. Here, you can indulge your senses with wellness therapies, and explore coffee country at your own pace.

Highlights

- **Emerge Spa:** Indulge yourself with one of the coffee therapies.
- **Yoga:** Start the day with yoga lessons in lush green environs.
- **Plantation Tour:** Get up and close with food ingredients.

153B, 174BL, 177T, 181T, 182 – 183T, 185B, 186TL, 189B, 191T, 192 – 193T, 192BL, 197BR, 201T, 202B, 204C, 206 – 207T, 208BL, 210B, 215BR, 226 – 227T, 226B, 228B, 230B, 239T, 266 – 267T, 267B, 268BL, 274BL, 300 – 301T.

Taj hotels – Kuteeram: 83T.

The Littlearth Group of Adventure Resorts & Theme Hotels: Destiny 17BR, 306 – 307T, 306B, 308B, 310T, 311B.

The Windflower Resort & Spa: 294 – 295T, 294BL, 296B, 298T.

Thiagarajan G: 162 – 163T, 164B.

Vani Ganpathy: 85BR.

Wikipedia: Creative Commons Attribution 2.0 Generic license/ earnest.edison9 70 – 71T; Creative Commons Attribution 2.5 Generic license/ L. Shyamal 154C\ 220 – 221T; Creative Commons Attribution-Share Alike 1.0 Generic license/ J.M.Garg 104T,/ Penarc 52BL; Creative Commons Attribution-Share Alike 2.0 Generic license/ Riju K 28BL; Creative Commons Attribution-Share Alike 2.5 Generic license/ Tamal Das 31B; Creative Commons Attribution-Share Alike 3.0 Unported license/ Adam Jones 55T,/ Amartyabag 36BL,/ Cks3976 236BL,/ D momaya 156BL,/ Dineshkannambadi 93C,/ Jmhullot 317B,/ Kousik Nandy 304C,/ Maheshkhanna 88TL,/ S.Gopinath Babu 161B,/ Sanjay Acharya 101T,/ Somaskanda 276B,/ Yathin S Krishnappa 232BL; Public Domain 98BL\ 113B.

Cover Images: Front – Getty Images: Lonely Planet Images/ Hira Punjabi.
Back – Getty Images: Riser/ Manoj Shah.

MAP CREDIT

Map my India, copyright © CE Info Systems

THIS GUIDE HAS BEEN RESEARCHED AND AUTHORED BY:

Supriya Sehgal has a penchant for travelling 'mapless and ungoogled'. Over the last 8 years, she has willingly got lost a number of times in the most obscure places of India. She lives on a healthy diet of anecdotes and tea with auto drivers, co-passengers and bewildered locals. Supriya currently runs a Bangalore-based travel photography outfit called 'Photography Onthemove' and writes regularly on travel.

Puneetinder Kaur Sidhu quotes Lao Tzu to best describe herself as a traveller with no fixed plans and no intention of arriving. She spends her waking hours executing the travel plans she dreams of.

Bikram Ghosh has been a traveller since he was very small, and though he is considerably larger now, he is still on the move. He likes to travel light and prefers more adventurous modes of transport. He used to maintain a backpacking blog many years ago, but had to give it up on account of backpacking.

LONELY PLANET INDIA TEAM
Commissioning Editor Kavita Majumdar
Design Manager Kavita Saha
Designer Harpreet Wadhwa
Layout Designer Arun Aggarwal
Picture Researcher Shweta Andrews

Although the authors and Lonely Planet have taken all reasonable care in preparing this book, we make no warranty about the accuracy or completeness of its content and, to the maximum extent permitted, disclaim all liability arising from its use.

PUBLISHED BY
Lonely Planet Publications Pty Ltd
ABN 36 005 607 983
1st edition – February 2013
ISBN 978 1 74321 539 5
© Lonely Planet February 2013   Photographs © as indicated 2013
10 9 8 7 6 5 4 3 2 1
Printed in India
All rights reserved. No part of this publication may be copied, stored in a retrieval system, or transmitted in any form by any means, electronic, mechanical, recording or otherwise, except brief extracts for the purpose of review, and no part of this publication may be sold or hired, without the written permission of the publisher. Lonely Planet and the Lonely Planet logo are trademarks of Lonely Planet and are registered in the US Patent and Trademark Office and in other countries. Lonely Planet does not allow its name or logo to be appropriated by commercial establishments, such as retailers, restaurants or hotels. Please let us know of any misuses: lonelyplanet.com/ip.